The Economics of Inflation

The Economics of Inflation

SECOND EDITION

Richard Jackman
Charles Mulvey and *James Trevithick*

MARTIN ROBERTSON · OXFORD

© Richard Jackman, Charles Mulvey, James Trevithick 1981

First published in 1975 and reprinted in 1976 and 1979 by
Martin Robertson & Co. Ltd., 108 Cowley Road, Oxford OX4 1JF.
Second edition published in 1981. Reprinted in 1982

British Library Cataloguing in Publication Data
Jackman, Richard
   The economics of inflation.
   1. Inflation (Finance)
   I. Title   II. Mulvey, Charles
   III. Trevithick, J.A.
   332.4'1   HG229

ISBN 0-85520-410-9
ISBN 0-85520-411-7 Pbk

Typeset by MHL Typesetting Ltd in 11/12 pt IBM Press Roman
Printed and bound in Great Britain by Camelot Press, Southampton

Contents

Preface

1 Introduction   1

The modern experience of inflation 1; Economic policy and inflation 3; The layout of this book 8

2 The Quantity Theory and the Keynesian Revolution   10

The traditional quantity theory of money 10; The income—expenditure approach to inflation 17

3 Wage Inflation and Excess Demand: The Phillips Curve   32

The Phillips Curve 33; The empirical evidence 46; Measurement problems 50; The breakdown of the Phillips Curve 53; Summary and conclusions 55; Appendix 1: The price equation 56; Appendix 2: Unemployment and vacancies in Great Britain 60

4 Cost Inflation and the Trade Unions   64

A simple model of cost inflation 65; Trade unions and the labour market 68; The nature and measurement of trade union power 70; Empirical evidence on the impact of trade unions on wage inflation 78; Incomes policies 84; Conclusions 86

5 Expectations and Inflation   88

The expectations hypothesis and the natural rate of unemployment 89; A microeconomic theory of the labour market 99; Empirical evidence on the expectations hypothesis 103; Policy implications 106; Summary and conclusions 113

6 Inflation and Monetarism   114

The stability of the velocity of circulation 115; Inflationary expectations, interest rates and the demand for money 120; The theory of nominal income 123; Money, inflation and causality 127 Conclusions 132

7   Inflation in an Open Economy   135

Purchasing power parity 136; The monetary theory of the balance of payments 138; The determinants of world inflation 142; World inflation and the Phillips Curve under fixed exchange rates 145, Flexible exchange rates 146; Conclusions 148

8   Inflation and Real Wages   150

The target real-wage hypothesis 151; Equilibrium real wages 157; Inflation and oil prices 162

9   The Effects of Inflation   171

The effects of anticipated inflation on investment and real interest rates 172; Anticipated inflation and economic welfare 179; The effects of unanticipated inflation 182

10 Conclusions and Policy Recommendations   188

The determinants of inflation 188; Recommendations for policy 190

Bibliography   194

Author Index   204

Subject Index   207

Preface

Since the first edition of this book was written, the problem of inflation has continued to preoccupy the governments of western nations. A variety of economic policies have been deployed against inflation but none has had more than limited success. The debate among professional economists has continued and the literature has grown apace. This edition is intended to incorporate these developments by building on the general framework of the first edition.

Our intention remains the same. This book is designed to be a survey of the literature on inflation which will serve as a text for undergraduates in the later years of their courses. We assume that the reader is familiar with elementary macroeconomic theory. However we have tried to offer an exposition which is as clear and simple as possible. To that end we have removed some of the more esoteric material which was included in the first edition.

This book is not merely an updated version of the first edition. While we have tried to retain the essential character of the previous edition, we have recognised the need to restructure many of the original chapters in order to provide an appropriate basis for introducing new material. In particular we have condensed the discussion of the Phillips curve and the debate which followed its discovery into a single chapter and we have expanded the exposition of the monetarist approach to inflation into two chapters. In the remainder of the book, chapters have variously been consolidated, expanded and reorganised to reflect the state of the current debate.

Although by far the major part of the book is given over to a survey of the technical literature on inflation, the last chapter contains some recommendations for anti-inflation policy which have a larger normative element than the chapters which precede it. It is here that differences of opinion and judgement arise. Indeed one of the authors — Trevithick — would lay far greater emphasis on a permanent incomes policy and correspondingly less emphasis on demand deflation as a cure for inflation than would the other two authors.

In addition to those people whose assistance we acknowledged in the preface to the first edition, we would like to thank Hali Edison for much-needed advice on chapter 7, and Marianna Tappas, June Jarman and Sheila Bullimore for typing the manuscript with great speed and efficiency.

Richard Jackman, London School of Economics
Charles Mulvey, University of Glasgow
James Trevithick, King's College, Cambridge
March 1981

CHAPTER 1

Introduction

Inflation surely helped to make Mr Edward Heath Prime Minister in 1970 and, even more surely, ex-Prime Minister in 1974. The popularity of Japan's Prime Minister, Mr K. Tanaka, is at an alltime low because of inflation. President Allende of Chile lost his life at least partly because of inflation. Throughout the world, inflation is a major source of political unrest. [Friedman, 1974]

1.1 THE MODERN EXPERIENCE OF INFLATION

Inflation is probably best defined as a persistent tendency for the general level of prices to rise. This definition is sufficiently elastic to embrace phenomena such as 'hyper-inflation', 'stagflation' and 'creeping inflation' while still remaining simple and precise. Inflation is not exclusively a modern phenomenon. It is well known that inflation was experienced in ancient times. However, we propose to concentrate for the moment on the modern experience of inflation in order to describe the phases of inflation that preceded the wage and price explosion that is presently raging throughout the non-communist world.

1.1.1 BEFORE THE SECOND WORLD WAR

Prior to the Second World War inflations tended to occur during and immediately after wars, when governments financed the war by resort to the printing press, or during periods when gold discoveries of a significant kind had been made. In other instances, such as the German hyper-inflation of 1923, weak governments have attempted to buy their way out of economic crises by printing vast sums of money. These inflations generally had two important characteristics:

1

(a)   they occurred in response to some particular event, such as a
      war, gold discovery or unmanageable economic crisis;
(b)   they lasted only as long as the event with which they were
      associated, and that was normally not very long.

Thus prior to the Second World War inflations tended to flare up from
time to time and then die down as the exceptional circumstances
that caused them ended.

1.1.2   THE SECOND WORLD WAR AND ITS AFTERMATH

The Second World War was accompanied, as were all wars, by a rapid
world inflation. As had happened often before, the wartime inflation
continued into the postwar period, and 'seemed part and parcel of
the process of postwar reconstruction' (OEEC, 1961). Before this
postwar inflation had had time to unwind itself as historical precedent
would lead us to expect, the Korean War broke out and another war
inflation was precipitated. By 1953 war and postwar hangovers were
behind us, and 'a new period of economic expansion began in which
persistent inflation was not generally anticipated or feared' (OEEC,
1961).

1.1.3   1953–59

Governments in the industrialized countries were now committed to
policies of rapid growth and full employment. These policies were,
on the whole, highly successful. Most European countries steadily
approached full employment during the 1950s, and many had achieved
this objective by the mid-1950s. At the same time growth rates were
running at satisfactorily high levels in most countries, although the
UK and the USA grew at markedly slower rates than the main European industrial countries. There were however disturbing signs that
inflation was not going to disappear. Between 1953 and 1959 retail
prices in the main industrial countries rose at an annual average rate
of about 2–4 per cent per annum. In addition to the persistence of
inflation, balance of payments problems became an increasing cause
for concern in some countries and were generally dealt with by sharp
bouts of deflation.

1.1.4 1960–74

In the first half of the 1960s the rate of inflation in many of the industrialized countries quickened. In most European countries prices rose between 1960 and 1966 at a rate of about 3—5 per cent per annum. In the USA and Canada inflation proceeded more slowly than in Europe and there is no evidence of any quickening during the early 1960s in those countries. From 1967 onwards however the rate of inflation in all the main industrial countries began to accelerate. By 1970 it was clear that a worldwide price and wage explosion was occurring, and by mid-1974 inflation had accelerated to levels ranging from 24 per cent in Japan to 7 per cent in Germany.

1.1.5   AFTER 1974

After 1974 the inflation rate moderated in most countries, although in the UK it reached its peak only in 1975. These more moderate rates of inflation were, however, generally above the rates that had prevailed during the early 1960s, and it was only in Germany and Japan that inflation fell to rates comparable with those of the previous decade. By 1979 inflation had begun to quicken again in most of the industrial countries, and by 1980 it had reached levels not seen since the first half of the 1970s in all of them. In figure 1.1 the inflationary experience of the UK, USA, Japan, France and Germany since 1960 is charted. (The data are set out in table 1.1)

Postwar experience of inflation in the main industrial countries may be briefly summarized as follows. Inflation ran at high rates from 1945 to 1953 and this was understood to be the result of postwar reconstruction followed by the effects of the Korean War; from 1953 to 1959 inflation persisted at relatively low rates, with much cyclical variation, and appeared to be tailing off in 1959; from 1960 to 1966 the inflation rate quickened in most countries; between 1967 and 1974 a worldwide acceleration of inflation occurred leading to a postwar peak by the end of the period; after 1974 inflation moderated and fell in most countries at first, but in 1979 and 1980 it again quickened and approached the rates that had been experienced prior to 1974.

1.2   ECONOMIC POLICY AND INFLATION

1.2.1   THE INFLATIONARY GAP AND COST-PUSH THEORIES

As we have seen, experience suggested to the observer in the early

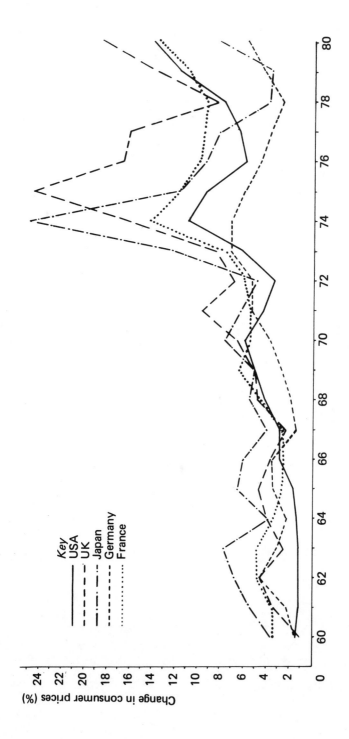

Figure 1.1 Rates of Inflation in Five Industrial Countries, 1960—80

TABLE 1.1   RATES OF INFLATION IN FIVE INDUSTRIAL
COUNTRIES, 1960–80

% per annum

Year	USA	UK	Japan	Germany	France
	%	%	%	%	%
1960	1.5	1.0	3.6	1.5	3.6
1961	1.1	3.4	5.4	2.3	3.4
1962	1.1	4.5	6.7	4.5	4.7
1963	1.2	2.5	7.7	3.0	4.8
1964	1.4	3.9	3.9	2.3	3.4
1965	1.6	4.6	6.5	3.4	2.6
1966	2.8	3.7	6.0	3.5	2.7
1967	2.8	2.4	4.0	1.5	2.7
1968	4.2	4.8	5.5	1.8	4.5
1969	5.0	5.2	5.1	2.6	6.4
1970	5.9	6.5	7.6	3.7	5.5
1971	4.3	9.5	6.3	5.3	5.5
1972	3.6	6.8	4.9	5.4	5.9
1973	6.2	8.4	12.0	7.0	7.5
1974	10.9	16.0	24.6	7.0	14.0
1975	9.2	24.2	11.7	5.9	11.7
1976	5.8	16.5	9.3	4.5	9.6
1977	6.4	15.9	8.1	3.7	9.4
1978	7.6	8.3	3.8	2.7	9.1
1979	11.4	13.4	3.6	4.1	10.7
1980	13.6	18.0	8.0	5.5	13.3

Source: *National Institute Economic Review.* Table 'Industrial Countries: Consumer Prices and the Labour Market

1950s that inflation was a phenomenon associated with particular events and would unwind itself as the event that occasioned it ended. The persistence of inflation through the 1950s therefore perplexed economists and governments alike. In a general way two schools of thought on the question of inflation emerged during this period. The neo-Keynesian school held that the inflation was caused by the existence of an 'inflationary gap', which in turn was the consequence of the inability of total output to satisfy the competing demands of consumers, investors and the government.

An opposing school of thought contended that inflation was caused by independent cost pressure on the price level — generally the consequence of trade union wage-push. There was no clear explanation of why the trade unions should have been capable of exercising a degree of power in the 1950s that they had apparently been unable to do in previous periods. In any case, these schools of thought vied with each other in the 1950s, although there was a middle ground which accepted a mixed demand-pull/cost-push hypothesis, and, since the policy prescriptions of each school differed, left policy-makers somewhat bemused. In the event policy tended to operate on the basis of short-run demand management, usually in response to balance of payments difficulties. The Netherlands was exceptional in that a statutory wages policy was operated continuously there from 1945 on. (For an excellent example of the agonizing that went on during the 1950s over the causes of inflation see OEEC, 1961.)

1.2.2 THE PHILLIPS CURVE

At the end of the 1950s and the beginning of the 1960s a new orthodoxy emerged. The 'Phillips Curve' was discovered in 1958 (Phillips, 1958) and given a theoretical rigour in 1960 by Lipsey (1960). The Phillips—Lipsey hypothesis held that, in the long run, the rate of change of money wages would be determined by the level of excess demand in the labour market (measured by the unemployment rate), while in the short run fluctuations in import prices and productivity growth would combine with excess demand in determining the rate of inflation. Thus according to this hypothesis there would be a long-run trade-off between wage inflation and unemployment, since the growth of import prices would tend to be equal to that of domestic prices and productivity would tend to grow at a steady rate. The Phillips Curve was quickly absorbed into the theory of inflation in its own right. The effect was to lend weight to the demand-pull explanation of inflation, although some writers have argued that the Phillips Curve is 'neutral' as between cost-push and demand-pull theories. The main proponents of the cost-push hypothesis did not normally deny the demand-pull implications of the Phillips Curve, but they still asserted the view that trade unions could and did push up the wage level independently of the level of excess demand.

The policy implications of the Phillips Curve posed acute political dilemmas for governments. The unemployment rate at which it was predicted that the rate of price inflation would fall to zero was considerably higher than that which was regarded as consistent with 'full employment'. Most governments responded to this unpalatable prospect by introducing 'incomes policies' or some form of wage control in order to bypass or at least shift the Phillips Curve in their efforts to contain inflation. However, if the inflation was in reality caused by the pressure of excess demand — as the Phillips Curve indicated — incomes policies were not a real alternative to a policy that eliminated the excess demand. In the event, incomes policies proved to have no lasting effects on the inflation rate when implemented in isolation, and, moreover, they attracted much political odium to the governments that introduced them.

With the demise of the simple Phillips Curve at the end of the 1960s, another new orthodoxy emerged in the form of the 'expectations-augmented Phillips Curve'. The policy implications of this hypothesis were even less palatable to policy-makers than its predecessor. While the 'natural unemployment rate', the rate of unemployment at which inflation would neither rise nor fall, was approximately the same as the unemployment rate that was associated with zero inflation in the simple Phillips Curve, lower rates of unemployment would be associated not simply with inflation but with ever-accelerating inflation.

At about the same time that the expectations-augmented Phillips Curve was absorbed into the demand-pull explanation of the inflation mechanism, the quantity theory of money re-emerged as the most acceptable account of the source of excess demand. The monetarism of Milton Friedman gained widespread credence among academic economists, although the cost-push school of thought remained unimpressed, and was absorbed in varying degrees of purity by most Western governments so that tight money policies became features of their macroeconomic policies in the latter half of the 1970s.

The background against which policy was formulated during the 1970s was a complex one. In the first two years of the decade the vast outflow of dollars from the USA resulted in an expansion of international reserves of over 50 per cent. The consequent monetary expansion in the rest of the world was followed in 1973 and 1974 by a wage and price explosion in all of the Western industrial countries. However, the system of fixed exchange rates which provides a mechanism for the transmission of monetary expansion from country to country was abandoned in 1971 and replaced with floating exchange rates. In theory, at least, this development ought to have made the battle against inflation easier in individual countries. However, the dramatic upsurge in world commodity prices (oil in particular) in 1973 and after was accompanied by a sharp rise in unemployment throughout the Western world which has persisted to the present day. Policy-makers were therefore confronted in the 1970s with a high rate of inflation proceeding against a background of historically high unemployment rates. This puzzling phenomenon of 'stagflation' heightened the dilemma facing policy-makers, and, at the time of writing, the puzzle remains unsolved.

1.3   THE LAYOUT OF THIS BOOK

In this introductory chapter so far, we have presented a sketch of some of the broad facts about modern inflation and described the sort of problems that have faced policy-makers. Because we have been concerned here to describe the facts of the inflationary experience, we have not compared theories or evaluated policies in any coherent way. Moreover, we have mentioned concepts that may be unfamiliar to many readers and that may therefore have mystified rather than enlightened. It is nevertheless useful to approach a subject as complex as inflation with a broad impression of the main issues that are involved, even though much of it is mysterious, and the scheme of the remainder of this book is intended systematically to develop and relate the principal themes touched on above.

In chapter 2 we introduce the Quantity Theory of Money, which was the classical approach to the theory of inflation and which has now been revived by Friedman. In addition, Keynes's view of the inflationary process as contained in *How to Pay for the War* is discussed. In chapter 3 the saga of the Phillips Curve is related and a number of issues that remain of considerable relevance at present are discussed.

In chapter 4 we examine the question of whether trade unions cause inflation. The empirical evidence is reviewed and we conclude that trade unions do affect the rate of inflation in certain circumstances. Chapter 5 outlines the expectations hypothesis and discusses job-search theory as a basis for the natural unemployment rate hypothesis. The empirical evidence is reviewed and some policy implications are considered.

Chapter 6 presents the monetarist approach to inflation, including a discussion of rational expectations. The question of causality in the monetarist theory is also discussed and empirical evidence on the relationship between money and prices is considered. In chapter 7 the area of debate is broadened to consider inflation as an international phenomenon. The issue of fixed versus flexible exchange rates in the international transmission of inflation is discussed in detail. Chapter 8 considers the phenomenon of 'real wage resistance' as a source of inflationary pressure. In addition, the role of international commodity prices, particularly oil, in the inflationary process is investigated. Chapter 9 considers the effects of inflation, both anticipated and unanticipated. In chapter 10 we present our conclusions and draw implications for economic policy.

CHAPTER 2

The Quantity Theory
and the
Keynesian Revolution

The idea that inflation is caused by an excessive quantity of money, of 'too much money chasing too few goods', can be traced back many centuries. The great classical economists – David Hume, Adam Smith, Ricardo and Mill – believed inflation could be explained purely in monetary terms. Their approach became known as the 'quantity theory of money' and culminated at the beginning of this century in the work of Fisher, at Yale, and of Marshall and other economists at Cambridge. In the 1930s the quantity theory was the orthodoxy that Keynes (1936) attacked in his *General Theory of Employment, Interest and Money*. In this chapter, to provide a context for the modern debate, we summarize the quantity theory and the Keynesian approaches to inflation.

2.1 THE TRADITIONAL QUANTITY THEORY OF MONEY

The classic exposition of the traditional quantity theory is Irving Fisher's (1920) *The Purchasing Power of Money*. The analysis is based on the famous equation of exchange:

$$Mv \equiv pT \qquad (2.1)$$

where M is the nominal stock of money; v its velocity of circulation, that is the number of transactions each unit of money finances over a period of time; T is the total number of transactions undertaken over that period of time; and p is their average price. The equation of exchange must hold, of necessity, because Mv and pT are two ways of measuring the same thing, the aggregate value of all transactions taking place over some given time period.

The equation of exchange is therefore an identity (that is, is true

10

by definition) and not a theory of how the economy works. Its purpose is to identify relevant variables and to define the relationships between them (in much the same way as the national income accounting identity provides an essential part of the structure of Keynesian analysis). To take an example, in cruder versions of the quantity theory v and T are assumed constant: the equation of exchange then tells us that a necessary implication of such assumptions is that any change in prices must be accompanied by an equal proportional change in the quantity of money.

What distinguishes the quantity theorists, therefore, is not so much their use of the equation of exchange as the theories they hold about the variables in it. Neither Irving Fisher nor other classical quantity theorists believed that v and T were constant. Rather, they argued that in equilibrium v and T were determined entirely by real forces and not by the quantity of money. To Fisher, v was determined by people's 'habits' and by the technology of exchange; T was determined in equilibrium by the free interaction of the forces of supply and demand, i.e. by real rather than monetary factors. If, on these assumptions, we double the quantity of money, the real forces that determine the equilibrium values of v and T will not be affected, and consequently, for a new equilibrium, prices must double also.

To go from a proposition about equilibrium states to a proposition about how an actual economy would behave over time, the quantity theorists made two further assumptions. First, they assumed that the real forces that determine the equilibrium values of v and T, while not being constant, would themselves change only slowly over time. Hence any substantial changes in the price level over time would have to result from a change in M rather than from changes in the real forces that determine v and T. Second, and this is the most contentious of the quantity theorist's assumptions, they assumed that after a disturbance the economy would quite quickly return to equilibrium. They recognized that, out of equilibrium, monetary disturbances would affect v and T — for example, an increase in money in circulation would be likely to lead to a greater volume of transactions in the short run — but they expected such disturbances to be short-lived (see Fisher, 1920, ch. 4). On these assumptions, then, a change in the quantity of money will initially affect v and T as well as p, but the economy will soon return to equilibrium with (approximately) unchanged values of v and T and hence with prices having changed in proportion to the change in the quantity of money.

We next consider what determines the equilibrium values of v and T.

To Fisher, the velocity of circulation was, in large part, a techno-logical matter depending on the nature of the transactions process in the economy. It was determined by institutional factors such as the use of the banking system, the availability of credit and the communi-cations system (which determines the speed with which funds can be transmitted from one place to another). Fisher recognized that money spent much of its time between transactions, rather than in the process of making them, and that people's habits would influence how long they held on to money they received before paying it out again. But his analysis of these habits was cursory, and not related to utility-maximizing decision-making on the part of individuals.

This deficiency was partially remedied in the Cambridge equation of the demand for money (Pigou, 1917):

$$M_d = kPy \qquad (2.2)$$

where M_d is the demand for nominal money balances, y is output, P is the average price of output (which is not the same as p in equation (2.1)) and k is the desired ratio of money balances to money income. In this formulation, the demand for money is the outcome of people's choices as to the average level of money balances they wish to hold, it being assumed that, other things equal, desired money balances will be proportional to money income.

The Cambridge equation differs from the equation of exchange in that it relates money to the more familiar concept of money income rather than to the value of all transactions. Given that money is the medium of exchange, it might seem more logical to relate the demand for it to transactions rather than to income, but the more useful income formulation can be defended on the grounds that there is probably a fairly stable relationship between income and total transactions, especially in the short run.

Formally, the Cambridge equation can be made equivalent to the equation of exchange, k being the reciprocal of the velocity of circulation. We may rewrite the equation of exchange, again as an identity, for income payments as

$$MV \equiv Py$$

where V is the income velocity of circulation ('the number of times per unit time that the money stock is used in making money income transactions' — Friedman, 1970a). Dividing this into (2.2) immediately gives $V = 1/k$.

The important innovation of the Cambridge approach is that k, the desired ratio of money balances to money income, is a choice variable. The amount of money people will want to hold will depend on the expected benefits of holding money (in terms of convenience, security, etc.) as against the returns on other assets, which depend on interest rates, expectations and so on. The Cambridge approach allows a wider range of economic variables, as well as institutional factors, to influence k and hence the velocity of circulation. However, these economic variables (such as the rate of interest) were themselves held to be determined in equilibrium only by real forces, and hence the Cambridge approach remained consistent with the quantity theory view of inflation as a purely monetary phenomenon.

To examine the determinants of the equilibrium level of transactions or income, it will be useful to introduce a highly simplified model of the neoclassical macroeconomic system.

Consider a labour market in which the supply of labour, N_s, is an increasing function of the real wage rate (W/P), where W is the money wage rate and P is the price level; that is, $N_s = N_s(W/P)$. Similarly, assume that the demand for labour, N_d, is also a function of the real wage rate, but this time a diminishing function reflecting the hypothesis that the marginal productivity of labour decreases with the level of employment; that is, $N_d = N_d(W/P)$. With flexible wages and prices, an equilibrium level of employment, N_F, and an equilibrium real wage rate, $(W/P)_F$, will be established simultaneously. These properties of labour market equilibrium are depicted in figure 2.1(a).

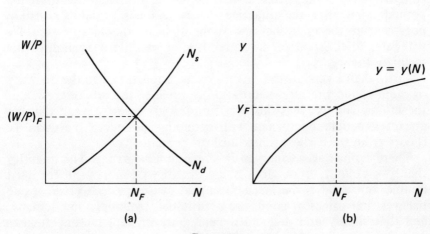

(a)   (b)

Figure 2.1

In order to determine the level of national income corresponding to the equilibrium level of employment, N_F, we need to introduce the notion of a short-run production function, $y = y(N)$: for a given state of technology and a fixed capital stock, the level of output, y, is positively related to the level of employment. The production function is concave to the N-axis, reflecting the presence of diminishing marginal productivity of labour.[1] This short-run production function is depicted in figure 2.1(b).

Figure 2.1 represents a completely self-contained subsystem of the neoclassical macroeconomic model. The characteristics of equilibrium in this subsystem depend solely upon: (a) the state of technology that provides information concerning not only the shape and position of the production function but also the properties of the labour demand function; and (b) the utility functions of individual suppliers of labour, which, in this highly simplified system, will provide information on the number of man-hours that workers are willing to work in return for a pre-specified real wage rate. It will be noted that the only price that enters the picture is a relative price, namely, the real wage rate (W/P). Absolute prices (the levels of W and P measured separately) cannot be ascertained from this subsystem alone but depend also on the quantity of money.

On the assumptions we have now set out, the velocity of circulation V (or k) and output (y) are determined only by real forces. These, then, are the basic assumptions underlying the quantity theory approach. Output (y) and velocity (V, or k) are determined, in equilibrium, independently of monetary factors, and are approximately constant over time. While something of an oversimplification, the popular view that the quantity theory assumes y and V constant does capture the main message of the quantity theory approach. We will refer to this popular interpretation as the 'naive' version of the quantity theory.

In the naive version the price level is proportional to the quantity of money, and the rate of inflation is equal to the rate of growth of the money supply. It is this very simple and powerful result that has attracted people concerned with economic policy to the quantity theory from the earliest times until the present day.

There is, however, one gap in the argument so far. The quantity theory says that, if we double the quantity of money, prices must double; but what is the mechanism that causes prices to rise? If one believes that prices of goods are determined by supply and demand, and that supply and demand depend only on real factors (such as preferences and technology), it would appear that an increase in the quantity of money would have no effect on the prices of individual goods, and hence no effect on the aggregate price level.

This apparent inconsistency has been resolved at some length in Patinkin's (1965) classic work *Money, Interest and Prices*. His argument may, however, be summarized quite briefly for present purposes. We start by examining the supply and demand for money balances. With the naive version of the quantity theory, the demand for money balances, for any given set of real variables, is proportional to the general level of prices and thus inversely proportional to the 'value of money' (that is, the price of money in terms of goods, $1/p$). This inverse relationship is depicted by the curve marked M_d in figure 2.2.

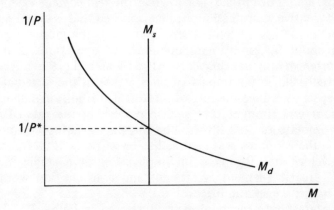

Figure 2.2

The supply of money in nominal terms is exogenously determined by the monetary authorities and is represented by the vertical line M_s in figure 2.2. The intersection of the demand for money function, M_d, with the vertical supply function determines the value of P at P^*. In other words, the only way in which desired real cash balances (M_d/P) can be brought into line with *actual* real cash balances (M_s/P) is by variations in the price level.[2] More specifically, if $(M_s/P) <$ (M_d/P), the price level will have to fall; and if $(M_s/P) > (M_d/P)$, the price level will have to rise.

The problem now arises as to how disequilibrium in the money market $((M_d/P) \neq (M_s/P))$ *generates* price changes. Let us assume the economy is initially in equilibrium with the price level at P^*, and suppose the government gives everyone a £10 Christmas bonus. Each individual would want to spend at least part of their £10; that is, they would want to finance extra purchases of goods by running down their holdings of money balances. But while each individual may wish to do this, collectively they cannot. Once there is more money in the economy, individuals taken together have no option but to hold that higher volume of money. However, the attempt by everyone to purchase more goods has the effect of increasing the prices of goods (because the output of goods is determined by real forces, as depicted in figure 2.1 above). As the prices of goods rise, people need higher nominal money balances to finance their trans-actions, and prices continue to rise until all the increased money supply is absorbed into higher (nominal) transactions balances. This mechanism, whereby a monetary disequilibrium affects the demand for goods, and hence prices, is known as the *real balance effect*.

An alternative transmission mechanism, one that is better suited to advanced monetary systems where changes in the money supply are brought about by government open-market operations, is provided by the *interest rate mechanism* of Alfred Marshall (1923). According to Marshall, the initial impact of an increase in the nominal supply of money is to reduce the rate of interest. On traditional neoclassical grounds, it was thought that such a decline in the rate of interest would stimulate desired investment and perhaps even consumption. But since the economy was assumed to be working at its full-employment level of output (as is an implication of a stable Walrasian system), greater planned investment and consumption would only issue in higher wages and prices.

The interest rate mechanism is illustrated in figure 2.3. The rate of interest, r, is measured on the vertical axis and the demand for and supply of real cash balances is measured on the horizontal axis. The

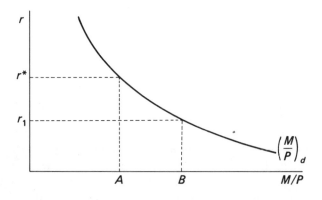

Figure 2.3

demand for real cash balances is shown by the $(M/P)_d$ curve in figure 2.3. Assume the economy is initially in equilibrium with the supply of real money balances equal to OA. If the government increases the nominal supply of money so that, at given prices, the real supply of money increases from OA to OB, the market, or short-term rate of interest will fall to r_1. With finance available at lower interest rates, planned investment will rise which will in turn lead to higher prices and a contraction in the real value of the money supply. The inflation will continue until the real money supply has been reduced back to OA, and the market interest rate returned to r^*. Monetary factors exert only a temporary influence on the rate of interest.

2.2 THE INCOME–EXPENDITURE APPROACH TO INFLATION

No student of economics can be unaware of the devastating theoretical impact which Keynes's (1936) *General Theory of Employment, Interest and Money* had in undermining the foundations of the neo-classical world, in which lapses from full employment were regarded as transitory deviations from an otherwise stable equilibrium. The powerful principle of *effective demand* attempted to demonstrate that the equilibrium[3] level of output and employment, X_E and N_E respectively, would in general not coincide with their full-employment values. By focusing upon the relationship between variations in *ex ante* expenditure and variations in real income and employment, Keynes established the *income–expenditure* approach to the determination of the level of economic activity. In this section we shall be concerned with the application of the extremely versatile principle of effective demand to the problem of inflation in the context of a fully employed economy. Section 2.2.1 will deal with the model of inflation contained in *How to Pay for the War* (Keynes, 1940) and with other inflationary gap models current in the early 1940s. In general, these models excluded any specific mention of the monetary forces that may be operative either in bringing inflationary pressure under control or in exacerbating the upward spiral of wages and prices. This omission is remedied to some extent in Section 2.2.2, in which money is explicitly incorporated into the Hicksian *IS–LM* interpretation of the complete Keynesian model. Finally, in Section 2.2.3 we shall examine another non-monetary theory of the inflationary process, Hansen's two-gap model, which is in direct line of descent from the earlier inflationary gap models but which expressly distinguishes between inflationary pressure emanating from the goods market on the one hand and that emanating from the factor market on the other.

2.2.1 INFLATIONARY GAP MODELS

Following upon the success of Keynes's *General Theory* in explaining the phenomenon of under-employment equilibrium, the onset of the Second World War appeared to undermine the claim to generality of the *General Theory*. The neoclassical world of full employment appeared to have made a startling comeback; capacity was being fully utilized and unemployment had been reduced to a minimum. From the economic point of view however there seemed to be one untidy blemish in an otherwise quite rosy picture: inflation was taking place at a rather alarming rate. The explanation of this pheno-menon was to pose an important challenge to Keynes and his followers, who had to answer the claim that the *General Theory* was nothing more than a description of the forces at work in a chronically de-pressed economy. In fact, the principle of effective demand was to exhibit remarkable robustness in the decade that followed. The notion of deficient aggregate demand had been advanced to explain the unemployment problem of the 1920s and 1930s; the notion of *excessive* aggregate demand was subsequently advanced to explain the phenomenon of inflation in the 1940s.

This is the essence of the inflationary gap approach to inflation. The problem of inflation could be explained in terms of an excess of aggregate *ex ante* real expenditure over producible real output. The real expenditure plans of consumers, investors and the government could not be met simultaneously since the equilibrium level of national income was unattainable. In terms of the familiar 'Keynesian cross' diagram of a closed economy, the problem was stated as follows. Let aggregate real expenditure be measured on the vertical axis and real income on the horizontal axis. According to traditional Keynesian taxonomy, real expenditure may be subdivided into consumption expenditure (C), investment expenditure (I) and government expendi-ture (G). The aggregate expenditure function, $C + I + G$, relates the level of desired real expenditure to the level of real income (see figure 2.4).

The intersection of the total expenditure function with the 45° line determines the equilibrium level of real national income, y_E. When national income is at y_E, the total amount of goods and services produced within the economy is equal to aggregate planned expendi-ture in real terms. But suppose now that y_E represents an unfeasible

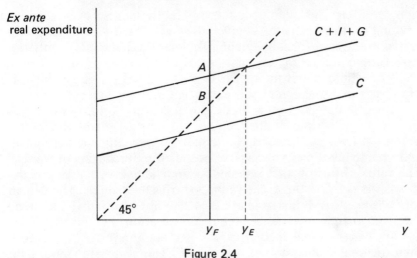

Figure 2.4

level of income; suppose, for example, that y_F represents the maximum level of output obtainable from the resources of capital and labour: it will represent an effective ceiling beyond which output cannot rise. The fact that y_E exceeds y_F will imply that *ex post* real expenditure will fall short of its *ex ante* value. There will consequently be upward pressure on prices, and an inflationary gap of magnitude AB will exist.

The Keynesian 'excess demand' theory of inflation is in some ways similar to the quantity theory approach, in that in both cases the immediate source of inflation is the excess of desired expenditures over full employment output. In the quantity theory approach the excess of expenditures derives from an excess of money balances, and the inflation of itself eliminates the excess demand by reducing the real value of money balances. In the Keynesian approach excess demand derives from real factors that are not necessarily affected by inflation. Thus it is not clear whether, in the Keynesian approach, the price level would converge automatically to some new higher level, or whether the process of inflation would continue indefinitely, and perhaps even degenerate into hyper-inflation. These are some of the questions that Keynes and his followers attempted to answer.

How to Pay for the War In his classic pamphlet *How to Pay for the War*, Keynes (1940) addressed himself to one central problem: how to finance the government expenditure and private investment necessary for the successful completion of the war effort while at the same time avoiding the evils of inflation. In the course of writing and advising on this problem, Keynes advanced a theory of inflation that served as the basis for subsequent inflationary gap models of inflation. An examination of the original model contained in *How to Pay for the War* would therefore appear to be a natural starting point for a more general discussion of subsequent inflationary gap models.

Keynes's argument runs along the following lines. Suppose that the values of output (valued, as are all the subsequent variables, at pre-war prices) is Q and that the value of government expenditure and private investment necessary for the effective waging of war is G. The value of output that remains for individuals to consume if they so wish is $Q - G$: this is the supply of consumer goods. The demand for consumer goods is arrived at by considering how individuals divide their disposable income between consumption and saving. If y is the level of national income and T is the amount paid in taxation, then disposable income will be $y - T$. The aggregate amount that individuals decide to save is denoted by S, so that desired consumption expenditure will be $y - (T + S)$. If $Q - G < y - (T + S)$, then the supply of consumer goods will fall short of the demand for those goods and an inflationary gap is said to exist.

Assuming that the ratio of real government expenditure plus private investment to real final output is constant, Keynes argued that the initial response of the system would be to hoist up the money value of $Q - G$ so as to clear the goods market. This initial response will lead to windfall gains which will benefit 'profiteers', who may either consume or save these gains. If they consume, the very high rates of personal and profits taxation will siphon off a sizeable amount – moreover, the increased consumption of profiteers could be offset 'by a modest increase of taxation on the general public'; if they save them, the inflation will be halted since the fall in aggregate consumer demand will bring about equilibrium between income and expenditure; if a mixture of the two effects occurs, it is clear that the inflationary process will cease and the price level will rise to a new high level.

These conclusions have been arrived at on the assumption that workers are willing to stand idly by and see the erosion of the real wage rate consequent upon an inflation in the price of final output. This is an extreme assumption even in times of war. In a situation of excess demand for labour resulting from the existence of an infla-tionary gap, profiteers may see no disadvantage in diverting some of their windfall gains to finance an increase in money wages rather than allow most of these gains to be taxed away. If wages are continually chasing prices, there would appear to be no escape from this wage–price spiral.

The distribution of national income plays an important role in Keynes's theory of inflation. An inflationary gap may be eliminated by a redistribution of national income away from those classes of society that save little and are taxed at low rates in favour of those classes that save a great deal and who are taxed quite heavily on the income they do not save. Wage-earners constitute the majority of the high-consumption–low-taxation group, whereas profiteers constitute the majority of the low-consumption–high-taxation group. We may write the marginal propensities to consume of profiteers and wage-earners as c_p and c_w respectively, where $c_p < c_w$. Assuming that non-consumption expenditure, G, is a constant proportion, g, of national income, the equation for income-expenditure equilibrium becomes:

$$y_t = c_w a_t y_t + c_p (1 - a_t) y_t + g y_t \qquad (2.3)$$

where a_t is defined as the equilibrium share of wages in national income. Since national income is assumed to be at its full-employment level, equation (2.3) defines a unique distribution of national income between workers and profiteers such that:

$$a_t = \frac{1 - g - c_p}{c_w - c_p} \qquad (2.4)$$

Clearly, the greater is the ratio of war expenditure to national income, the lower will have to be the share of wages if equilibrium is to be maintained. But suppose that

$$a_t > \frac{1 - g - c_p}{c_w - c_p} \ .$$

In this case an inflationary gap exists. The way in which the share of wages falls in response to inflationary pressure to an equilibrium level defined by equation (2.4) is the subject of chapter 9 of *How to Pay for the War*. Essentially, Keynes believed that, because of lags in the adjustment of wages to prices, real wages could be reduced by inflation. Assume that prices respond instantaneously to wage increases, but that wages react with a one-year lag to price increases

(Trevithick, 1975). We can write these assumptions as:

$$P_t = \frac{N_t}{a_t Q_t} W_t \tag{2.5}$$

and

$$W_t = \frac{a_t^* Q_t}{N_t} P_{t-1} \tag{2.6}$$

where N is employment, Q is output, a is the actual share of labour and a^* is the share of output that workers are content to achieve in wage bargaining. Hence

$$a_t = a_t^* \frac{P_{t-1}}{P_t} = \frac{a_t^*}{1 + \dot{P}_t} \tag{2.7}$$

where $\dot{P}_t$, the rate of inflation, is defined conventionally as

$$\dot{P}_t = \frac{P_t - P_{t-1}}{P_{t-1}}$$

Thus, if workers bargain for a given target share of output, but always bargain on the basis of last year's prices (or bargain for next year's wages on the basis of current prices), their actual share of income can be reduced by inflation so as to satisfy equation (2.4). In *How to Pay for the War* Keynes (1940, p. 72) analyses a numerical example, in which a 15 per cent reduction in wages is brought about by a 15 per cent inflation.

In this model we have the rather paradoxical result that persistent inflation becomes the means whereby the inflationary gap is eliminated. It is the process of inflation that redistributes income from workers (with a low propensity to save, or to be taxed) to profiteers (with a high propensity to save or to be taxed), hence depressing demand sufficiently to remove the original excess of real expenditure over real national income.

Neo-Keynesian developments Keynes was not alone in inquiring into the repercussions of an exogenous increase in aggregate expenditure at full employment. The resource strains experienced by an economy at war had already become apparent in the USA in the early 1940s, and the great fear at this time was, quite naturally, that inflation would erupt and wreak unacceptable havoc. Many American economists turned their attention to the development of formal models of the inflationary process which took as their foundation the income–

expenditure approach, suitably modified to cater for situations of excess demand.

A typical example of how basic Keynesian principles were applied to the question of inflation is to be found in a celebrated article by A. Smithies (1942). Once again, Smithies was concerned with the situation depicted in figure 2.4, in which *ex ante* expenditure exceeds the productive capacity of the economy. There is one important difference, however, between Smithies's model and the scheme outlined in *How to Pay for the War*: instead of deflating by an appropriate price index, Smithies defined all of his expenditure functions in *money* terms. That is, the total expenditure functions may be written in the following manner:

$$E' = \sigma + \epsilon Y + G' \qquad (2.8)$$

where Y is *money* national income ($= P \cdot y$), and the 'prime' superscripts indicate the money values of aggregate expenditure (i.e. $E' = P \cdot E$) and government expenditure plus private investment (i.e. $G' = G \cdot P$), ϵ is the marginal propensity to consume and σ is the level of autonomous consumption. The fact that σ is fixed in *money* terms is of cardinal importance to the model, for it implies that inflation will gradually erode the real value of autonomous consumption until the point has been reached at which full-employment equilibrium has been established. Thus, by couching the aggregate expenditure function in money terms, Smithies has indicated one possible escape route from a situation of chronic excess demand: the value of the intercept of the consumption function will decline in real terms in the presence of inflation (see figure 2.4).

Unfortunately, there is no economic reason to assume that real autonomous expenditure will in fact decline in an inflationary situation. By framing all of his expenditure functions in money terms, Smithies inserted an arbitrary assumption concerning the behaviour of aggregate expenditure.

Fortunately, one alternative escape route remains in Smithies's model. This is the conventional neo-Keynesian assumption that the presence of money illusion in the labour market will serve to redistribute income away from high-consumption groups (workers) and in favour of low-consumption groups (non-wage-earners).[4] This hypothesis introduces an asymmetry into the expenditure plans of different groups: capitalists and rentiers are not subject to money illusion but workers are. Inflation will therefore tilt the distribution of income in favour of the former group, which, on average, saves a greater proportion of its real income than the latter group. The consequent flattening of the consumption function will bridge the inflationary gap and save the day.[5]

Many of the features of the Smithies model were incorporated into subsequent theoretical studies on inflation. For example, the assumptions of money illusion in the labour market and of differential consumption patterns between wage-earners and non-wage-earners were common elements in later models. For instance, passive economic groups who live on incomes fixed in nominal terms and whose expenditure figures significantly in total spending will find their real purchasing power eroded by inflation. Once again *ex ante* expenditure will gradually be brought into line with full-employment income. A similar result can be produced by assuming that some sort of Pigou effect is operative. If consumption varies directly with the real value of liquid assets, inflation may reduce consumption by diminishing the value of such assets. The scope for elaboration on the same theme is without limit.

Most of the models that followed *How to Pay for the War* are formally very similar to each other. As in the Smithies model, they in general reduce to a first- or second-order difference equation in either the price level or equivalently (since output was assumed constant) in money national income. Conclusions concerning the existence and stability of the equilibrium levels of these variables are drawn through an examination of the magnitudes and signs of the original structural parameters. On the whole, the economic justification for restricting the parameters to taking certain values or ranges of values does not receive extensive treatment, with the result that such models are vulnerable to the criticism of being somewhat arbitrary; greater emphasis tended to be laid, for example, on how different lag structures affected the mathematical properties of the solution.

In general, neo-Keynesian theories predict either that the rate of price inflation will eventually fall towards zero or (less commonly) that it will accelerate progressively; very rarely do they predict that the rate of inflation will remain constant over time as in Keynes's own model. Moreover, nearly all such theories (Keynes's being no exception) predict that, provided certain key parameters have the right sign and magnitude and that the system is characterized by the existence of lags of sufficient length, then equilibrium will be restored *automatically*: The inflationary gap would be closed even in the absence of discretionary government intervention, although a contractionary fiscal policy would considerably accelerate the process and would therefore be desirable.

2.2.2 MONEY IN A SIMPLE KEYNESIAN MODEL

One feature that these early income—expenditure models have in common is that they provide theories of inflation in which money plays no part. Keynes's own criticisms of the quantity theory approach can be found in chapter 21 of the *General Theory*. There, Keynes suggests two reasons why an increase in the quantity of money may not lead to an equal proportional increase in prices. First, as we have seen, the quantity theory argument depends on the assumption that the economy is always at, or close to, full employment equilibrium. In the Keynesian model, by contrast, output is typically not at full employment, so changes in the quantity of money alter the level of output rather than prices. Second, the Keynesian analysis of the demand for money suggests it may be highly interest-elastic, implying that the velocity of circulation will vary substantially as the interest rate changes. Further, away from full employment, the interest rate will be determined by monetary as well as real forces. A change in the quantity of money may then affect interest rates and the velocity of circulation, rather than prices or output.

Clearly, the first of these reasons can hardly be relevant in the context of an excess demand inflation, when the economy's resources can be assumed to be fully employed. With full employment, changes in the money supply will affect prices unless they are fully offset by changes in the velocity of circulation.

To explore this point further, we must first introduce the familiar Hicksian *IS—LM* framework. The interest rate, r, is measured on the vertical axis and the level of real income, y, on the horizontal axis. Full employment output is again denoted y_F. In figure 2.5 we

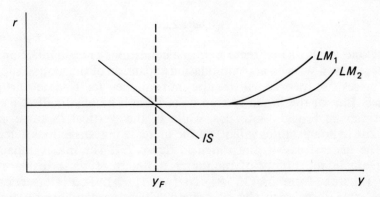

Figure 2.5

assume the economy is at full employment equilibrium with the interest rate in the liquidity trap. An increase in the money supply will shift the *LM* curve from LM_1 to LM_2. The demand for money is infinitely interest-elastic and an increase in the money supply is simply held in idle balances rather than driving down the interest rate and stimulating expenditure. The inflationary gap is therefore unaffected. Put in another way, the velocity of circulation simply slows down to accommodate any increase in the money supply.

There is one other situation in which an increase in the money supply will not affect the inflationary gap. This is the case in which the *IS* curve is vertical at the full employment level of output. Even though the *LM* curve may be positively sloped, an increase in the supply of money will simply depress the rate of interest and will not raise the level of demand. In this case, the rate of interest will fall until it has reduced the velocity of circulation sufficiently to absorb the initial increase in the money supply (figure 2.6).

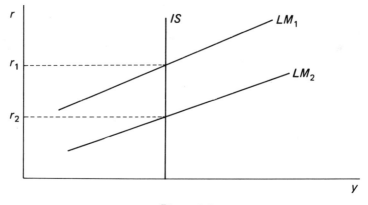

Figure 2.6

If one (or both) of these extreme conditions prevail, inflation can proceed even with no accommodating expansion of the money supply. As prices rise, people will require more money for transactions purposes. But, in the liquidity trap case, there is money in idle balances that can be brought into use, while in the 'vertical *IS* curve' case, the rise in interest rates will offset the increase in transactions demand.

The general case is illustrated in figure 2.7. The initial impact of increase in the supply of money from M_0 to M_1 is to displace the *LM* function from $LM(M_0/P_0)$ to $LM(M_1/P_0)$. The intersection of this latter curve with the *IS* curve produces an equilibrium level of real income in excess of y_F. In other words, an inflationary gap

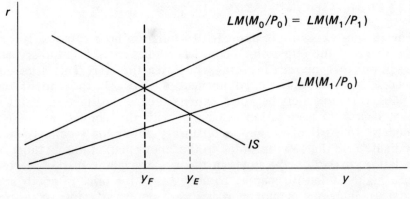

Figure 2.7

will exist. Prices will continue to rise for as long as y_E exceeds y_F. Prices will stabilize only when the new supply of money, M_1, has been deflated in real terms by a sufficiently large price increase. Full employment equilibrium will be restored when $(M_1/P_1) = (M_0/P_0)$, that is, when the *LM* curve has drifted back to its initial position.

But the above prediction is perfectly consistent with the quantity theory approach, for in equilibrium the level of real balances remains a constant proportion of real income. Indeed, as it stands it is simply a more elaborate way of presenting the Marshallian transmission mechanism outlined in section 2.1. It must therefore be concluded that 'money does not matter' in an income–expenditure model: (a) if the liquidity preference function is infinitely elastic with respect to the rate of interest; and/or (b) if the investment function is completely interest-inelastic.

If neither of these conditions is fulfilled, an increase in the money supply (at full employment) raises prices proportionately, as in the quantity theory. It likewise follows that, in the general case, a sufficient contraction in the money supply (or its rate of growth) can bring an excess demand inflation to a halt. Nor can inflation continue, in the general case, in the absence of an accommodating increase in the money supply. It is interesting to note that, in the general case, changes in the quantity of money always alter the equilibrium price level proportionately. Even if the economy is near to an extreme case, for example with a very steep *IS* curve, the proportionality relationship remains. The neglect of monetary factors in early Keynesian inflationary gap models thus seems, in retrospect, difficult to justify.

2.2.3 THE HANSEN TWO-GAP MODEL

The income-expenditure approach to inflation bore copious fruit in the shape of the numerous theoretical studies in the inflationary gap tradition that appeared during and after the war. This apparent success however did not go unchecked. Towards the end of the 1940s, certain writers began to express their dissatisfaction with the high degree of aggregation associated with the simplest Keynesian models. In particular, they were uneasy about the seemingly subordinate role that was accorded to the labour market during times of inflation. In early neo-Keynesian theories, the labour market reacted in a highly defensive manner to increases in the price of goods and services. Increases in money wages were simply attempts to restore the initial level of real wages in the face of rising prices. The role of the labour market in *initiating* price increases was seldom investigated. An important contribution to our understanding of how demand conditions in both the product market and the labour market affect the rate of inflation is contained in the writings of the Swedish economist, Bent Hansen (1951).

The essence of Hansen's model is illustrated in figure 2.8. The real wage is measured on the vertical axis and the level of real national income is measured on the horizontal axis. The $\eta(W/P)$ function relates the *demand* for real output to the real wage rate. The higher the real wage rate, the higher is the level of real *ex ante* demand (i.e. $\eta' > 0$). This proposition is justified on the basis of two assumptions:

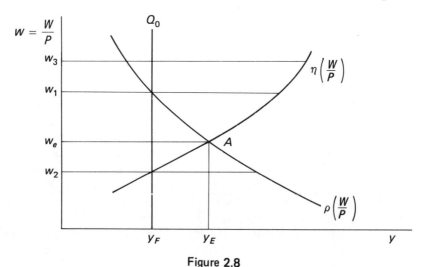

Figure 2.8

first, that as the wage rate rises, the real wage bill will rise; and, second, that as the real wage bill rises relative to other incomes, real demand will rise owing to the higher marginal propensity to consume of wage-earners. The $\rho(W/P)$ function, on the other hand, indicates how the output decision of entrepreneurs is affected by rising real wages. Its negative slope reflects the phenomenon of diminishing marginal productivity of traditional neoclassical theory. The higher the real wage rate, the lower will be the demand for labour; if this lower demand translates itself into a lower level of employment, as is assumed in elementary comparative static analysis, the supply of real output will fall. The equilibrium level of output, y_E, occurs at the intersection of the η and ρ functions at point A.

But suppose that y_E represents an infeasible level of output. Assume instead that there is a ceiling to output given by the vertical line Q_0.[6] The fact that the capacity curve Q_0 lies to the left of point A will give rise to either a goods gap or a factor gap or both, depending upon the level of the real wage rate. On the assumption that real wages are the most important component of factor incomes, an *index* of the factor gap may be obtained by measuring the horizontal distance between the Q_0 curve and the ρ function. The size of the goods gap is measured by the horizontal distance between the Q_0 curve and the η function. An inspection of figure 2.8 reveals that, at all wage rates between w_1 and w_2, there is both a positive factor gap $((\rho - Q_0) > 0)$ and a positive goods gap $((\eta - Q_0) > 0)$.

Two further behavioural assumptions are required to complete the model. The first is an equation linking the rate of change of prices to the size of the goods gap, so that

$$\frac{dP}{dt} = f(\eta - Q_0) \text{ where } f'(\ ) > 0 \text{ and } f(0) = 0. \quad (2.9)$$

The second is an equation linking the rate of change of money wages to the index of the size of the factor gap, so that

$$\frac{dW}{dt} = g(\rho - Q_0) \text{ where } g'(\ ) > 0 \text{ and } g(0) = 0. \quad (2.10)$$

The equation for the rate of change of *real* wages is therefore

$$\frac{d\left(\frac{W}{P}\right)}{dt} = \frac{g(\rho - Q_0) - \frac{W}{P} f(\eta - Q_0)}{P}. \quad (2.11)$$

Quasi-equilibrium is said to prevail when $d(W/P)/dt = 0$. For this to occur, the following condition must be satisfied:

$$\frac{W}{P} = \frac{g(\rho - Q_0)}{f(\eta - Q_0)}.\tag{2.12}$$

The real wage rate that satisfied condition (2.12) is the quasi-equilibrium real wage rate, w_e. Its magnitude will depend upon the relative sluggishness of response of the money wage rate and the price level. The faster the speed of response of the money wage rate to that of the price level, the higher will be w_e. Moreover, it can be easily verified that w_e will be located in the interval $w_1 > w_e > w_2$. Further inspection of the properties of the model will reveal that w_e is a stable quasi-equilibrium in the sense that, if any other real wage rate were to prevail initially, the process of money wage/price inflation will drive the real wage rate towards w_e. For example, if the initial real wage rate is w_3, there will be a positive goods gap and a negative factor gap. The dynamic adjustment functions (equations (2.10) and (2.11)) will imply a continuous depression of the real wage rate to the point where equation (2.12) is satisfied, i.e. where the real wage rate is w_e. Once the real wage rate has been driven below w_1, the size of the goods gap will have been reduced but a positive factor gap will have emerged. It is for this reason that Hansen states that a necessary condition for full inflation is the existence of both a positive goods gap and a positive factor gap.

Hansen's separation of the goods and factor markets and his investigation of the role of excess demand for factors of production in pushing up money wages independently of prices provided a useful starting point for subsequent empirical studies of the determinants of the rate of change of money wages. Indeed, much of the early theorizing on the Phillips Curve relation owed a great deal to his dynamic treatment of the factor market. Excess demand for labour services has always played a central part in determining the rate of change of aggregate money wages, even in highly sophisticated theories that have appeared since the late 1960s. His separate treatment of the labour market was a distinct improvement on most neo-Keynesian models, which tended to treat the behaviour of money wages in a fairly arbitrary manner (*vide* Smithies). Viewed in this light, his model may be seen as bridging the gap between neo-Keynesian theory and the more empirically orientated models that were to follow.

NOTES

1. Note that the demand curve for labour, $N_d(W/P)$, is simply the first derivative of the production function at different levels of employment.

2. Note that the choice of a price deflator, in our example the average price level P, is immaterial since all *relative* prices (e.g. the real wage rate) have been determined in the real sector of the economy and the choice of a *numéraire* to characterize the equilibrium vector of relative prices is arbitrary.

3. Note that Keynes defined equilibrium in respect of the laws of motion of the economic system. An economy in which markets *persistently* fail to clear may be regarded as being in a state of rest and hence in equilibrium.

4. We have seen that, when writing on inflation at this period, Keynes made no such assumption. The term 'neo-Keynesian' is a catch-all category designed to include economists who would tend on balance to subscribe to the income—expenditure method.

5. Smithies introduced money illusion as a theoretical possibility in a more general model. His article is concerned more with investigating the mathematical conditions for the existence of a stable equilibrium at full employment and less with advancing tentative empirical estimates of the values of particular parameters.

6. The capacity constraint as we have drawn it is vertical. Alternative shapes for the constraint are clearly possible. For example, Bronfenbrenner and Holzman (1963) assume that capacity will increase with the real wage rate up to a certain point, after which further increases in the real wage rate reduce the level of capacity.

CHAPTER 3

Wage Inflation and Excess Demand: The Phillips Curve

The Keynesian income—expenditure model provides a theory of output at less than full employment, and, through the inflationary gap mechanism discussed in the previous chapter, a theory of inflation in times of generalized excess demand. But what was required in the decades of relative prosperity after the Second World War was a theory of the inflationary process in economies at, or close to, full employment, and this is something the Keynesian model fails to provide. An extreme Keynesian might want to argue that, up to full employment, changes in demand will be fully taken up in changes in output with no effect on prices, and that only when demand exceeds full employment, and an inflationary gap develops, will prices begin to rise. More realistically, one might argue that, because of rigidities and bottlenecks in some sectors, as demand increased prices would start to rise in some sectors before full employment had been reached in others. Thus the economy would be prone to some inflation even before full employment was attained.

A second major development at this time was the key role attributed to labour and to wage determination in the inflationary process. Most Keynesian economists were of the view that the prices of goods were not determined in competitive markets, but rather were administered by producers. Prices, they believed, were set by producers on the basis of 'normal' costs plus a profit markup. (For evidence on pricing behaviour, supporting this view, see appendix 1 to this chapter.) Firms faced by an increase in demand for their goods would increase production, which would in turn increase their demand for their inputs. Over the economy as a whole the main impact would be an increase in the demand for labour. If wages rise as a result, firms' costs will rise, and the higher costs will be passed on to consumers in the form of higher prices. On this approach, the key to inflation clearly lies in the responsiveness of wages to changes in the demand for labour.

The relationship between the rate of increase of money wages and unemployment (or some other measure of the pressure of demand in the labour market) is known as the 'Phillips Curve', in recognition of Phillips's (1958) pathbreaking statistical study. In this chapter, we first outline Phillips's work and results, and then discuss some of the more important theoretical and empirical issues it gave rise to. In so doing, we are examining the inflation debate of the 1960s; for, by the end of that decade, the Phillips Curve appeared to have broken down. In subsequent chapters of the book, we consider theories that have been put forward to replace, or modify, the Phillips Curve approach. However, the central Phillips Curve relationship — between money wage increases and the pressure of demand for labour — remains an essential part of a number of the new approaches, and continues to be one of the most controversial aspects of the inflationary process. We therefore examine the Phillips Curve debate here in some detail.

3.1 THE PHILLIPS CURVE

Phillips's work consisted of statistical tests of the relation between the level of unemployment and the rate of change of money wages in the UK over the period 1861–1957. His results were quite striking. He obtained, by means of rather unorthodox statistical methods, the graphic relationship shown in figure 3.1, which has come to be known as the 'Phillips Curve'. The fitted curve was taken to indicate the rate of money wage inflation that would occur at different levels of

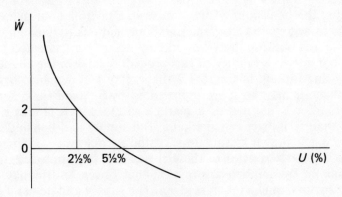

Figure 3.1

aggregate unemployment, which in turn are proxies for different levels of excess demand for labour.

The curve has some interesting aspects. For example, it may be seen from figure 3.1 that at a rate of unemployment of about 5½ per cent wages would remain static. Of more relevance to policy-makers, the curve shows that at a rate of unemployment of about 2½ per cent wages would rise at around 2 per cent per annum, which is consistent with price stability, since the trend growth rate of productivity was then thought to be about 2 per cent per annum. The possible policy implications of these findings were quickly recognized. (See for example Paish, 1968). At its crudest, the chief implication to be drawn from the curve is that price stability can be achieved if policy can somehow stabilize the level of unemployment at around 2½ per cent. In practice, this prescription purports to refer to a long-run situation; it was accepted that in the short run fluctuations in productivity growth and import prices would be reflected in price changes.

The Phillips Curve quite clearly had important implications for both the theory of inflation and for economic policy. There was therefore a need to examine its theoretical foundations more rigorously and to subject the data to more sophisticated statistical testing.

3.1.1 LIPSEY ON THE PHILLIPS CURVE

Phillips had argued that a relationship between the rate of change of money wages and excess demand for labour was consistent with general economic principles, but he did not offer any theoretical analysis of this proposition. The most significant early attempt to give theoretical and statistical rigour to the Phillips Curve concept was made by Lipsey (1960). Lipsey began his theoretical analysis by examining the behaviour of wage rates in a micro-labour market. He went on to aggregate across micro-labour markets to derive a macro-economic relationship between money wages and unemployment, and we consider the validity of this procedure later in the chapter.

Following Lipsey, in figure 3.2 the supply and demand curves for a micro-labour market, i, are represented by S_iS_i and D_iD_i. A micro-labour market is defined as a market within which labour is more mobile than it is between markets. The supply and demand curves for labour are drawn as functions of the money wage. (Lipsey provides no explicit derivation of these curves, but this approach suggests he is making the implicit assumption that prices, and money wages in other sectors, can be taken as given. The supply and demand curves are then orthodox neoclassical microeconomic functions. It is this

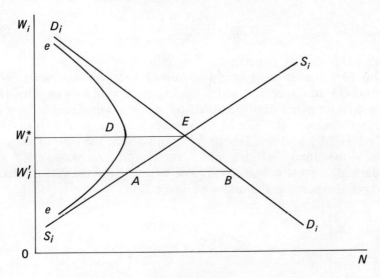

Figure 3.2

implicit assumption, that wages and prices elsewhere in the economy can be taken as given, that can create difficulties in going from the micro- to the macro-analysis, as we shall see later.)

The equilibrium wage, which equates supply and demand, in market i is OW_i^*. Suppose however that the current wage is only OW_i'. There is now excess demand of AB units of labour, and hence upward pressure on the wage rate. To equilibrate the market, wages must rise from OW_i' to OW_i^*. We must now consider what determines the speed with which wages rise in response to excess demand. The simplest and most intuitively plausible assumption to make is that the speed of the wage reaction is dependent on the ratio of excess demand to total labour supply.

$$\dot{W}_i = f\frac{(D_i - S_i)}{S_i} \qquad f' > 0 \qquad (3.1)$$

where

$$\dot{W}_i = \frac{dW_i}{dt} \times \frac{1}{W_i} \, .$$

Thus, the larger is the excess demand for labour, the faster will be the rate of adjustment in the wage rate. The simplest form of this relationship is a linear one, as assumed by Lipsey:

$$\dot{W}_i = a\frac{(D_i - S_i)}{S_i} \tag{3.2}$$

where a is a positive constant.

This function is illustrated in figure 3.3. If we start with excess demand OX in figure 3.3, which might correspond to wage OW_i' (and hence to excess demand measured by $AB/W_i'A$) in figure 3.2, money wages will increase at a rate $\dot{W}_{i1}$. As wages increase, as shown in figure 3.2, excess demand for labour falls, and hence the rate of wage increase slows down. After a while, the equilibrium wage, OW_i^*, will be reached. Excess demand will now be zero, and the rate of change of wages also zero, at the origin of figure 3.3.

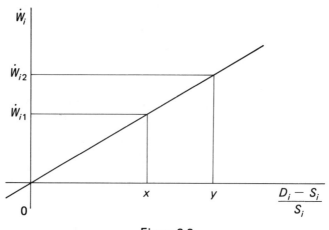

Figure 3.3

3.1.2 THE MEASUREMENT OF EXCESS DEMAND

Equation (3.1) relates the rate of change of money wages to the excess demand for labour, but there is, of course, no direct way of measuring the level of excess demand. Phillips and Lipsey both used the aggregate unemployment rate as a proxy measure of excess demand. In principle, unemployment could be quite a good proxy. The supply of labour consists of those in work (N) and those unemployed (U), while the demand for labour consists of jobs filled (which is the same as employment, N) and job vacancies (V). It follows that the excess demand for labour

$$D - S = (N + V) - (N + U) = V - U.$$

In the absence of reliable data on job vacancies, if it can be assumed that vacancies bear a stable (and inverse) relationship to unemployment rates, unemployment will be a good proxy for excess demand. The next step therefore is to examine the relationship between unemployment and vacancies.

3.1.3 UNEMPLOYMENT IN THE MICRO-LABOUR MARKET

Let us start by assuming the market is in equilibrium with wage OW_i^* (figure 3.2). This means that the demand for labour (the number of jobs available) is exactly equal to the supply (the number wanting to work) at that wage rate. If there were no frictions of any sort in the market, there would be no unemployment at the equilibrium wage. But as long as some workers are changing jobs, and it takes time for them to find a new job, there will be both unemployment and job vacancies in equilibrium. We call such unemployment 'frictional unemployment'. The curve *ee* in figure 3.2 illustrates the frontier of effective employment once frictional unemployment is allowed for, *DE* measures the equilibrium level of frictional unemployment, and also of job vacancies.

At a wage OW_i', where there is excess demand for labour, the level of frictional unemployment falls. The argument is that, as the surplus of jobs over the number of people looking for work increases, the average time it takes to find a suitable job will fall. But, however much the level of excess demand increases, frictional unemployment can never become negative: the *ee* curve can come very close to the S_iS_i curve but can never cross it. It follows that, in conditions of excess demand, the relationship between excess demand and unemployment is nonlinear.[1]

This relation is illustrated in figure 3.4. In equilibrium $(D_i = S_i)$

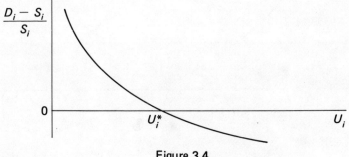

Figure 3.4

unemployment is positive, and the equilibrium level of frictional unemployment is denoted U_i^*. As excess demand increases unemployment falls, but the relationship is nonlinear, as illustrated by the part of the curve to the left of U_i^* in figure 3.4.

If the wage is higher than OW^* there is an excess supply of labour, and unemployment is measured by the distance between the *ee* curve and the S_iS_i curve in figure 3.2. In so far as unemployment is now largely a consequence of market disequilibrium (the gap between the S_iS_i and D_iD_i curves), the level of unemployment itself becomes quite an accurate measure of excess supply. We can therefore assume that, in conditions of excess supply, the unemployment excess demand relationship becomes approximately linear. This is shown by the position of the curve on the right of U_i^* in figure 3.4.

It is now only necessary to combine the two relationships:

$$\dot{W}_i = a\frac{(D_i - S_i)}{S_i} \quad a > 0$$

and

$$U_i = f\frac{(D_i - S_i)}{S_i} \quad f' < 0$$

in order to yield a testable relationship between the rate of change of wages and the level of excess demand. These relationships are combined graphically in figure 3.5. This figure illustrates another form of

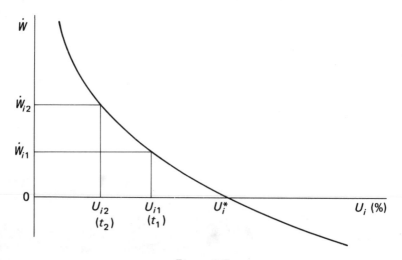

Figure 3.5

the market reaction function, which is essentially the same as that illustrated in figure 3.3, the difference between the two being that in figure 3.5 the unemployment rate is used as an approximate indicator of the true level of excess demand used in figure 3.3. The formulation of the reaction function illustrated in figure 3.5 is theoretically inferior to that in figure 3.3 but yields a testable relation. The main part of this function is nonlinear, but in the range $U_i > U_i^*$ will be linear by assumption (i.e., both of the functions combined to yield this reaction function were linear in that range). In functional form this relation will be described by some equation of the general form $\dot{W}_i = \alpha + \beta U_i^{-c}; U_i < U_i^*$.

Consider how to interpret this reaction function. At time t_1 we observe that the unemployment rate is U_{i1} and that wages are increasing at a rate of $\dot{W}_{i1}$. This means that the market is in disequilibrium during period t_1 with unemployment (which is an index of excess demand) of $U_i^* - U_{i1}$, and that wages are rising to equilibrate the market at a rate $\dot{W}_{i1}$. In period t_2 we now observe that unemployment has fallen to U_{i2} and the rate of increase of wages has increased to $\dot{W}_{i2}$. We may say here that over the period shifts in the supply or demand schedules must have occurred at a faster rate than the equilibrating increase in wages and that the disequilibrium has increased as a result. If no shifts in the supply and demand schedules had occurred after the initial disequilibrium in period t_1 was observed, then in some subsequent period t_2, $\dot{W}_i$ would be zero and unemployment U_i^*; i.e., the disequilibrium would have been eliminated by the equilibrating rise in the wage rate, and unemployment and vacancies would be equal at U_i^*.

3.1.4 PERSISTENT EXCESS DEMAND

In order to explain the continuous tendency for wages to rise where positive excess demand exists, we have been required to conceive of a situation in which the demand curve is displacing more rapidly in time than the supply curve. This is not entirely satisfactory, but it is an inevitable consequence of partial equilibrium analysis. While it is true that the nature of the continuous inflationary process does involve a persistent growth of labour demand in excess of the growth of labour supply in individual markets, it is helpful to recall the analysis contained in the income—expenditure models. That analysis showed that, when real expenditure exceeded real output (usually as a consequence of government policy), money wages and prices would inflate. (Persistent inflation can, of course, occur for other reasons, such as those discussed in relation to the expectations hypothesis and cost-push models.) At the macroeconomic level this is a simple concept. However, while it is the case that this process must operate in the micro-markets, it is difficult to conceptualize the disaggregation. With this caveat in mind, we shall continue to conceive of persistent excess demand in micro-labour markets as a process of dynamic displacement of supply and demand curves at differential rates.

3.1.5 LIPSEY'S AGGREGATION PROCEDURE

Assume that there are only two labour markets in the economy, and that mobility within each market is greater than between the markets. Further, assume that in each labour market the $\dot{W} = f(U)$ reaction function is identical and that labour supply in each market is equal. Aggregation of the two markets, a and b, is very simple under these assumptions:

$$U = \frac{U_a + U_b}{2} \quad \text{and} \quad \dot{W} = \frac{\dot{W}_a + \dot{W}_b}{2}.$$

Now, if both markets experienced the same proportional rate of unemployment, aggregate unemployment would be equal to each market rate; i.e., $U_a = U_b = U$. Similarly, since the reaction function is identical for both markets, the rate of change of wages in each market would be the same and would also equal the macro-rate of wage increases; i.e., $\dot{W}_a = \dot{W}_b = \dot{W}$. Thus the macro-reaction function would be identical to each of the micro-functions for all situations in which $U_a = U_b$. A different situation would arise however where U_a was not equal to U_b.

Assume that aggregate unemployment, U, is equal to U^* in figure 3.4. Now by definition

$$\frac{U_a + U_b}{2} = U = U^*.$$

Now let $U_a < U_b$. Taking a simple hypothetical example, we may specify that $U_a = U^* - x\%$, and that $U_b = U^* + x\%$. Obviously, the average unemployment rate is U^*, and U_a is less than U^* by the same number of percentage points as U_b is greater than U^*.

Figure 3.6 illustrates this situation. The reaction function illustrated in the diagram is the micro-function for both market a and market b.

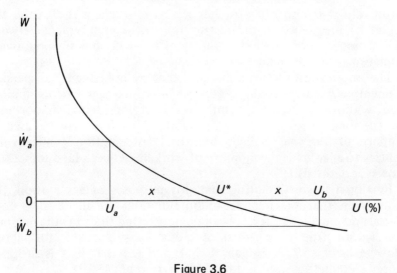

Figure 3.6

If unemployment rates in each market were equal, this reaction function would also obtain for the macro-market. It may however be seen by inspection that, when average unemployment is U^* but unemployment in market b is U_b and in market a is U_a, then the average rate of increase in wages will be positive.[2] This is so because the positive rate of increase in wages in market a is numerically greater than the negative rate of reduction in wages in market b, and this in turn is a phenomenon that derives from the nonlinear configuration of the reaction function to the left of a. The macro-reaction function will therefore intersect the axis not at U^* but instead at some unemployment rate greater than U^*. Thus, because the rate of unemployment is unequally distributed between the two micro-markets, the macro-reaction function will be displaced upwards.

This phenomenon will obviously be true for all situations in which some markets experience an excess demand for labour whilst in others there is excess supply, that is, when structural unemployment exists. The foregoing analysis suggests therefore that at the macro-level it is not only the rate but also the distribution of unemployment that determines the location of the macro-reaction function. Thus, for any set of micro-markets with identical reaction functions, the macro-function that will be traced out to relate the average rate of change of wages as unemployment varies will be systematically above the micro-functions when unemployment is unequally distributed.

Intuitively it is also obvious that if this is so then, the greater the degree of inequality in the distribution of unemployment between the various micro-markets, the greater will be the rightward displacement of the macro-function.

The implication of this argument, that by reducing the dispersion of unemployment it should be possible to reduce aggregate unemployment without an increase in inflation, is of considerable importance for economic policy. Arguments along these lines can be used in support of regional policy, industrial intervention policies and policies to encourage the mobility of workers between labour markets (however defined).

Finally it is worth noting that, for purposes of aggregation, the assumption that the micro-reaction functions are identical is both crucial and unrealistic. It has been demonstrated that: (a) the assumption is not true of regional or industrial submarkets for labour (Bowers *et al.*, 1970; Sargan, 1971); and (b) that if it is dropped Lipsey's prediction need not hold (Bowers *et al.*, 1970).

3.1.6 THE LIPSEY APPROACH AND MACROECONOMICS

A more fundamental problem, as indicated earlier, is that one cannot necessarily go from a microeconomic to a macroeconomic relationship simply be aggregating over the individual micro-markets. The microeconomic analysis assumes that wages and prices in the rest of the economy can be taken as given, but this assumption is not valid when macroeconomic changes are being considered.

For example, if there is an increase in the price of coal (relative to the prices of other goods), the demand curve for coal-miners will shift out, there will be an excess demand at the existing wage, and wages will then rise to restore equilibrium, just as the Lipsey anslysis describes. But what if there is an inflationary gap in the economy as a whole, and a tendency for the prices of all goods to rise? Firms in market i will be able to charge higher prices for their output, so their demand for labour at each money wage will rise and there will be an excess demand for labour at the existing money wage in market i. Money wages in market i will then rise. In the Lipsey analysis, a new equilibrium is then reached and that is the end of the story. But, with a macroeconomic disturbance, as firms in market i raise their wages, they will find wages in other markets rising as well. The supply of labour to firms in market i, which with a neoclassical supply function will depend on relative wages to the different sectors, will then not increase. The supply curve S_iS_i in figure 3.2 will shift up because of the increased wages being offered in other sectors. There is also a possibility that aggregate monetary demand in the economy as a whole may rise as a result of a general increase in money wages, thus shifting out the demand curve D_iD_i.

The implication is that, while in a microeconomic context, a rise in wages in response to excess demand will restore the market to equilibrium, the same does not follow for a macroeconomic disturbance. While excess demand in each market may still lead to wage increases in each market, consistent with the Lipsey analysis, these wage increases will not necessarily eliminate the excess demand. Lipsey's analysis is misleading in that, by neglecting the macroeconomic context, it gives the impression that adjustments in money wages can be relied on to return the system to full employment. But this does not, of course, detract from the model's value in analysing the relationship between excess demand and wage changes.

The discussion of the macroeconomic context suggests another point. If firms find their supply of labour curves shifting because of wage increases in other sectors, they may find it worthwhile to attempt to anticipate such shifts when deciding what wage to offer. If they do, the wage increases in each sector depends in part on the expected level of wage increases in other sectors. The development of this line of argument has been the most important advance in the analysis of inflation in recent years, and we will return to it in chapter 5.

In this section, we next examine the two other variables that Phillips found to influence money wage increases in his 1958 article. As well as finding a relationship between the rate of change of wages and the level of unemployment, $\dot{W} = f(U)$, Phillips found a relationship between the rate of change of unemployment and wage changes, $\dot{W} = g(\dot{U})$. Diagrammatically, this relation appeared in the form of 'loops' around the Phillips Curve. Lipsey explained the 'loops' in terms of unequally distributed unemployment in submarkets.

3.1.7 THE 'LOOPS'

Phillips noted that, in the course of a cycle, unemployment would be falling on the cyclical upswing and rising on the cyclical downswing. This is what we would expect if the rate of unemployment is an indicator of the level of demand. He further observed that when unemployment was rising the rate of change of wages was lower than would be expected at that rate of unemployment, and that when unemployment was falling the rate of change of wages was higher

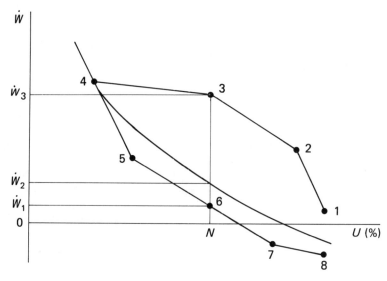

Figure 3.7

than would be expected at that rate of unemployment. This phenomenon can best be illustrated by observing a hypothetical cycle and
observing the relations sequentially.

In figure 3.7 the average macro-reaction function is shown with
eight annual observations, comprising a complete cycle, individually
illustrated. Each annual observation is linked to the observation for
the following year by a line. Two observations, for years 3 and 6,
were made for the same unemployment rate ON. Unemployment
is falling from year 1 to year 4 and rising from year 4 to year 8. The
rate of change of wages in years 1, 2 and 3 is systematically higher
than the average for those rates of unemployment as indicated by
the reaction function. The rate of change of wages is systematically
lower than the average for the years 5, 6, 7 and 8, when unemployment is rising.

Hence we have a loop around the macro-function and an apparent
relation between $\dot{W}$ and the rate of change of unemployment, $\dot{U}$.
Consider observations 3 and 6. Both observations were made at the
same level of unemployment ON at which the macro-function predicts
a rate of change of wages of $\dot{W}_2$. Observation 3 occurs when unemployment is falling (demand rising) and the actual $\dot{W}$ is $\dot{W}_3$. Observa-
6 is made when unemployment is rising (demand falling) and the
actual $\dot{W}$ is $\dot{W}_1$. This implies, as well as $\dot{W} = f(U)$, that $\dot{W} = g(U, \dot{U})$.
Phillips explains this phenomenon in terms of expectations. He says:

in a year of rising business activity, with the demand for labour in-
creasing and the percentage unemployment decreasing, employers
will be bidding more vigorously for the services of labour than they
would be in a year during which the average percentage unemploy-
ment was the same but the demand for labour was not increasing.

Conversely in a year of falling business activity, with the demand
for labour decreasing and the percentage unemployment increasing,
employers will be less inclined to grant wage increases, and workers
will be in a weaker position to press for them than they would be in
a year during which the average percentage unemployment was the
same but the demand for labour was not decreasing. [Phillips, 1958]

Phillips thought, then, that wage increases would be responsive not
only to current but to expected future labour market conditions, the
rate of change of unemployment being a good guide to the latter.
This raises the difficulty, as Lipsey has pointed out, that, if expected
future labour market conditions affect current wage settlements,
one might also expect them to influence firms' recruitment behaviour.
If so, the observed level of unemployment, as well as the observed
level of wage increases, would be shifted, and nothing could therefore be said, *a priori*, as to whether an expected tight labour market
in the future would lead to observations above or below the Phillips
Curve.

Lipsey (1960) suggested an alternative, but also rather unsatisfactory, explanation. He argued that the loops resulted from an
upward shift of the Phillips Curve during the upswing associated with
a greater dispersion of unemployment across micro-labour markets.
There is however no obvious reason why the dispersion should be
greater in the upswing than in the downswing. An empirical study
by Archibald (1969) found no support for Lipsey's suggestion, the
evidence indicating no correlation between the direction of change of
unemployment and its dispersion.

It must also be noted that Phillips had shown that loops were no
longer to be observed after the Second World War. A theory that
accounts for the loops in terms of very general arguments, such as
those mentioned above, cannot easily explain their apparently
sudden disappearance.

3.1.8 PRICE CHANGES

Phillips also observed a relation between changes in the cost of living
and the rate of change of money wages. He postulates a 'threshold
effect' in this relation. Basically, Phillips suggests that it is only when

the cost of living rises more rapidly that money wages (as a result of an increase in import prices) that this factor will influence the rate of change in wages. Where money wages are rising more rapidly than the cost of living, then 'employers will merely be giving under the name of cost of living adjustments part of the wage increases which they would in any case have given as a result of their competitive bidding for labour' (Phillips, 1958). In other words, he appears to suggest that, when demand factors induce rises in wages greater than the rise in the cost of living, there is already full compensation for price rises provided for in the wage rise; but that, when a reduction in the real wage is threatened by a faster rate of increase in the cost of living than in wages, then a cost of living adjustment on top of what would be induced by demand pressure will be added to wage rates. The evidence provided by Phillips on this hypothesis is very much of the nature of casual empiricism and is not particularly convincing.

The Phillips model therefore postulates three basic relations between the rate of change of money wages and its determinants. The rate of change of money wages is determined predominantly by the level of unemployment but also by the rate of change of that level, and by the rate of change of the cost of living when this rate exceeds the rate of change of wages that would be induced by demand pressures.

3.2 THE EMPIRICAL EVIDENCE

We turn now from the theoretical analysis underlying the Phillips Curve to the empirical estimates. Phillips's own estimation procedure (in the original 1958 article) was rather unorthodox, and we first outline his approach. Phillips started with the presumption, which was confirmed by his observations of inflation and unemployment over the whole period 1861–1957, that the relationship between unemployment and the rate of change of wage rates would be 'highly nonlinear'. He postulated a relationship of the form:

$$\dot{W} = a + bU^{-c} \tag{3.3}$$

or

$$\log(\dot{W} - a) = \log b - c \log U \tag{3.3a}$$

where a, b and c ($a < 0$; b, $c > 0$) are coefficients to be estimated.

Neither equation (3.3) nor (3.3a) can be estimated directly by standard linear regression analysis. If, however, we knew the value of a, equation (3.3a) might appear to be a straightforward equation, linear in logarithms, and b and c could be estimated by standard techniques. The immediate difficulty is that for some observations $\dot{W} < a$, so that the dependent variable in equation (3.3a) is the logarithm of a negative number, which does not exist. Of course, if equation (3.3a) were to hold exactly, for all observations, there would be no observations of $\dot{W} < a$. But equation (3.3a) does not hold exactly, in part because of random errors but in part also because it omits the change in unemployment terms. Phillips's procedure was to group the observations in class intervals based on the level of unemployment, each group including years in which unemployment was increasing and years in which it was decreasing. Hence, by taking group averages, the impact of changes in unemployment tends to be cancelled out, and the group averages can therefore be expected to fit equation (3.3a) more closely than the original observations.

Phillips then fitted equation (3.3a) on group averages for the period 1861–1913, after choosing the value of a by 'trial and error'. His estimated equation was:

$$\dot{W} + 0.900 = 9.638 \ U^{-1.394} \tag{3.4}$$

or

$$\log (\dot{W} + 0.900) = 0.984 - 1.394 \log U \tag{3.4a}$$

There are no standard tests of the statistical significance of the overall fitted relationship, or of the coefficients in the Phillips study. Inspection of the section diagrams plotted for each of the trade cycles suggests, however, that the relationship provides a good fit. (For a recent examination of Phillips's estimation procedures making use of modern econometric techniques, see Gilbert, 1976. Gilbert's paper also provides a rigorous account of the standard interpretation of Phillips's estimation set out above, and originally due to Lipsey, 1960, as against an alternative 'revisionist' interpretation suggested by Desai, 1975.)

3.2.1 LIPSEY'S TEST

An alternative estimation approach is to return to equation (3.3) and assume a particular value for the coefficient c. Equation (3.3) can then be estimated by standard techniques; there are no problems with negative logarithms necessitating the use of grouped data; and other explanatory variables can be included without difficulty. This was the basis of Lipsey's (1960) approach. Using much the same data as Phillips, he estimated an equation of the form

$$\dot{W} = \alpha_0 + \alpha_1 \, U^{-1} + \alpha_2 \, U^{-2} + \alpha_3 \, \dot{U} + \alpha_4 \, \dot{P}$$

with the coefficients on the unemployment terms selected on the basis of Phillips's estimates. The best fit for the 1861–1913 period was given by:

$$\dot{W} = -1.21 + 6.54U^{-1} + 2.26U^{-2} - 0.019\dot{U} + 0.21\dot{P} \quad R^2 = 0.85$$

Each of the variables in this equation has the sign suggested by the theoretical argument, and overall 85 per cent of the variation in the increase in wages can be associated with changes in unemployment and price increases (with the bulk of the variation being associated with changes in unemployment).

3.2.2 THE PERIOD 1923–57

The parameters of the equations set out above were estimated on data relating to the period 1862–1913. The application of these equations to data for the subsequent period yielded some interesting results, and these are set out briefly below.

(a) The basic equation that explains the variance in $\dot{W}$ in terms of U, $\dot{U}$ and $\dot{P}$ continues to perform well throughout the period.
(b) The variables U and $\dot{U}$ prove to be considerably less significant in explaining the variance in $\dot{W}$ after 1923 and especially so in the period 1947–57.

In general, the fitted macro-function relating $\dot{W}$ and U, which was the basic relation postulated by Phillips, changes over the period. For levels of U greater than 3 per cent the new relation lay above the old one, but for values of U less than 3 per cent the new curve lay below the old one. This shift is illustrated in figure 3.8.

It should be noted here that, while the general explanatory power of the three-variable model did not deteriorate in the postwar period, the explanatory power of U did deteriorate significantly. Indeed, the predictive power of the equation in the later years of the period depended more on the $\dot{P}$ variable than on any other. This change has some interesting implications, and we shall consider these in a more general context in chapters 5, 6 and 8.

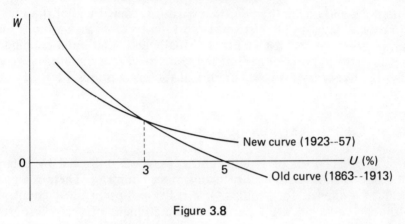

Figure 3.8

3.2.3 TESTS OF THE INTER-MARKET UNEMPLOYMENT DISTRIBUTION HYPOTHESIS

A prediction of the Lipsey model is that, the greater the inequality in the distribution of unemployment between submarkets, the greater will be the rate of wage inflation for a given level of average unemployment. Various tests of this hypothesis in different guises have been made. There are however a number of practical difficulties involved in devising a test. First, of course, there is the problem of defining a 'labour market'. Certain researchers have chosen to define a submarket in regional terms and have devised tests accordingly. (See Brechling, 1972; McKay and Hart, 1974a; Archibald, 1969; Thomas and Stoney, 1972.) Only Thomas and Stoney (1972) have claimed satisfactory results. Other work has concentrated on industrial labour markets (Sargan, 1971), but again has not produced conclusive results. We have tested a variant of the model in which specific institutional criteria are incorporated and an occupational definition of labour submarkets is used with modest success (Mulvey and Trevithick, 1974).

The second difficulty probably explains why no one has found empirical support for the Lipsey hypothesis. That is that the hypothesis depends crucially upon certain assumptions which may or may not be met in practice. We noted earlier that Bowers *et al* (1970) have shown that the predictions of the Lipsey model are accurate only when there exists a particular configuration of micro-reaction functions and a particular distribution of unemployment associated with them. Since it is virtually impossible to sort out the expected behaviour of the model from the actual structure of micro-reaction functions and unemployment that exists, a straight test of the Lipsey hypothesis is more likely to test the validity of its assumptions than its predictive power. The fact that virtually all of the empirical models based on the hypothesis have little predictive power therefore suggests that the hypothesis is based on unrealistic assumptions.

3.3 MEASUREMENT PROBLEMS

The original work of Phillips and Lipsey was followed by a large number of similar studies for many other countries. There is a good deal of evidence for Phillips-type relationships in most countries, although quite wide differences in the strength of the relationship and the slope and location of the curve (OECD, 1970; and for a discussion of this literature, see Santomero and Seater, 1978, section IV). An immediate issue raised by some of these studies concerned the appropriate measurement of the variables. The USA is an area of particular interest in this regard. A number of early attempts to relate $\dot{W}$ to U for the US economy yielded rather poor results, suggesting the presence of only a weak inverse relationship. This was especially the case for the postwar period (see Bhatia, 1961). But later studies, using refined data (Simler and Tella, 1968) and refined definitions of the variables (Perry, 1966), do appear to evidence a reasonably strong Phillips relation, including the postwar period. We first consider the excess demand for labour variables.

3.3.1 THE MEASUREMENT OF EXCESS DEMAND

Ideally, as we have shown earlier in the chapter, excess demand in the labour market is measured by the difference between 'true' vacancies and 'true' unemployment. The main problem in attempting to calculate such a measure is that the recorded vacancies data are often deficient. For example, in the UK data are collected on vacancies notified to employment offices. Firms are not compelled to register vacancies, and often there is no incentive for them to do so, so that the number of recorded vacancies falls far short of the true figure. It is for this reason that most empirical work has been based on the unemployment data alone, as a proxy for excess demand.

The data on unemployment, however, may themselves not be entirely reliable. Again referring to the UK, people have to register as unemployed in order to qualify for unemployment benefit, and for this reason one might expect the data on unemployment to be quite accurate. But the figures may none the less be misleading, because some unemployed people, though looking for work, may not be eligible for unemployment benefit (for example many married women in the UK), and because some people drawing unemployment benefit are not (or not very actively) looking for work.

Augmented unemployment variables The ideal unemployment series with which to proxy the excess demand for labour is one that measures the actual numbers of persons who are effectively not in employment but who are willing and able to work. Several studies have attempted to estimate the 'hidden unemployed' who are not registered as unemployed. Simler and Tella (1968) made estimates of this kind for the USA; Taylor (1970) has made similar estimates for the USA. The results of augmenting the unemployment data in this way have had mixed results in improving the explanatory power of unemployment in the wage equation. While Simler and Tella found the fit was improved for the USA, Perry (1970) found hidden unemployment to be insignificant. Taylor (1970) found the augmented unemployment variable did not perform better in the US wage equation than the straightforward unemployment variable. This suggests that hidden unemployment is related to registered unemployment in some fairly stable way over time. Taylor (1972) has introduced a different augmentation of the registered unemployed into the wage equation for the UK. He has made estimates of the rate of labour hoarding by employers (i.e., labour retained by employers which is surplus to current requirements) and has added this to the rate of registered unemployment. This augmented unemployment variable performs well in explaining the rate of change of earnings corrected for overtime, but does nor perform any better than registered unemployment as a regressor in the wage rate change equation.

Related to the idea of labour hoarding is the notion that employers adjust employment slowly to changes in demand. It follows that the level of unemployment at any period of time reflects the pressure of demand in previous periods, rather than that of the current period. On this argument, a good measure of the current pressure of demand will be the unemployment rate in the next period. MacKay and Hart (1974b) have examined, and found some support for, the hypothesis that wage increases should be related to future, rather than current, unemployment rates.

Unemployment and vacancies Dicks-Mireaux and Dow (1959) measured excess demand as the difference between vacancies and unemployment (as a proportion of the labour force). Though theoretically the correct construction, the inadequacies of the recorded vacancies data must throw some doubt on the value of this procedure in practice. In fact, Dicks-Mireaux and Dow achieved quite good results with their excess demand measure, though during their data period (the immediate postwar years in the UK) unemployment and vacancies tended to move rather consistently, so that different measures of excess demand could be expected to give similar results.

Generally, however, the unemployment measure was preferred to vacancies because of the more reliable data. It was only after the 'breakdown' of the standard Phillips Curve relationship (in the mid-1960s in the UK) that vacancy data (and other measures of excess demand) were taken seriously. We return to this point in section 3.4 below.

The measurement of wage changes So far we have used the term 'wages' in a loose way. Wages refer to negotiated wage rates (minimum or standard, time or piece) or to actual earnings (hourly or weekly), and certain issues arise in relation to which definition we use when we talk about wage inflation. The main such issue concerns the economic nature of the relationship between wage-rate changes and earnings changes. One school of thought (see Hines, 1964) holds that earnings inflate continuously in response to the continuous pull of excess demand, and that the periodic process of collective bargaining simply serves to consolidate the wage drift so generated in inter-bargaining periods into negotiated wage rates. Another school of thought (see OEEC, 1961) contends that wage drift tends to 'float' on top of negotiated wage rates, since it tends to be a largely institutionalized additive to basic rates, and that the rate of earnings inflation is determined mainly by wage rate inflation. Empirical tests have produced mixed results which suggest a certain amount of 'consolidation' and a certain amount of 'floating' in the wage rate— earnings change relation. A sophisticated study was carried out by Dicks-Mireaux and Shepherd (1962) for the UK (wage drift is not a significant phenomenon in the USA), and they found evidence of a significant consolidation effect but by no means as strong an effect as estimated by the OEEC study (1961). Ashenfelter and Pencavel (1974) have argued that the determinants of weekly earnings change in the UK since the war have been wage rate changes together with increased overtime working.

If the Phillips Curve relationship is thought to derive from a Lipsey-style model of the labour market, the wage variable should measure the price per unit of labour input. No one variable is self-evidently the correct measure. Changes in earnings per worker, for example, may indicate changes in the amount of labour input per worker (as a result of overtime working) rather than changes in the price per unit. Wage rates are the major (but by no mean always the only) determinant of the price per unit of labour input, and are thus usually the preferred measure. A problem with wage rates, though, is that, once negotiated, they are fixed until they are due for re-negotiation, and hence they do not respond at all to changes in the pressure of demand during the contract period. For this reason, Ashenfelter and Pencavel (1974) have suggested that the wage index should take account of the fraction of workers receiving wage increases in each period. (For further discussion of these points see Taylor, 1972, and Ashenfelter and Pencavel, 1974.)

3.4 THE BREAKDOWN OF THE PHILLIPS CURVE

During the mid-1960s the Phillips Curve appeared to lose almost all its explanatory power. This phenomenon was observed in almost all industrialized countries, but was most marked in the UK. We have already set out some of the evidence in chapter 1. Suffice it to say here that during the late 1960s and 1970s inflation has shown a tendency to persist and to accelerate, while at the same time unemployment has risen to levels far higher than those experienced in the 1950s and early 1960s. This turn of events has caused a great deal of consternation among economists, initially because they had no explanation for what was happening or any agreed policies for dealing with the new problems. There was therefore a need to re-formulate the theoretical analysis of inflation — and its relationship with unemployment — in a way that would account for the recent experience.

It is useful to distinguish the approaches that were considered at this stage under four main headings. First was the argument that unemployment was no longer an adequate indicator of the pressure of demand in the labour market. It was noted, for example, that the relationship between unemployment and other labour market variables, such as vacancies, had also shifted. While we do not intend to go into great detail on these issues here, in Appendix 2 to this chapter we discuss briefly the shift in the unemployment—vacancies relationship in the UK. It does, however, seem possible to draw two general conclusions, both for the UK and for other countries. The tendency for unemployment rates to rise relative to other labour market indicators does seem to be a general phenomenon, which would be associated with an outward shift of the Phillips Curve. But, whatever the labour market indicator one chooses, by no stretch of the imagination can the 1970s be described as a period of permanent and massive excess demand. The rapid inflation of recent years requires some other explanation.

In chapter 4 we consider a second explanation. This is the 'cost-push' approach, according to which inflation depends not so much on market forces as on the power or militancy of the trade unions. The power of organized labour, on this approach, enabled trade unions to force through whatever wage increases they decided upon, which their employers could, in turn, pass on in higher prices, almost irrespective of market conditions. On this approach there need be little, if any, relationship between inflation and unemployment, and its proponents regarded the apparent breakdown of the Phillips Curve as a confirmation of their views. The main weakness with the 'cost-push' approach, however, was that its adherents were for a long time unable to offer any alternative theories to account for differences in inflation rates over time or across countries (other than by *ad hoc* references to various social, political or industrial events). We consider these issues in chapter 4, leaving discussion of the new incarnation of cost-push – the 'real wage resistance' hypothesis – to chapter 8.

The third explanation for the breakdown of the Phillips Curve is based on the idea that wage claims take account not only of excess demand but also of expected inflation. On this approach, there are two components to any wage change: one, based on excess demand, being an adjustment to an existing market disequilibrium, and one, based on expectations, being an adjustment to anticipated future changes in supply or demand. This approach leads to the 'expectations-augmented' Phillips Curve:

$$\dot{W} = f(U) + \dot{P}^e$$

where $\dot{P}^e$ is the expected rate of inflation. We consider the expectations approach in much more detail in chapter 5.

The expectations approach has, perhaps, been the major theoretical development in the economics of inflation in the postwar period. One particular development, embodying the concept of rational expectations, has led to a reinstatement of the classical monetary theory of inflation. We examine the monetarist revival in chapter 6.

Finally, there is the view that inflation is an international pheno-menon, to be explained not by domestic demand pressures but by supply and demand for goods in world markets. This approach gained support from the fact that inflation accelerated in most countries of the world at about the same time, during the late 1960s, and this could be associated with the very rapid growth in international liquidity at that time (caused by the financing of the Vietnam War). Similarly, the upsurge in inflation in many countries in the mid-1970s, following the increase in oil prices imposed by the OPEC countries in the autumn of 1973, suggests an international, rather than a purely domestic, perspective. We discuss these issues in chapters 7 and 8.

3.5 SUMMARY AND CONCLUSIONS

We began by noting that, if prices are determined as a mark-up on cost, rather than by supply and demand in product markets, price increases are mainly the result of cost increases and in particular of wage increases. A theory explaining the determinants of wage in-creases is thus the key to understanding the inflationary process. Phillips, proceeding by applying the general idea that excess demand causes prices to go up to the labour market, empirically derived a nonlinear relationship between the rate of change of money wages and the level of unemployment standing as a proxy for excess demand for labour. In addition, he suggested two subsidiary hypo-theses: (a) that the rate of change of unemployment affects em-ployers' expectations and therefore the rate of wage change; and (b) that price changes over a certain threshold also affect the rate of change of wages. The main prediction of Phillips's work therefore was that there would exist a trade-off between wage inflation and the level of excess demand for labour.

Lipsey supplied a theoretical underpinning for Phillips's work by considering an adjustment mechanism that would function within a micro-labour market and then proceeding to aggregate the micro-markets. As well as vastly improving the statistical specification of the Phillips Curve, which permitted more detailed analysis of its properties, Lipsey attempted to explain the phenomenon of the loops and advanced an additional prediction of the model: that the distribution of unemployment between submarkets as well as its overall rate would affect the rate of change of wages.

Phillips and Lipsey believed they had established the existence of a trade-off between wage inflation and excess demand for labour. Recent experience appears to have exploded this relationship, in that rapid inflation has been accompanied by high unemployment and a depressed demand for labour. It seems possible to explain the breakdown of the Phillips Curve in part by the fact that the relationship between unemployment and the pressure of demand in the labour market appear to have altered. But even when this, and other, measurement problems are allowed for, there is no doubt that a simple Phillips Curve relationship between money wage increases and the excess demand for labour no longer fits the facts. In subsequent chapters, we examine recent theoretical and empirical developments. In some — those based on the expectations or monetarist approach — the Phillips Curve relationship still has a central role, though only as part of the inflation theory. In other developments — those based on cost-push or 'real wage resistance' theories — the Phillips Curve relationship appears to play a much smaller part in accounting for recent inflationary experience.

APPENDIX 1 : THE PRICE EQUATION

So far we have concentrated our attention on the wage-change equation, but now we must consider the determinants of price changes. It was noted earlier that many models of the inflationary process appear to assume a passive price-change mechanism, where prices adjust in response to increases in unit costs, and there are two general versions of this model.

THE PURE MARK-UP MODEL

The first version of this model postulates that prices are fixed by summing unit prime costs and adding a fixed percentage mark-up to cover overheads and the profit margin. Dow (1956) employs such a model, and the main independent variables are changes in unit labour costs and import prices, both lagged and weighted. The change in the unit labour costs variable is calculated as changes in average money wages deflated by changes in output per man, which implies that prices will be responsive both to changes in the trend of the ULC (unit labour cost) index, and to short-run fluctuations, owing to cyclical factors, around that index. This is a significant point, since a model utilizing such a variable implies that the mark-up is on all non-capital costs rather than simply on prime costs. Nield (1963), as we shall see, makes an explicit distinction between these two possibilities.

In any case, the mark-up model takes the following general form on the assumption that the relative share of profits in the value of output is constant:

$$\dot{P}_t = \alpha_0 + \alpha_1 \dot{W}_t - \alpha_2 \left(\frac{\dot{X}}{N}\right) + \alpha_3 \dot{P}_{mt} \qquad (3.5)$$

where $\dot{P}$ is the rate of change of prices, $\dot{W}$ is the rate of change of money wages, $\dot{P}_m$ is the rate of change of import prices and $(\dot{X}/N)$ is the rate of change of average output per man. Hines (1964), Dicks-Mireaux (1961) and Klein and Ball (1959) have tested variants of this basic equation. In all cases the fit tends to be good.

THE 'NORMAL-COST' MODEL

Nield (1963) has adopted a slightly different approach to the construction of a price equation. Instead of accepting the pure mark-up hypothesis, he has postulated the idea of 'normal-cost' pricing. Normal cost pricing is a process of price-fixing based on the cost of some notional 'normal' output level rather than on actual current costs. Thus, when output and costs fluctuate in response to cyclical or other short-term factors, prices will not be adjusted. If on the other hand the costs of producing the 'normal' level of output change, prices will be adjusted accordingly. The most significant source of change in normal costs is likely to be the trend of unit labour costs, which are determined jointly by money wages per man-hour and the trend of output per man-hour. This implies that in the price equation the long-term trend of unit labour costs, rather than the simple money wage deflated by an output-per-man variable, should be included. This yields the following basic equation:

$$P = \alpha_0 + \alpha_1\beta_1 (ULC) + \alpha_2\beta_2 P_m ; \quad \beta_1 + \beta_2 = 1 \qquad (3.6)$$

where P is the price level (wholesale), ULC is the trend value of unit labour costs and P_m is the import price level (material and fuel). β_1 and β_2 are weights. Nield tested three extended forms of equation (3.6), using manufacturing index number series employing a complex system of geometrically declining weights to take account of all previous values of each series. (The weights therefore ensure that, the more distant in time any observation is, the less will be its impact on the value of the observation.) The three equations tested permitted a distinction to be made between productivity change resulting primarily from technological change (the trend of the *ULC* index) and changes in productivity resulting from short-term changes in demand (fluctuations around the trend of the *ULC* index). His results indicated that:

(a) the effect of changes in output per man on prices is symmetrical;
(b) only changes in the trend of the *ULC* index affect prices;
(c) short-run changes in productivity do not affect prices, probably because they reflect labour hoarding and dishoarding effects at different points in the cycle.

FURTHER TESTS OF THE 'NORMAL-COST' MODEL

The 'normal-cost' model has been subjected to careful analysis by Godley and Nordhaus (1972) and by Sargan (1980b). Godley and Nordhaus assume that prices are based on a mark-up on historic costs, so that output price increases lag behind input price increases because of the time taken for the inputs to go through the various stages of the production process. On the basis of observation of the length of these production lags, Godley and Nordhaus calculate a notional output price index as a mark-up on historic costs, given the levels of input prices. They find their calculated price index correlates closely with the actual behaviour of output prices. They then consider whether the actual price index (or mark-up) was affected by the pressure of demand in the goods market. They consider a number of different measures of excess demand, but none appears to be correlated with the mark-up. They deduce that firms' prices are entirely cost-determined, and are not affected by the pressure of demand in the market.

A rigorous econometric examination of the UK price equation has recently been carried out by Sargan (1980b). In his analysis, the time lag between changes in input prices and changes in output prices is computed by statistical techniques, rather that being derived from empirical observation. His conclusions as to the effects of the pressure of demand are, however, the same: namely, that firms price on the basis of costs and take no separate account of market demand.

PRICE EXPECTATIONS

We will argue in chapter 5 that expected inflation should influence wage increases, and on similar grounds one might argue that expected price changes should influence firms' pricing decisions. Solow (1969) was the first to attempt to incorporate price expectations in the UK price equation. His results suggest a more significant role for demand pressures than was the case with the 'normal cost' studies. We discuss studies incorporating price expectations in more detail in chapter 5.

PRICE EQUATIONS FOR OTHER COUNTRIES

A good survey of the state of knowledge on the price equation in the early 1970s is to be found in Eckstein (1972). Price equations for the USA appear generally to support the normal-cost hypothesis, with pressure of demand effects appearing rather erratically. There are, however, in many of these studies difficulties in interpreting whether particular variables (such as actual, rather than normal, unit labour cost) represent supply-side or demand-side effects. The conclusion to be drawn from a survey of these studies is that a significant impact of demand on the mark-up of prices over costs has not been identified (Nordhaus, 1972). Studies on European countries and on Canada (also surveyed in Eckstein, 1972) show a similarly mixed picture.

CONCLUSION

The evidence both for the UK and other countries suggests that there is no clearly identifiable effect of the pressure of demand on the mark-up of prices over normal costs. This evidence is normally interpreted as meaning that firms set their prices 'passively' to cover their costs and without reference to market demand. The implication is that, to understand why prices change, one need only discover why costs change, and in particular why wages change.

Such an interpretation is consistent with the UK studies, which identify a lag between cost increases and price increases. In a number of the US studies, however, prices are found to be a mark-up on current cost. This evidence is consistent with the view that prices respond to demand, but wages respond immediately to changes in prices.

More generally, the finding of a constant mark-up might be regarded as evidence not so much of the absence of an effect of demand on prices, but rather as an indication that prices and costs adjust to changes in demand at approximately the same speed. The logic of this argument implies that a properly specified price

equation should exclude endogenous cost factors (such as wages)
Some such equations — generally identified with the monetarist
approach — are discussed in later chapters.

APPENDIX 2 UNEMPLOYMENT AND VACANCIES IN GREAT BRITAIN

The belief that the relationship between unemployment and the
pressure of demand in the labour market has changed has received
some support from the fact that in Britain the relationship between
unemployment and vacancies also changed at about the same time.
Normally, one would expect that, because unemployment and
vacancies are both related to the pressure of demand in the labour
market, they will bear a stable, and inverse, relationship to one
another. In figure 3.9, male unemployment and vacancies are plotted

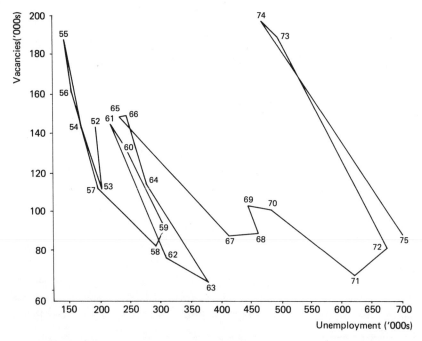

Figure 3.9 Male Unemployment and Vacancies, Great Britain, 1952–75.
'Vacancies' are those suitable for adults (since April 1974, those
notified to Employment Offices). June figures are shown (in thousands),
seasonally adjusted.
(Source: *Department of Employment Gazette*, 1976)

for the years 1952–1975: from 1952 to 1965 a relatively stable inverse relationship is observed, but after 1965 the relationship breaks down.

To account for this break-down one can argue that the relationship between the pressure of demand in the labour market and either unemployment or vacancies (or both) has changed since 1965. An official analysis of this question (Department of Employment, 1976) examined the various hypotheses that had been put forward to account for a rise in 'voluntary' unemployment, such as more generous unemployment or redundancy pay, but found the number of unemployed in receipt of such improved benefits too small to account for a significant shift in the relationship. The conclusion therefore was that it must be primarily the relationship between vacancies and the pressure of demand that had shifted, and a possible reason might be that the government had been encouraging employers to register vacancies at employment exchanges. The shift in the unemployment – vacancies relationship is thus attributed to an increase in the proportion of vacancies registered, and hence recorded in the statistics.

The official explanation, set out above, is however not very convincing. First, there are other indicators of the pressure of demand in the labour market, and these tend to show that it is the unemployment figures, rather than the vacancy figures, that are out of line. Figure 3.10 shows unemployment, vacancies and a Confederation of British Industries (CBI) series recording the proportion of manufacturing firms reporting that their production was constrained by shortages of skilled labour. To the extent that the CBI series can be taken as an indication of actual labour shortages, there appears to have been no significant shift in the relationship between such shortages and notified vacancies.

Second, the official explanation, which suggests a massive excess supply in the labour market throughout the 1970s – a period of rapid and often increasing inflation – entails a complete abandonment of the idea that wage increases might be related to the pressure of demand. As figure 3.10 shows, the vacancy series suggests some periods of excess demand during the 1970s, and these periods (1973/4, 1978/9) did in fact precede increases in the inflation rate.

If one accepts, from the evidence of other labour market indicators and from the evidence from the inflation rate, that the relationship between vacancies and the pressure of demand has not changed at all significantly, one is thrown back to the problem of accounting for the rise in unemployment. It seems clear that purely economic

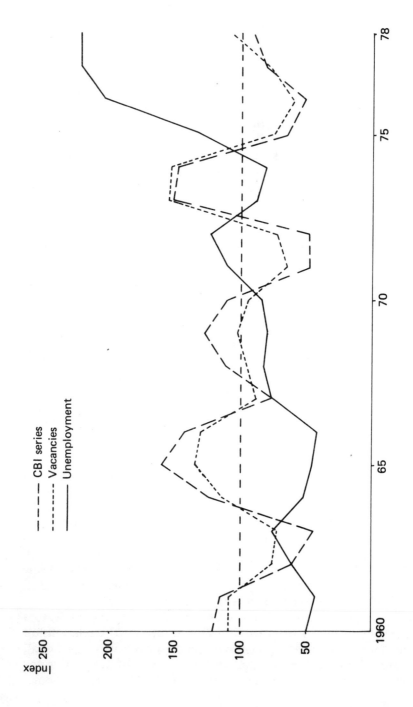

Figure 3.10   (Source: *Department of Employment Gazette, 1976*; CBI surveys)

arguments cannot explain the size of increase that has been observed (for a recent study of the impact of unemployment benefit, see Nickell, 1979). A change in social attitudes may have been much more important. For example, in the 1950s there was much more of a stigma attached to drawing unemployment benefit than there was during the 1970s (in part a result of government policy encouraging those eligible to unemployment benefits to claim them). If the stigma had deterred people from claiming benefit in the 1950s and early 1960s, data on registered unemployment would be artificially depressed relative to the true level of unemployment during those years.

This very brief account has served to raise some of the main issues in the discussion, rather than to provide a full analysis. None the less, it does appear reasonable to conclude that the level of unemployment accompanying any given level of excess demand in the labour market has been rising steadily since the mid-1960s, for reasons that are not well understood, and that this drift in the relationship between unemployment and excess demand is one factor in the breakdown of the conventional Phillips Curve relationship.

NOTES

1. Figure 3.2 carries the implication that, as excess demand increases, not only does unemployment fall but employment decreases also. This is a consequence of drawing the supply curve upward-sloping, which is consistent with economic theory for a micro-labour market. The aggregate supply curve of labour need not be upward-sloping, however. For example, if it were vertical we can draw an *ee* locus downward-sloping throughout its length, so that an increase in excess demand would be associated both with a fall in unemployment and with a rise in employment.

2. This result, though it appears intuitively obvious, does not necessarily always hold. In deriving aggregate unemployment rates, individual sectors are, implicitly, being weighted according to the size of their labour forces, while in deriving the aggregate inflation rate individual sectors are, implicitly, being weighted according to their wage bills. Peston has shown that, because of the different weights being employed, a greater dispersion in unemployment could in fact be associated with a lower aggregate rate of wage increases. However, this appears to be a statistical curiosum of little practical significance (see Peston, 1971).

CHAPTER 4

Cost Inflation and the Trade Unions

Central to the model of Keynes's General Theory is the proposition that money wages do not fall rapidly even in the face of massive unemployment. Social and institutional factors, such as workers' concern with their relative wages and the power of the trade unions, can, according to Keynes, have more influence on wage bargains than the pressure of demand in the labour market. In times of deep depression these institutional forces can prevent cuts in money wages, as shown by the experience of the 1930s. As a natural extension of this argument, one might suppose that these same institutional forces could bring about an increase in money wages when the economy is nearer to full employment, even before the appearance of excess demand. Inflation that results from this process is called cost-push inflation (the increase in costs pushing up prices in the absence of excess demand in the market), as distinct from demand-pull inflation (where excess demand pulls up prices and wages).

Since the war, the most important controversy concerning the sources of inflation has been between the cost-push and the demand-pull camps. Within each camp there are, of course, many differences of opinion. But the demand-pull camp are united in the belief that the main cause of inflation is excess demand in the economy as a whole. It follows that a policy of demand restraint is essential for the control of inflation. In the cost-push camp, on the other hand, the main causes of inflation are believed to be social and institutional, and largely if not completely independent of the level of demand in the economy. Inflation can be controlled, on this interpretation, only by devising an institutional framework to restrain individual wage claims in the common good. A prices and incomes policy may seem to offer most hope in these circumstances.

The rival camps have disputed with each other over both the theoretical analysis of the inflationary process and the formulation and interpretation of empirical hypotheses. In the process each camp has developed its position. The demand-pull group have in particular stressed the role of expectations in the inflationary process (see chapters 5–7), while the cost-push group have increasingly come to emphasize the importance of 'real wage resistance' (chapter 8). In this chapter, however, we are concerned with some of the earlier theories of cost-push inflation, which give particular emphasis to the role of trade unions in the labour market.

4.1 A SIMPLE MODEL OF COST INFLATION

The current inflation consists of a social dispute about the distribution of the national income; persistent attempts by many social groups to increase their consumption faster than is consistent with the aims of other groups or with macroeconomic stability; persistent consequential bidding up of the price level in a wage–price or wage–wage spiral. [Posner, 1973]

The logic of this position may be formalized by considering the following highly simplified model in which W_B is the money wage bill, Z_B is the money profit bill, the real value of national income is constant, and money national income, Y, is totally exhausted by the incomes of wage-earners and profit-earners; i.e., $Y = Z_B + W_B$. Moreover, let the subscript t denote the magnitude of any variable at time t. A condition for zero inflation is that the following relationship should hold *ex ante*:

$$Y_t = (\alpha_1 + \alpha_2)Y_t \qquad (4.1)$$

where α_1 and α_2 are the shares of wages and profits in national income. Clearly, $(\alpha_1 + \alpha_2) \equiv 1$, *ex post*. What is important is that each income-receiving group should be satisfied with the realized division of national income. Should one group be dissatisfied with its income share, then the sum of the desired shares in national income may exceed unity; i.e., $(\alpha_1 + \alpha_2) > 1$.

In order to determine the dynamic properties of this model, we shall assume that equation (4.1) is initially satisfied *ex ante* but that one group (in our example, wage-earners) becomes dissatisfied with its share of national income. More specifically, we shall assume that, in period 1, the money wage bill rose in an attempt to establish the following relationship between wages and money income:

$$W_{B1} = \alpha_1' \, Y_0$$

where α_1' is the new *ex ante* wage share. It is now assumed that profit-earners, in an effort to restore the *status quo ante*, raise prices by an amount just sufficient to maintain the initial share of profits in national income. If profit-earners react instantaneously in defence of their income shares, the following equation will hold:

$$Z_{B1} = \alpha_2 \, Y_1.$$

If a similar reaction pattern persists for all succeeding periods, the resulting equation for money national income will be:

$$Y_t = \alpha_1' \, Y_{t-1} + \alpha_2 \, Y_t = \left(\frac{\alpha_1'}{1 - \alpha_2} \right) Y_{t-1}. \tag{4.2}$$

The first-order difference equation (see Baumol, 1951) is of the simplest possible nature and produces a solution:

$$Y_t = Y_0 \left(\frac{\alpha_1'}{1 - \alpha_2} \right)^t. \tag{4.3}$$

Since we have been assuming throughout that real income is constant, equation (4.3) is also an equation in the price level, P_t. By the appropriate manipulation we may derive the following expression for the rate of inflation:

$$\dot{P} = \frac{\alpha_1'}{1 - \alpha_2} - 1. \tag{4.4}$$

The rate of inflation will be zero if and only if $\alpha_1' = 1 - \alpha_2$. That is, $\dot{P} = 0$ if the amount claimed by labour is equal to the amount conceded by capital. Should the two groups be engaged in some sort of class struggle for shares in national income, then $\alpha_1' > (1 - \alpha_2)$ and the claims on national income cannot be satisfied simultaneously. The more intense the struggle for income shares (i.e., the larger is the discrepancy between α_1' and $(1 - \alpha_2)$), the higher will be the rate of inflation.

The basic model can be elaborated and extended in a number of directions. For example, the introduction of fixed income groups who are unable to defend themselves against the ravages of inflation could provide an important stabilizing factor in reconciling the competing claims of other economic groups (see Holzman, 1950). Money illusion could also fill a similar role. Moreover, a complex model could be devised in which competitive and non-competitive markets coexist side by side and in which inflationary inpulses are transmitted from one group of markets to the other (see Duesenberry, 1950).

The cost-push hypothesis may also be expressed in what is possibly a more familiar guise by disaggregating the analysis to take account of rivalry, not between different broad categories of income recipient, but between different groups within the same broad income category. For example, a notable feature of recent British experience has been the growing friction between members of different unions, each union vying with others to establish or maintain a 'fair' pattern of wage differentials between comparable groups of workers. The evidence in support of this 'comparability' hypothesis will be surveyed later in this chapter. At this stage all that is necessary is to restate the cost-push hypothesis in terms of a more disaggregated model.

Consider n different categories of labour so that there are $(n-1)$ wage differential ratios W_2/W_1, W_3/W_1, ... W_n/W_1. Define

$$\frac{W_2}{W_1} = \beta_2, \frac{W_3}{W_1} = \beta_3, \ldots, \frac{W_n}{W_1} = \beta_n$$

(note that $\beta_1 = 1$). If the set of differentials $\beta_2, \beta_3, \ldots, \beta_n$ is generally regarded as just and equitable by all of the participants in the wage bargain, then there will be no tendency for one group to make a wage claim so as to improve its relative position on the scale of differentials. On the other hand, if one group, dissatisfied with its own relative position in the pecking order, unilaterally attempts to leapfrog some other groups, this will set in motion a chain reaction among all other groups in an effort to restore what was generally considered to be a fair structure of differentials. All money wages will tend to move in sympathy with that of the dissatisfied group. Such behaviour bears a close resemblance to the simple model outlined above, since the inflationary impulse arises from the fact that the *ex ante* and *ex post* values of at least one element of the vector $(1, \beta_2, \beta_3, \ldots, \beta_n)$ are out of line.

In simple models of this type the rate of inflation is determined by the excess of the total claims of the various groups in the economy over the total of income available. The main weakness of these models is that they offer no theories as to what determines the total of claims in the economy. The models thus have no empirical content: they cannot explain why inflation rates vary over time or across countries, nor can the models be refuted by any empirical evidence.[1] Further, the notion of people being satisfied or dissatisfied with their share of the national income, though intuitively quite plausible, is at odds with the normal axioms of economic behaviour. Normally one assumes that households maximize utility and firms maximize profits, each subject to various constraints, and it is not clear how a struggle for shares of income fits into this framework.

We have spoken of cost-push inflation as resulting from the impact of social and institutional forces on the wage bargain. It seems logical therefore to attempt to build up a theory of cost-push inflation from these institutional factors in the labour market. Most obvious is the role of the trade unions, to which we now turn.

4.2 TRADE UNIONS AND THE LABOUR MARKET

Almost half of the labour force in the UK, and about a quarter in the USA, are members of trade unions, and their wages are fixed in collective bargaining between the unions and employers. Moreover, many of those employees who are not members of trade unions effectively have their wages fixed in accordance with the outcome of collective bargaining by way of convention, third-party decision or defensive employer tactics. While there is no way of estimating the extent to which collective bargaining determines wage rates in practice, it is safe to say that a majority of wages are effectively determined by the outcome of collective bargaining. We must now therefore recognize that wage inflation is largely the result of the outcomes of a series of collective bargains.

To recognize that wage inflation is largely the outcome of a collective bargaining process is not to suggest that the bargaining process itself affects the process of inflation. The market requires that there be some kind of administrative machinery (however atomistic) whereby market-determined wage adjustments are translated into actual pay changes and wage offers. There is no reason to suppose that such machinery will necessarily affect the process of wage inflation. Collective bargaining is however a rather special form of machinery for fixing pay, since it is intended to reduce or eliminate the competitive element in the supply of labour and to affect the market adjustment process as a result.

In chapter 3 we had assumed that wages would adjust at a rate determined by the excess demand for labour (pp. 34–6). We may write this 'competitive' wage adjustment relationship in the form

$$\dot{W} = aE \tag{4.5}$$

where

$$E = \frac{D-S}{S}$$

where E is the proportional excess demand for labour, D is the demand for, and S the supply of, labour.

We now hypothesize that the effect of collective bargaining is to alter the wage adjustment equation, which we now write as

$$\dot{W} = bE + z \quad b \leqslant a \quad z \geqslant 0. \tag{4.6}$$

Equation (4.6) differs from (4.5) in two ways. First, it allows for the possibility that collective bargaining may bring about wage increases even in the absence of excess demand in the labour market (represented by $z > 0$). Second, it suggests that collective bargaining may dampen the responsiveness of wage bargains to changes in the pressure of demand in the labour market (that is, $b < a$). In the extreme cost-push case, wage increases are independent of excess demand ($b = 0$).

In figure 4.1, these wage adjustment hypotheses are translated into Phillips Curves (drawn as straight lines for convenience). Case (a) is where the activities of trade unions are neutral and the process of collective bargaining yields the same outcome as competitive market prices ($b = a$, $z = 0$). In case (b), the trade union achieves a higher

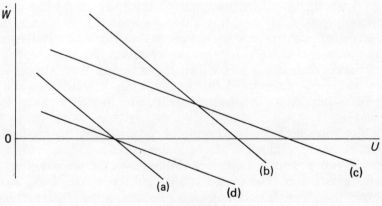

Figure 4.1

money wage increase at each level of demand through the exercise of market power, but the outcome of the wage bargain remains as responsive to the pressure of demand as in the competitive market ($b = a, z > 0$). In figure 4.1 case (b) is thus drawn parallel to case (a), and vertically above it. Case (c) has the trade union affecting the slope as well as the position of the Phillips Curve ($b < a, z > 0$), corresponding to the idea that wage settlements are less responsive to market conditions under collective bargaining than modern competitive conditions. By obstructing market forces, the trade union may do better for its members when the pressure of demand is low, but in times of very high demand it may get in the way of its members securing as rapid a rate of wage increases as market forces would have brought about. In case (d), trade unions do not impart on inflationary bias but serve only to slow down the responsiveness of wage increases to the pressure of demand ($b < a, z = 0$). This view of the impact of collective bargaining has been put forward by Friedman (1951).

4.3 THE NATURE AND MEASUREMENT OF TRADE UNION POWER

Trade unions derive power from the exercise of collective (as against individual) bargaining over wages. This power enables unions to fix wages at a level higher than that which could be obtained in the absence of collective action, and may enable unions to secure a more rapid rate of wage increases at some levels of excess demand than would result in their absence. The advantages of collective bargaining can best be explored within the context of a 'bargaining model' of wage determination. Bargaining models normally postulate a bilateral monopoly model of the firm, which places limits on the maximum wage the firm can pay, and the minimum the union can accept (derived from the market demand for the firm's product and from competition for workers from other employers, respectively). Within these limits the outcome is determined by the bargaining strength and skills of the two sides. A good survey of bargaining models is given by de Menil (1971).

While bargaining models are useful for analysing the implications of collective bargaining, it is important to stress at the outset that they do not provide a theory of the impact of trade union activity on wage inflation. The reason is that collective bargaining enables workers to achieve a once-and-for-all increase in their wages (relative to the non-unionized level), but it does not enable them to achieve a permanently faster rate of wage increases. There is the analogy with the conventional theory of monopoly: once the monopolist has set his profit-maximizing price he has no incentive to go on pushing up his price further. His most profitable course, having set the profit-maximizing price, is to change it only in response to increases in demand or in costs. Each increment of monopoly power in the economy brings about a once-and-for-all increase in prices, but subsequently price increases are independent of the amount of monopoly in the economy. On the basis of bargaining models, increases in unions' collective bargaining power have similar once-and-for-all effects. It is for reasons of this sort that many economists (see, e.g., Parkin, 1975) have concluded that the predictions of bargaining models concerning inflation are no different from those of excess demand models.

In this section we consider the mechanisms through which collective action can increase wages within the framework of a bargaining model. We also discuss the relationship between this approach and the representation of union power as shifts in the Phillips Curve (as sketched out in the previous section).

The advantages of collective bargaining are generally held to fall into three categories:

(a) information and expertise: the union negotiator will have more skill and experience in bargaining and better knowledge of the market and the employer's circumstances than individual workers;

(b) power: the ability to impose substantial costs on the employer through strikes or other forms of collective action (whereas the only sanction available to the individual worker is to quit);

(c) militancy: because of its greater size and impact, a union's wage policy may be motivated in part by political or institutional considerations, which would be futile for an individual worker.

We next consider these points in a little more detail. (For more extensive discussion, see Holt, 1971; Levinson, 1966; and Purdy and Zis, 1974.)

4.3.1 INFORMATION AND EXPERTISE

A trade union has greater capacity to gather and marshal information relevant to a wage demand, and will have greater skill in using this information in bargaining, than an individual worker. This advantage derives simply from the fact that trade unions have greater resources and more specialized bargaining expertise than individuals.

In particular, trade unions will have access to more accurate and up-to-date information on the profitability of companies, and of developments in the market and in productivity, so they can better evaluate what the employer can afford to pay, and the likely strength of employer resistance to wage claims. Additionally, trade unions may have a better idea of likely developments in retail prices, and wage claims elsewhere in the economy, than would individual workers.

The information advantage of a trade union, taken on its own, appears to imply that wages of unionized workers would adjust more quickly to changes in economic circumstances — both upwards and downwards — than would wages of non-unionized workers. To set against this is the point that, because of trade unions' organization and formal procedures, it will actually take longer for wages to adjust in the union sector. In times of labour shortages, for example, employers of non-unionized labour may bid up wages rapidly in an attempt to recruit more workers, while employers of unionized labour will be bound by agreements reached through collective bargaining procedures. In terms of the speed of adjustment, an 'organizational lag' introduced by the trade unions may well exceed the reduction in the 'information lag', with the result that trade union-negotiated wage rates react more slowly to market forces than non-union wage rates. It may be suggested that the trade union 'organizational lag' provides a possible justification for the belief that the Phillips Curve will be flatter if the labour force is unionized (pp. 69—70 above). It is true that, if the pressure of demand in the labour market fluctuates, the observed Phillips Curve will be flatter if there is a lag in wage adjustment. (In figure 4.1 we would observe curve (d) rather than curve (a).) But one cannot, of course, infer from this that if demand were maintained at a high level wage increases would be permanently lower with a unionized labour force. To take a simple example, we might write the non-union wage equation as

$$W_t = a\,E_t \tag{4.7}$$

which is equation (4.5) with subscripts to denote that wage increases in time t depend on excess demand in time t. The union wage equation might then be written

$$W_t = a.\ \left(\frac{E_t + E_{t-1}}{2}\right) \tag{4.8}$$

the lagged excess demand term representing the organizational lag introduced by the trade unions.

If excess demand fluctuates through a cycle, say $(0, 1, 0, -1, \ldots)$ then wage increases will also fluctuate through a cycle, which is in the non-union case (from equation (4.7)), $(0, a, 0, -a, \ldots)$ and in the union case (from equation (4.8)), $(-\frac{1}{2}a, \frac{1}{2}a, \frac{1}{2}a, -\frac{1}{2}a, \ldots)$, giving the flatter Phillips Curve.

If, however, excess demand is zero up to time t, and 1 thereafter, wage increases will also be zero up to time t, with or without unions, and will rise to a in period $t + 1$ in the non-union case (equation (4.7)) but only to $\frac{1}{2}a$ in period $t + 1$ in the unionized case (equation (4.8)). But in period $t + 2$ and all subsequent periods wage inflation will be a according to either equation. The flatter union Phillips Curve is only a transitory phenomenon.

4.3.2 POWER

By means of collective action such as strikes or other forms of disruption of production, trade unions can impose much larger costs on employers than can workers acting individually. While a firm can normally replace, or do without, individual workers, it cannot replace or do without its entire labour force. A firm facing an all-out strike can produce nothing and hence will have no income. All firms have some fixed costs, and hence make a loss during the period of a strike. Such losses can force firms into bankruptcy. Thus a union armed with the strike threat has considerable power.

At the same time, of course, a strike entails cost for the union's members in the form of loss of pay during the strike, and potential future losses of pay or employment opportunities resulting from orders or customers the firm may lose during the course of the strike. It can be argued that, at times of full employment, workers can easily find jobs elsewhere, and hence the cost they incur as a result of a strike − even one that results in their employer's bankruptcy − can be minimal. In this extreme case, the unions will clearly have the upper hand in wage bargaining and can to a large extent lay down terms for wages and employment. Even in a completely union-dominated firm, the wages that can be paid are limited by the firm's revenue and its investment requirements. The union-dominated firm behaves rather like a textbook monopoly, except with the monopoly profits being diverted to the union.

The more normal case, however, is one in which workers have skills specific to, or preferences for working in, their particular firm, and hence have an interest in its future prospects. Strikes now impose serious costs on both employer and workers; both have an incentive to settle a dispute quickly, and each side tries to trade on the costs of a strike to the other side by trying to negotiate a settlement to their own advantage. Situations of this sort can be analysed with the use of bargaining models, of which one of the first, and best known, is that of Hicks (which was originally developed in the mid-1930s but reformulated in the 1960s — see Hicks, 1968).

We do not have the space here to do more than sketch the outlines of Hicks's model. It is based on the idea that the costs of a strike, both for employer and for the union, increase with the duration of the strike. In figure 4.2. the curve marked *CC* is the 'employer's concession curve', indicating that the longer the strike lasts the higher is the wage that the employer is prepared to concede. The curve *RR* is the 'union resistance curve', indicating that the longer the strike goes on for, the lower is the wage the union is prepared to accept. Thus, in figure 4.2, after a strike of length D_E employer and union will be prepared to settle for a wage of W_E.

If the employer's concession curve were known to the union, and the union resistance curve known to the employer, both would recognize that they would settle at W_E, and it would be in the interests of both parties to agree to that outcome immediately and without a strike. However, as the figure shows, it is in the interest of each side to attempt to deceive the other as to the position of its curve. For example, if the union were able to persuade the employers that its

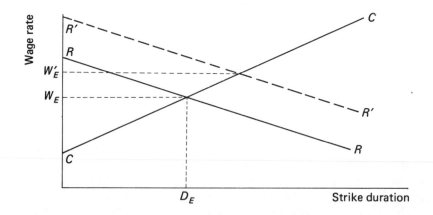

Figure 4.2

resistance curve were $R'R'$ the employers might agree to a wage of W'_E without a strike. But given that each side knows that the other has an incentive to misrepresent its position, negotiations may break down and strikes result, which enable each side to find out what the other's true position is.

A final implication of this model is that, if there is an increase in union power, so that RR actually rises to $R'R'$, but employers do not realize this shift has occurred, we would expect to observe both more (or longer) strikes and an increase in wages. In empirical work, strikes have often been used as an indicator of union power and this analysis provides some theoretical justification for such a procedure. (For further development of bargaining models of strikes see Ashenfelter and Johnson, 1969; Hieser, 1970; Pencavel, 1970; and Johnston, 1972).

4.3.3 MILITANCY

By militancy we refer to political or institutional factors which may cause a union to press for a wage increase greater than that which is in the economic best interests of its members. A major institutional determinant of trade union behaviour is the concern over relative wages. Workers may judge their trade union leaders by comparing their wage increases with those of workers in different unions. The idea that unions are particularly concerned with relative wages was a major element in Keynes's analysis of money wage rigidity (Keynes, 1936, p.14), and was developed in a classic study by Ross (1948; and see also Levinson, 1966).

More recently, the idea of relative wage rigidity has been examined within the context of 'wage leadership' models. The wage leadership hypothesis postulates that some particular group of workers will strike a 'key bargain', which will then be imitated by other groups of workers in order to re-establish the *status quo ante* in the relations between the wage rates of the groups involved. The process by which the terms of the key bargain are generalized — the transfer mechanism — is invariably connected either with trade union attachment to notions of horizontal and vertical equity in wage fixing, or with situations in which inter-union competition makes it imperative for each union to be seen to perform at least as well as its rivals. This is an essentially political process, leading to upward adjustments of a large number of wage rates in response to some key bargain which may or may not have been struck according to criteria common to the whole employment group embraced by the transfer mechanism.

An interesting question here is what determines the key bargain. It may very well be that the key bargain reflects the economic circumstances of the particular employment in which it was struck, for example, a local excess demand for labour (Mulvey and Trevithick, 1974) or a productivity agreement (Jackson *et al.*, 1972), while its generalization into other sectors may reflect only the institutional or political force of the transfer mechanism. The wage leadership hypothesis has been the subject of a large number of empirical studies, which we discuss in section 4.4.

A more recent development is to relate militancy not so much to internal trade union politics as to national political issues. The government is necessarily drawn into pay bargaining in its role as employer in the public sector. Public sector unions face an employer who can always afford to pay more, and who can never go bankrupt. Their bargaining strength seems to depend on the support they can get from other unions and from public opinion − that is to say, ultimately on political rather than economic considerations. In the UK, for example, it is thought that the widespread economic disruption brought about by strikes in support of higher wage claims (but in part at least politically inspired by hostility to government policies) brought down both the Heath government of 1974 and the Callaghan government of 1979.

Incomes policies draw governments into private sector wage negotiations, often creating conflict between private sector unions and government (rather than the employer). These conflicts can again become politicized, with the union's attitudes being determined as much by its views on government policies in general as by purely economic considerations.

4.3.4 UNION POWER AND THE PHILLIPS CURVE

We have examined how unions may influence the wage bargain. We now consider the way in which these effects influence the Phillips Curve. It will help to start from a situation in which inflation is zero, all labour markets are in equilibrium, and there are some unions in the economy while part of the labour force remains non-unionized. Let us now assume that, for some external reason, the power of the unions increases, and that they are therefore able to achieve increases in the wages of their members. We now ask two questions: (a) what happens to the wages of non-unionized workers? and (b) can the increase in union power lead to continuing inflation, or has it only a once-and-for-all effect?

(a) There are two effects of the union wage increase on non-union workers. First, employers of non-union labour may not wish to allow an increase in the union–non-union differential, if only because a large differential is likely to lead to the unionization of their labour force. Likewise, customary wage relativities, arbitration awards and so on may help raise non-union wages along with the increase in union wages. But, second, the higher union wages will, in principle, reduce employment in the union sector, hence increasing the supply of workers looking for jobs in the non-union sector, and this factor will tend to push down wages in the non-union sector.

If the first of these effects predominates, there will be an increase in wages throughout the economy, and at the same time, if the level of aggregate demand remains constant (in nominal terms), unemployment will rise. If the second effect predominates, the union wage increase will have led to no increase in average wages, being offset by the fall in non-union wages. Nor will unemployment rise, for those losing jobs in the union sector will find new employment in the non-union sector.

(b) The effects of the union wage increase after the first period depend, ultimately, on the response of government policy. If union wage increases are matched by the non-union sector, the more wages are pushed up the more unemployment will result, and this must at some stage weaken the unions' power. (The higher is unemployment, the less willing their members will be to risk their jobs for further wage increases.) In this sense, the unions can only achieve once-and-for-all wage increases. In figure 4.1, this is equivalent to arguing that the unions can shift the Phillips Curve from (a) to (b) or (c), meaning that wages will rise at the original level of unemployment, but that the effect of wage increases will be to raise unemployment until it reaches a level (where curve (b) or (c) crosses the horizontal axis) at which inflation again falls to zero.

The outcome sketched above has, however, assumed that the government is willing (and able) to hold aggregate demand constant. If the government is reluctant to see unemployment rise, and therefore allows an expansion of aggregate demand, inflation can proceed indefinitely. The accommodating expansion in demand is now a necessary condition for, though not the original cause of, the inflation. Proponents of the cost-push school are normally prepared to accept that, as a logical proposition, a sufficiently high level of unemployment will stop inflation, but they argue that the required level of unemployment would cause such serious social and political problems as to be an unacceptable policy option. The government's policy options are thus limited to endeavouring to control the exercise of union power or to allowing continuing inflation.

4.4 EMPIRICAL EVIDENCE ON THE IMPACT OF TRADE UNIONS ON WAGE INFLATION

Tests of the impact of trade unions on wage increases have taken three main forms. First, and most direct, are studies that have attempted to incorporate a variable (or variables) purporting to measure trade union power or militancy in an aggregate wage equation. Second are the studies testing the 'wage leadership' hypothesis. Third, there are a number of investigations of the determinants of the union–non-union wage differential which provide some insight into the transmission of inflationary impulses in the economy.

4.4.1 TRADE UNION WAGE PUSH VARIABLES IN AGGREGATE WAGE EQUATIONS

This approach amounts to a direct empirical test of equation (4.6) (p. 69 above); that is,

$$\dot{W} = bE + z$$

where E is again the level of excess demand and z represents the trade union wage push factor.

There is of course no direct measure of trade union militancy or wage push. A variety of proxy indicators have been considered, the main ones being (a) the proportion of the labour force unionized (or its rate of change); (b) strikes; (c) industrial profitability; and (d) political variables.

Proportion of the labour force unionized   In a celebrated article, Hines (1964) found strong econometric evidence that the rate of change of the proportion of the labour force unionized was a significant explanatory variable in the UK wage equation. His hypothesis was that trade union pushfulness is manifest both in recruitment campaigns to increase membership and in higher wage demands.

Hines's hypothesis is generally regarded as rather implausible. The variations that have taken place in trade union membership in the UK since the war have been minute, and may plausibly be related to a number of other factors (e.g., changes in the industrial structure) as well as the level of current trade union pushfulness. The measure can obviously take no account of changes in pushfulness in sectors that are already fully unionized. While allowing that there may be some loose relationship between recruitment drives and wage push, it seems hard to believe that there is a sufficiently close and systematic link between the two variables that one can be used as an accurate measure of the other (Godfrey, 1971; Purdy and Zis, 1973).

These doubts have led to a re-examination of the statistical validity of the Hines model. Thomas and Stoney (1970) have argued that the model may be mis-specified. Considered as a stochastic difference equation system, the model is dynamically explosive and this limits the use of standard significance tests. Purdy and Zis (1973) have redefined the change-in-unionization variable in order to bring it more closely into line with Hines's own hypothesis, have redefined the wage and price variables to make them consistent with each other, and have re-estimated the equation using annual rather than quarterly data. Their findings reduce the significance of the change-in-unionization variable, but it nevertheless remains significant.

A more recent study of the Hines model (Henry, Sawyer and Smith, 1976) sets out to assess how well the model performs outside the data period of Hines's original calculations. The postwar data period examined by Hines (1964) was 1949–61; however, some estimates up to 1969 were reported by Purdy and Zis (1973) and also in a separate study by Hines (1971). Both found that the change-in-unionization variable performs less well in the 1960s than in the earlier period. Henry *et al.* (1976) test the Hines model on data from 1949 to 1974. They find the change in unionization variable almost totally insignificant, not only for the more recent period but also for the 1949–61 data period which Hines had examined. It is, unfortunately, not clear why these contradictory results should have been obtained.

An interesting, and sometimes neglected, section of Hines's original (1964) paper examines the factors influencing changes in trade union membership. A major finding (which is confirmed by Henry *et al.*, 1976) is that inflation 'causes' increases in trade union membership. The argument here is that, the faster the rate of inflation, the greater the impetus for workers to join trade unions in an attempt to ensure they do not fall behind in the inflationary scramble (Robinson and Wilkinson, 1977, especially p. 9).

One interpretation of these findings is, therefore, that inflation leads both to higher wage claims and to increases in trade union membership. Changes in unionization may, therefore, be associated with higher wage claims, but are not the cause of them. Such an interpretation would be consistent with the 'single-equation' estimates of Hines (1964) and Purdy and Zis (1973), and with the results of Henry *et al.* (1976). Only the simultaneous equation estimates in Hines (1964) appear to find a role for changes in unionization or wage increases over and above the effects of inflation.

Further support for the view that changes in unionization have no significant impact on wage increases once the effects of inflation have been allowed for can be drawn from an international study by Ward and Zis (1974). Of European countries, data on trade union membership appear available only for Germany and the Netherlands. Their wage equations for both countries incorporate price inflation, and for both they find a negative coefficient on the change in unionization variable.

Strike activity   The bargaining model discussed in section 4.3 has the implication that, if changes in trade union militancy can be represented by shifts in the union resistance curve (*RR* in figure 4.2), we will observe a positive correlation between strike activity and wage increases. A finding that strikes have an independent influence in the wage equation might then be taken as evidence of union militancy effects.

The evidence on strikes is rather mixed. Studies carried out on a number of countries suggest that strike activity leads to significantly higher wage increases in Italy, France, Belgium and Australia but appears to have no effect on wage increases in Germany, the Netherlands and Switzerland (Ward and Zis, 1974; Laidler, 1976; Phipps, 1977). In the UK, Godfrey, (1971), Taylor (1972) and Laidler (1976) find a significant impact of strike activity, while Johnston and Timbrell (1973) and Ward and Zis (1974) find that there is no effect.

It is, however, not surprising that there are difficulties in identifying a stable empirical relationship between strike activity and wage increases. In a classic study, Ashenfelter and Johnson (1969) showed that strike activity was itself affected by the pressure of demand and by the rate of growth of real wages. Thus, one can argue that excess demand strengthens the bargaining position of the trade unions and thus leads to higher wage claims, supported by the threat of strikes. In this picture, strikes are a part of the transmission mechanism through which excess demand leads to higher wage increases. One might then argue that, while the power of the strike threat plays an important part in this transmission mechanism, the number of strikes that actually materialize is not important, but simply depends on the proportion of employers who are slow to recognize that their bargaining position has worsened. Wage equations, such as those in the studies cited above, that include an excess demand measure as well as strike activity may find that wage increases are well explained by excess demand, with no independent role for strikes, when possibly it is the strike threat that brings about the relationship between excess demand and wage increases.

More generally, as argued in section 4.3, bargaining theory suggests that strikes will occur when there are differences in the perceptions of the unions and the employers about the level of its final settlement. If there is, for any reason, an increase in the bargaining power of the unions, which is perceived in the same way by both unions and employers, the outcome will be a higher wage settlement without a strike.

The bargaining model suggests that strikes will be related to events the consequences of which are perceived differently by employers and unions. But to the extent that people learn from experience, such differences in perceptions in relation to any given type of exogenous change are likely to diminish over time.

Industrial profitability   A number of studies have indicated that the level (and changes in the level) of profits is a significant explanatory variable in the wage-change equation (see Bowen, 1960). The most common interpretations placed on the profit variable are (a) that it indicates the balance of bargaining power in the labour market (Bowen, 1960; Kaldor, 1959); (b) that profits-push inflation has evoked a defensive wage response (Ackley, 1958); and (c) that profits and wages will rise together when there is excess demand in both goods and labour markets. It should be said at the outset that the studies that indicate an association between wage changes and a profit variable normally do not include a price-change variable, and the inclusion of such a variable generally reduces the significance of the profit variable (Bowen and Berry, 1963). Further, Lipsey and Steuer (1961) for the UK and Bodkin (1966) for the United States have found only a weak association between wage changes and profit variables. It should therefore be borne in mind in any discussion of the role of a profit variable that its statistical credentials are by no means impeccable.

The bargaining power hypothesis depends on the notion that when profit levels are high trade unions will feel that a favourable opportunity exists to press for higher wages, since these can be financed out of high profits with a minimum of employers' resistance. At the same time the opportunity cost (in terms of lost profits) to the employer of facing a strike is greatest when profits are high, and his ability to buy off a dispute is in any case enhanced by high profits. Hence we might expect a large number of wage claims to be advanced by trade unions and successfully negotiated when profits are high and a small number to be advanced with less success when profits are low.

The main difficulty with establishing the role of profits is that profitability is not an independent variable, but is itself determined by the state of demand, productivity levels and so on. One could indeed argue that profits are a good proxy measure for excess demand. Finally, one may note that the generally depressed profit levels of the 1970s seem to have been accompanied by higher rather than lower wage claims, which appears to cast doubt on the view that profits are a major factor in wage bargaining.

Political variables   There is a well-established political belief, at least in the UK, that the militancy with which the trade unions pursue their wage demands can be influenced by the attitude of trade union leaders towards the government in power. In particular, if a Labour government pursues general economic policies favoured by the trade union movement, the trade unions will co-operate with it by moderating their wage demands. They will, by contrast, shown no such restraint under a Conservative government. To test this hypothesis, Klein and Ball (1959) introduce a politicial dummy variable into their wage equation, and find it to be highly significant, with wages rising at a rate 3 per cent per annum faster under Conservative governments than they would have done, other things equal, under a Labour government. However, their data period extends only up to 1957, and more recent studies have not incorporated this particular variable.

4.4.2 THE WAGE LEADERSHIP HYPOTHESIS

Trade unions can affect the rate of wage inflation by creating a 'wage transfer mechanism', based on criteria of horizontal and vertial equity in the structure of relative wages. Such a mechanism implies the existence of 'wage-leaders' and 'wage-followers' in the labour force. Numerous efforts to substantiate this intuitively plausible hypothesis have been made for both the USA and the UK (see Sargan, 1971; Brechling, 1972; Eckstein and Wilson, 1962; Thomas and Stoney, 1972; Seltzer, 1951; Mulvey and Trevithick, 1974; Jackson *et al.*, 1972; Levinson, 1960). In general, these studies have yielded findings that tend to support some type of wage leadership transfer mechanism hypothesis in a wide variety of contexts. In particular, Seltzer (1951) and Levinson (1960) have produced convincing evidence of a wage leadership process in the US steel and automobile industries. Similarly, Eckstein and Wilson (1962) have found that, for a group of inter-related US heavy industries, including automobiles and steel, wage leadership and 'wage rounds' could be clearly identified. In those studies, however, the key bargain was always taken as given and its determinants remained unknown.

An immediate difficulty with the wage leadership hypothesis is that its main prediction—that wages in different sectors will tend to go up by the same amounts—is not inconsistent with the predictions of standard economic theory where wages are determined in competitive markets. It is indeed a standard proposition of general equilibrium theory that relative wages in different occupations will be unaffected by changes in the general price level. This is not to say that the wage leadership hypothesis is empirically indistinguishable from standard price theory, but simply to note that rigidity in wage relativities could be consistent with either approach. (For further discussion, see Addison and Burton, 1979).

Even if one were to accept that the structure of relative wages were determined entirely by institutional forces, the implications for the overall inflation rate depend crucially on the factors that determine the 'key bargain'. A number of writers suggest that it is the group of workers in the strongest bargaining position that set the pace, by securing for themselves a large wage increase which then becomes the 'going rate' for that wage round. For example, Mulvey and Trevithick (1974) showed that, in Ireland, the rate of overall wage inflation was related to conditions prevailing in the tightest labour market (in their case, skilled manual workers). Similarly, Jackson *et al.* (1972) and Eatwell *et al.* (1974) have argued that it is workers in the industries with the fastest growing productivity that are able to secure the highest pay increases, and these pay increases are then transmitted to other sectors of the economy.

Theories of this type are, however, unable to account at all satisfactorily for the great surge of inflation in the mid-1970s.

4.4.3 THE UNION—NON-UNION WAGE DIFFERENTIAL

Earlier in the chapter we discussed the hypothesis that the Phillips Curve for unionized works would be flatter that that for non-union workers (pp. 68—73). Such an hypothesis implies that, in times when the pressure of demand is high, the differential between union and non-union wages would fall, while in times of slack, the differential would rise. Now this implies that, if inflation is of the excess demand variety, the onset of inflation should be associated with a reduction in the union–non-union wage differential. By contrast, if inflation were initiated by trade union cost-push, one would expect the onset of inflation to be accompanied by a widening of the differential.

Arguing along these lines, Layard *et al.* (1978) suggest that the acceleration of inflation in the UK, at least during the period 1968–72. can be given a cost-push interpretation. They show that the union–non-union differential remains approximately constant up to 1968, then starts to rise quite rapidly until 1972, after which it appears to stabilize at the higher (1972) level. The increase in the differential, they suggest, can be attributed to an increase in trade union power, or militancy (perhaps influenced by the Paris riots of May 1968, in which the French trade unions successfully challenged the authority of the government, and were awarded large pay increases as a result). While Layard *et al.* may well be correct in ascribing the increase in the union–non-union differential to greater union militancy, it does not follow that the higher rate of inflation must also be given a cost-push interpretation. There is an alternative explanation, based on international monetary developments in this period. On this interpretation the devaluation of the pound in November 1967 would generate inflation in the UK, which was then compounded by a surfeit of international liquidity. (We discuss this interpretation more fully in chapter 7, where we argue that the inflation rate in an economy that is part of a fixed exchange rate system must ultimately be determined by the 'world inflation rate', rather than by domestic factors.)

4.5 INCOMES POLICIES

If the cause of inflation lies in the excessive wage claims by trade unions, it may seem that the best hope for controlling inflation lies in incomes policies aiming to restrain or control the rate of wage increases. We cannot attempt even to survey the substantial literature on incomes policy here, and we instead confine ourselves to a few key theoretical and empirical propositions.

First, it may reasonably be asked why, if a union has the power to secure a large wage increase and it is in its members' interests for it to do so, it will agree to an incomes policy that prevents it from gaining that increase. (In the light of recent experience, it seems reasonable to assume that the government cannot enforce an incomes policy by law against the opposition of the trade unions.) Yet, trade unions are often willing to co-operate with incomes policies. The reason seems to be that trade unions recognize that, while it is individually rational for them to pursue high wage increases, it may be collectively irrational; for the result of higher wage claims by all unions may simply be a faster rate of inflation, with no increases in real wages. If one assumes that the real wages of union members are unaffected by inflation, and that union members dislike inflation, it is in the best interests of unions, acting collectively, to agree to a low rate of growth of money wages.

The analysis, however, is rather like that of a cartel. In a cartel, each member benefits if all the members reduce their output, but each has an incentive to cheat by reducing his own output by less than the agreed amount. Likewise, with an incomes policy, each union may agree to the policy believing that it will help reduce the rate of inflation, but it will still have an incentive to get a money wage increase for its own members greater than that allowed for in the policy, hence improving their real wage. This suggests that incomes policies are likely to work only in a system of highly centralized wage bargaining where the policy can be enforced closely and 'cheating' can be prevented.

Historical experience suggests that incomes policies do not last for very long. In the UK three years has been about the maximum. Whether incomes policies collapse because they are inherently unstable as suggested by the cartel analogy, or because they fail to allow for necessary adjustments in relative wages, or for some other reason is not altogether clear. Supporters of incomes policy argue that, with changes in institutional arrangements, incomes policies could become a permanent feature of wage bargaining. One would require, for example, a permanent body, operating according to agreed criteria, to assess whether relative pay adjustments should be allowed. Arrangements such as synchronizing the date of all pay settlements could be introduced to strengthen awareness of the collective interest in wage bargaining.

We turn finally to econometric studies of the effects of incomes policies. The major studies relating to the UK economy up to 1970 are published in Parkin and Sumner (1972). The bulk of these studies find the effects of incomes policy, typically measured by introducing a dummy variable for periods when incomes policies were in operation into the wage equation, small or insignificant. In more recent work, Henry and Ormerod (1978) report a 'rebound' effect, whereby wage increases are slowed down during the time of operation of an incomes policy, but then rebound at the end of the policy to catch up for what was lost while the policy was in force.

To conclude this section, we would argue that, given the institutional structure of the UK (and in particular the importance the unions attach to 'free collective bargaining') both *a priori* reasoning and empirical estimates suggest that incomes policy can play only a very secondary role in controlling inflation. Indeed, in our final chapter we will argue that there may be times when incomes policies are useful, but their value is more in the effect they may have on expectations than in bringing about voluntary restraint in the exercise of trade union power.

4.6 CONCLUSIONS

Our main conclusions can be summarized briefly. Trade unions have an important influence on the conduct of wage bargaining, and on the relative wages of different groups of workers. More controversially, it seems to us that a number of studies suggest that trade unions can inject an inflationary bias into the system in the sense that, for a given pressure of demand in the economy, the rate of wage increases may be higher with trade unions than in their absence. (One might equivalently argue that trade unions raise the rate of unemployment consistent with the maintenance of any given rate of inflation.)

We have, however, been critical of a number of cost-push hypotheses. Many such theories fail to provide a coherent picture of the overall inflationary process. Some are proposed on the basis of empirical evidence, which is in no way inconsistent with the excess demand approach. Most, however, have simply failed to produce convincing empirical support. An exception is the 'target real wage approach', to which we return in chapter 8.

NOTE

1. A model with no empirical content may none the less be 'true'. If, in fact, there are no general or systematic factors influencing wage claims, it is better to recognize that fact than to attempt to force the data to fit some preconceived theoretical pattern. Wiles (1973), for example, holds that wages are determined 'by the whim and fancy of trade union leaders'. The attitudes of trade union leaders may be influenced by political, social or cultural factors, and also by the organization of the trade unions themselves (which affects who becomes a trade

union leader, and the pressures that can be brought to bear by shop stewards and the rank and file members on the leadership), but it is consistent with Wiles's approach to expect a substantial unpredictable component in wage inflation.

CHAPTER 5

Expectations and Inflation

The theories of inflation we have discussed up to this point have been concerned with the relationship between increases in money wages and unemployment (or some other measure of the pressure of demand in the labour market) and, perhaps, some additional explanatory variables. Such theories suggest the existence of a stable trade-off between wage inflation and the pressure of demand. The government can, in accordance with its policy objectives, choose either to maintain a high level of demand in the economy, with low unemployment but a relatively high rate of inflation, or, alternatively, to maintain a low level of demand, with higher unemployment but greater price stability. The Phillips Curve, as Rees (1970) put it, appeared to offer the authorities a 'menu of policy choices'.

The most important development in inflation theory in recent years, however, suggests that this picture is seriously misleading if not wholly incorrect. This new development is the argument that expectations play a crucial role in the inflationary process. Once expectations are taken into account, it is argued, the government cannot influence the rate of unemployment in the long run through maintaining a higher (or lower) level of aggregate demand. There is an equilibrium in the labour market, and if the government attempts to reduce unemployment below the 'natural rate' (implied by the labour market equilibrium) it will be faced by ever-accelerating inflation. The Phillips Curve, as described in chapter 3, is to be regarded as a strictly short-run phenomenon; in the long run the Phillips Curve is vertical.

This chapter is in four sections:

(a) the theoretical argument underlying the expectations hypothesis;
(b) a microeconomic theory of the labour market;
(c) empirical evidence on wages and expectations;
(d) policy implications of the expectations hypothesis.

We assume here a closed economy: we consider the role of expectations in an open economy in chapter 7. Finally, we note that, while the expectations hypothesis has been pioneered by Friedman and other monetarist economists, it carries with it no commitment to the view that money is the only (or even a major) influence on aggregate demand. In terms of the distinction set out in chapter 2, the expectations hypothesis is consistent with both quantity theory and Keynesian approaches to the determination of aggregate demand.

5.1 THE EXPECTATIONS HYPOTHESIS AND THE NATURAL RATE OF UNEMPLOYMENT

Following upon the initial enthusiasm that greeted the largely empirical work of Phillips (1958), Lipsey (1960) and others, there has arisen a growing scepticism concerning the long-run properties of the trade-off relation $\dot{P} = f(U)$. Long before the crude, closed-economy version of the Phillips Curve had been exposed to criticism by the facts of national and international experience, it had come under increasing attack on basically theoretical grounds from economists working within a more strictly neoclassical tradition. Many writers (Friedman, 1968; Phelps, 1967; Cagan, 1969) contend that, if the authorities attempt to maintain a level of unemployment that does not coincide with the 'natural' unemployment rate, then the inevitable outcome will be either accelerating inflation or accelerating deflation.

This concept of the natural rate of unemployment plays a central role in Friedman's assault upon the notion that there exists in the long run a Phillips Curve of the conventional type:

> *At any moment of time, there is some level of unemployment which has the property that it is consistent with equilibrium in the structure of real wage rates. . . . The 'natural rate of unemployment', in other words, is the level that would be ground out by the Walrasian system of general equilibrium equations, provided there is imbedded in them the actual structural characteristics of the labor and commodity markets, including market imperfections, stochastic variability in demands and supplies, the cost of gathering information about job vacancies and labor availabilities, the costs of mobility and so on.*
> *[Friedman, 1968]*

In highly simplified terms, the natural unemployment rate, U^*, can be regarded as the rate that, once certain realistic modifications are made to the basic model, will be consistent with an *employment* rate

N_F in figure 2.1 above. To this extent it may be regarded as a *full employment level of unemployment.* If the demand for labour exceeds N_F, the actual unemployment rate will be below U^* and there will be upward pressure on the real wage rate. Similarly, deficient aggregate labour demand will produce an actual unemployment rate in excess of U^* and will put downward pressure upon the real wage rate. Only when the actual and natural rates coincide will the real wage rate clear the labour market. From that point onwards real wages will rise in line with labour productivity.

But does not the foregoing analysis closely resemble the theoretical relationship embodied in the Phillips Curve? To this question Friedman gives a resounding No. Whereas Phillips's original contribution to the study of wage inflation was couched entirely in terms of *money* wage rates, Friedman maintains that the central object of study should be the behaviour of *real* wage rates at various levels of unemployment. The Phillips procedure of examining how money wage rates respond to varying levels of aggregate demand may not be too misleading when the average rate of change of prices has been negligible over a substantial period of time. On the other hand, where the rate of price inflation has been appreciable over some relevant time horizon, the Phillips exercise loses all meaning.

The logic of Friedman's position may be clarified if we start from the simplest possible version of the Phillips Curve, where the rate of increase of money wages depends only on the level of unemployment. We may thus write

$$\dot{W} = f(U). \tag{5.1}$$

Friedman's objection to the existence of the stable trade-off relationship described by equation (5.1) is that it relates *money* wage rather than *real* wage changes to the level of excess demand. If the market is in equilibrium, according to Friedman, money wages will not remain constant; rather, real wages will remain constant, which implies increases in money wages equal to the expected rate of inflation of prices. This means that equation (5.1) must be replaced by

$$\dot{W} = f(U) + \dot{P}^e \tag{5.2}$$

where $\dot{P}^e$ is the expected rate of inflation. Equation (5.2) is often described as the 'expectations-augmented Phillips Curve'.

It follows from (5.2) that for any given expected rate of inflation there remains a trade-off between unemployment and wage increases,

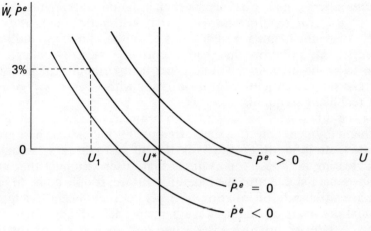

Figure 5.1

but that the position of that trade-off depends on the expected rate of inflation. This proposition is illustrated in figure 5.1, in which three different trade-off relations correspond to three different expected rates of inflation. Each curve is an identical copy of all other curves but is displaced in either an upward or a downward direction. For example, the highest curve of the three (the one corresponding to a positive expected rate of inflation) is an image of the middle curve (corresponding to zero expected inflation); the vertical distance between the two curves measures the difference between their two expected rates of inflation.

Let us now suppose for the sake of argument that prices have been stable over a long period of time and are generally expected to remain stable. In such circumstances the expected rate of inflation will be zero and the middle curve will be the relevant trade-off relation. If prices are to remain stable, it is clear that the authorities will have to exercise restraint in the use of the monetary and fiscal instruments at their disposal and maintain an unemployment rate U^*. If on the other hand it is assumed that the authorities have a change of heart and decide that the cost of price stability in terms of unemployment is too high, they may use the very same instruments to drive the unemployment rate down to U_1. In the short period the pursuit of such a policy will produce a rate of inflation of, say, 3 per cent, which may seem at the time to be an acceptable price to pay for a lower unemployment rate. As prices continue to rise, however, individuals and groups who have entered into contracts framed in *nominal* terms come to recognize that inflation is depriving them of part of the *real* remuneration that they had anticipated. They will rightly place the blame for such losses upon their failure to anticipate correctly the inflation that had occurred. Gradually, people will begin to abandon their erstwhile belief in the stability of prices and will take steps to anticipate future inflation with a view to safeguarding their real living standards.

On the other hand, as long as the government persists in maintaining an unemployment rate U_1, such attempts by individuals and groups to anticipate inflation on the basis of their past mistakes can only be self-defeating. Suppose for example that, after assuming that prices would remain stable into the indefinite future, people come to terms with a realized rate of inflation of 3 per cent and begin to adjust all nominal contracts, including wage bargains, accordingly. That is, the expected rate of inflation rises from zero to 3 per cent. In these circumstances the rate of inflation will rise to 6 per cent, for the relevant trade-off relation will be one that corresponds to an expected rate of inflation of 3 per cent. Once again, inflation will have been under-anticipated by a margin of 3 per cent, and once again there will be a tendency to revise expectations in an upward direction. By maintaining an unemployment rate U_1, the authorities will eventually plunge the economy into a headlong decline into hyper-inflation. Only by managing demand in such a way as to maintain unemployment at a level U^* will the authorities be able to prevent any acceleration in the rate of inflation. This unemployment rate is, of course, the 'natural' rate. The upshot of this line of reasoning is that accelerating inflation or deflation can be avoided only by setting the unemployment rate at its 'natural' rate. Inflation can still occur at this rate, depending upon the initial state of price expectations, but it will be taking place at a *constant* rate.

To develop the analysis further it will be helpful to make two further assumptions. We will assume that both labour productivity and the mark-up of prices over wages are constant. We can thus assume that the rate of wage inflation and the rate of price inflation are equal, and equations (5.1) and (5.2) can be rewritten:

$$\dot{P} = f(U) \qquad (5.1')$$

$$\dot{P} = f(U) + \dot{P}^e. \qquad (5.2')$$

Equation (5.2') can then be rearranged so that

$$\dot{P} - \dot{P}^e = f(U). \qquad (5.3)$$

The current rate of inflation can be divided into two parts: that part which is fully anticipated, $\dot{P}^e$; and that part which is unanticipated, $\dot{P} - \dot{P}^e$. The expectations hypothesis states that only *unanticipated* inflation will vary with the unemployment rate. A further implication of this hypothesis is that the only situation in which inflation is fully anticipated is when unemployment is at its natural rate. The natural rate of unemployment may be found very easily (in theory at least): when inflation is fully anticipated, $\dot{P} - \dot{P}^e = 0$, so that the natural rate of unemployment is found by evaluating the root of the equation $f(U) = 0$.

But the idea of a *rising* rate of inflation cannot be deduced from the foregoing analysis. It depends upon an assumption, implicit in the verbal account, concerning the formation of expectations. The current expected rate of inflation is supposed to depend systematically upon the actual rates of inflation experienced in the past. Symbolically, this may be written

$$\dot{P}^e_t = h(\dot{P}_{t-1}, \dot{P}_{t-2}, \ldots, \dot{P}_{t-n}). \tag{5.4}$$

The exact manner in which the expected rate of inflation depends upon past rates of inflation needs to be spelt out in greater detail. Since expectations are unobservable and unquantifiable in their own right, *a priori* restrictions must be imposed upon the formation of a variable such as $\dot{P}^e$. One convenient and therefore common way of describing the emergence of inflationary expectations is that of *adaptive* expectations. The adaptive expectations model states that the expected rate of inflation in period t is a weighted average of all past rates of inflation. The weights are seldcted in such a way that greater importance is attached to more recently experienced rates of inflation; more specifically, $\dot{P}_{t-1}, \dot{P}_{t-2}, \dot{P}_{t-3}$ are assigned the respective weights $(1-\psi)$, $\psi(1-\psi)$, $\psi^2(1-\psi)$, etc., where ψ is greater than or equal to zero but less than one; a weighting system that follows this pattern is described as being one of geometrically decreasing weights, since the coefficients of the distributed lag equation (5.5) below decline in geometric progression. The adaptive expectations model therefore postulates that expectations are formed according to the following scheme:

$$\dot{P}^e_t = (1-\psi)\dot{P}_{t-1} + (1-\psi)\psi\dot{P}_{t-2} + (1-\psi)\psi^2\dot{P}_{t-3}\ldots. \tag{5.5}$$

or

$$\dot{P}^e_t = (1-\psi) \sum_{j=1}^{\infty} \psi^{j-1}\dot{P}_{t-j}.$$

The assumption that ψ satisfies the property that $0 \leqslant \psi < 1$ is important on two counts. First, it ensures that the expression (5.5) has a finite limit, i.e., that the geometric progression converges. Second, it produces the economically meaningful result that, the more distant is the rate of inflation, the less is the importance attached to it.

It can be easily verified that the adaptive expectations model described in equation (5.5) is equivalent to the following statement:

$$\dot{P}^e - \dot{P}^e_{t-1} = (1-\psi)\,(\dot{P}_{t-1} - \dot{P}^e_{t-1}). \qquad (5.6)$$

This description of how expectations evolve is extensively used in the theory of inflation (see, for example, Cagan, 1956; and Solow, 1969).

If it can be assumed, as the adaptive expectations model postulates, that the current expected rate of inflation depends systematically upon past rates of inflation and reacts most sensitively to the most recently experienced rates of inflation, then the notion of an acceleration in the rate of price change at unemployment rates other than the natural rate becomes clearer. When the actual rate of inflation exceeds the expected rate of inflation in a given period, as would be the case where the government maintained $U < U^*$, a higher expected rate of inflation will be generated in the subsequent period, leading to a higher *actual* rate of inflation in this period. Since there is no tendency for the unanticipated part of inflation to vanish over time if the government pursues a policy of maintaining unemployment at a level below its natural rate, there will always be a tendency for expectations to be revised upwards in a vain attempt to catch up with the actual rate of inflation. It is this continuous upward revision in the expected rate of inflation that produces the acceleration in the actual rate of inflation. The only situation in which such revision will not occur is when unemployment is at its natural rate.

While the idea that people's expectations about inflation are strongly influenced by past experience seems intuitive and plausible, the adaptive expectations formulation (as set out in equation (5.5)) cannot be regarded as entirely satisfactorily. To illustrate, consider an economy in which the rate of inflation, for whatever reason, rises steadily year after year; that is, the inflation rate is, say, 5 per cent one year, 6 per cent the next, 7 per cent the year after and so on. On the adaptive expectations model, people's expectations of future inflation will be based on a weighted average of past inflation rates, and hence each year their expectation of inflation will be below the rate that actually materialises. In these circumstances, it seems likely that people would take into account not only the average level of the inflation rate in the past, but also whether it has been increasing or decreasing.

This example suggests that we will want to impose a further condition on the expectations formation process, namely, that it should be efficient in the sense of leading to reasonably good forecasts. It can be shown that, if the underlying trend rate of inflation changes only slowly, while there are substantial random transitory influences (both positive and negative) on year-to-year price movements, the adaptive expectations mechanism is the best way of forecasting future inflation on the basis of past inflation rates. If, however, the inflation rate is on a rising trend, the adaptive expectations mechanism is inefficient because it will generate inflation forecasts that will generally turn out to be too low.

We will not pursue these points in any more detail here (for a fuller account, see Flemming, 1976, chapter 7). The conclusion we would stress is that the expectations formation mechanism may itself be influenced by the experience of inflation, and that this has implications both for econometric analysis and for government policy, to which we return later in the chapter.

Before leaving the subject of expectations formation, we should mention that a very different approach has gained considerable support in recent years. This is the theory of 'rational expectations', which is based on the idea that the price expectations formation mechanism assumed in any economic model should be consistent with the predictions of that model. For example, those who believe in a crude quantity theory model, so that inflation is determined by the growth of the money supply, should, if they are to be consistent, argue that inflation expectations are also determined by the growth rate of the money supply, rather than by past inflation rates. We discuss the rational expectations approach in more detail in chapter 6.

5.1.1 KEYNESIAN OBJECTIONS

There is no doubt that the expectations hypothesis, if correct, undermines the whole basis of Keynesian economics. It implies, first, that in the long run the rate of unemployment is independent of the government's macroeconomic policy, and, second, that even in the short run the government can influence unemployment only by generating a rate of inflation different from that which people were expecting (that is, by 'fooling' workers into accepting money wage increases lower than the rate of inflation).

One type of Keynesian objection was to argue that Friedman's concept of the natural rate of unemployment had no theoretical basis. As Hahn argued,

> *[Friedman] wants to speak of the natural level of unemployment as that level 'which would be ground out by the Walrasian system of general equilibrium equations' which he takes for this purpose to cover market imperfections, stochastic variability in demands and supplies, costs of mobility, etc. As far as I know, no one has ever succeeded in writing down such equations, nor in 'grinding out' the natural level of unemployment from them. I also doubt that such a task is well formulated. [Hahn, 1971, p. 62]*

A rigorous microeconomic theory of the labour market has, however, been developed (Phelps, 1971) which does support Friedman's position on the expectations hypothesis and on the natural rate of unemployment. We examine this theory in more detail in section 5.2.

In a sense though, the problem for Keynesian economists goes even deeper. For if equation (5.2) is a correct description of the determinants of wage increases, then unemployment must be held at a level where $f(U) = 0$ whether or not that level of unemployment corresponds to any labour market equilibrium concept. It may be better to speak not of the natural rate of unemployment (which suggests some equilibrium properties), but rather of the NAIRU — the 'non-accelerating inflation rate of unemployment' — which makes clear that we are concerned with the rate of unemployment that holds inflation constant, rather than that which, in some sense, equilibrates the labour market.

The NAIRU result depends, however, not on the general proposition that price expectations affect wage settlements, but on the more precise proposition that price expectations affect wage settlements with a coefficient of unity, or in other words that the wage bargain is concerned only with the expected value of real wages. Thus it runs counter to one of the most basic of Keynesian notions, the idea that there may be some degree of 'money illusion' in the wage bargain (Tobin, 1972). In such circumstances, wage bargains might take expected inflation into account, but only partially rather than fully. That is, the Phillips Curve could be written in the form

$$\dot{P} = f(U) + \phi \dot{P}^e \quad 0 < \phi < 1 \tag{5.7}$$

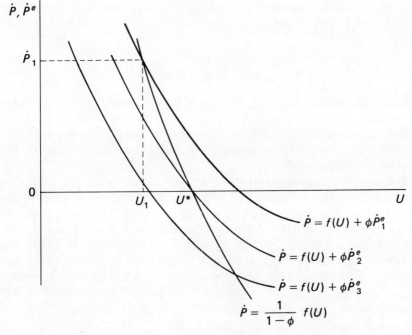

Figure 5.2

In equilibrium, as before, $\dot{P} = \dot{P}^e$, and hence

$$\dot{P} = \frac{1}{1-\phi} f(U). \tag{5.8}$$

There is, then, a long-run Phillips Curve trade-off between fully anticipated inflation and unemployment that is steeper than the short run trade-off, as depicted in figure 5.2. Clearly, $\dot{P}_1^e > 0$, $\dot{P}_2^e = 0$ and $\dot{P}_3^e < 0$. Should the government decide to run the economy at some unemployment rate U_1, then eventually the rate of inflation would converge upon $\dot{P}_1$ where inflationary expectations are fulfilled.

It does none the less seem extremely difficult to justify a coefficient of less than unity on price expectations. If we consider two economies identical in every respect except that in one the actual and expected inflation rate is a steady 10 per cent while in the other it is a steady 20 per cent, it is hard to see why workers should be prepared to accept a lower expected real wage for any given level of unemployment in the latter (as equation (5.7) would imply). While there may

be wage and price rigidities in the economy, it seems logically unsatisfactory to model them by means of a less than unit coefficient on
price expectations.

5.1.2 COST INFLATION AND EXPECTATIONS

Up to this point we have been analysing the role of inflationary
expectations within the context of what is essentially an excess
demand theory of inflation. Inflationary expectations were seen as
exerting an important influence in determining the position of the
short-run Phillips Curve.

By far the largest proportion of the theoretical and empirical
research into the influence of price expectations in an inflationary
process has been undertaken by the monetarists. However, it would
be highly misleading to infer from this that price expectations do not
play an important part in other approaches to inflation. In particular,
if one accepts a basically cost-push analysis of inflation, one might
become very alarmed at the prospect of the buildup of inflationary
expectations. For example, one could incorporate a model of expectations formation identical to the analysis of section 5.1 into the
cost-push theory outlined in section 4.1 above. In this case the equation
for the rate of inflation would no longer be (4.4) but (4.4'), set out
below:

$$\dot{P} = \left(\frac{\alpha_1'}{1 - \alpha_2} - 1 \right) + \phi \dot{P}^e. \qquad (4.4')$$

The series for $\dot{P}^e$ could be generated by a mechanism such as the
adaptive expectations process of equation (5.6). Nor does the
monetarist assumption of the absence of money illusion undermine
the validity of this model; i.e., the restriction that ϕ be equal to unity
leaves the theory underlying (4.4') unaffected. What the cost-push
approach denies — and this does set it apart from monetarist and
other demand-pull approaches — is that there will exist within the
range of 'acceptable' rates of unemployment a particular rate at which
an inflation will cease to accelerate. In other words, the search for
U^* will prove to be futile. But the key word is 'acceptable': few
cost-push theorists would deny that, if a massive deflation of aggregate
demand were produced by monetary and fiscal restriction, and if this
deflation were maintained for long enough, then inflation will start
to decline. However, they argue that the level of unemployment at
which this fall in the rate of inflation would start to take place is
likely to be unacceptably high.

5.2 A MICROECONOMIC THEORY OF THE LABOUR MARKET

As we have seen, Friedman's arguments concerning the role of price expectations in the Phillips Curve and the natural rate of unemployment were based on general economic principles (such as the absence of money illusion) rather than on a specific analysis of the labour market. But at about the same time a number of economists, in particular Phelps, Holt, Alchian and Mortensen (see Phelps, 1971), were developing a microeconomic theory of the labour market which implied a macroeconomic relationship between unemployment and unanticipated inflation, as in equations (5.2) and (5.3) above. This theory is generally known as the 'search theory' of unemployment. In this section we first discuss the assumptions and analysis of search theory, and then consider its implications in the analysis of unemployment and inflation.

5.2.1 SEARCH THEORY

Search theory is based on two very plausible assumptions. First, it is assumed that workers differ from one another in their skills and preferences and that jobs differ from one another in their requirements and characteristics. It follows that workers will not be indifferent between job opportunities, and firms will not be indifferent between job applicants. Second, it is assumed that information is imperfect, so that, for example, a newly unemployed worker does not know what types of jobs may or may not be open to him.

It follows that it will often be sensible, or rational, for a newly unemployed worker not to take the first job he comes across, but instead to investigate first what types of jobs are available. The unemployed, in this view, are looking not for any job, but for an *appropriate* job, given their skills, preferences, etc. Even if jobs are reasonably easily available, the unemployed worker is always faced with the choice between accepting a current job offer or remaining unemployed and continuing to search for a more desirable job.

An immediate objection to the search theory is that it seems to pose too extreme a choice. Why cannot the unemployed worker both take the current job offer and continue searching for a better job? In fact, may not workers in employment find it easier to find better jobs, in so far as their existing employment acts as a recommendation to future employers (Tobin, 1972)? For some types of jobs these seem reasonable arguments, but in general the considerations that job search takes time and energy (travelling, attending interviews, etc.), and that the hiring and set-up costs with each new job can be quite high, support the idea that the unemployed can search more efficiently.

A model along these lines has been formalized by Mortensen (1971). Mortensen shows that, given the distribution of potential wage offers that a worker believes to exist (which may, of course, differ from the true distribution because the worker has incomplete information), and given the greater efficiency of searching while unemployed, a worker will accept or reject a current job offer according to whether the wage is above or below a critical value (known as the 'reservation wage').

Each worker's view of the wage distribution is held to depend primarily on his own recent experience of the labour market, and hence these wage distributions will differ between workers. Thus, at any moment of time different workers will have different reservation wages. Furthermore, if workers are unemployed for a while, they will acquire a lot of additional information on wages, which may alter their perception of the wage distribution (and hence their reservation wage).

We turn now from workers to employers. Employers are assumed to have a steady stream of job vacancies (owing to retirements, resignations, etc.), and they receive a steady stream of job applicants. Because the applicants all have different reservation wages, the higher the wage the firm offers, the greater the proportion of applicants it can recruit. Thus a firm that wishes to expand will set a wage in excess of the average to allow it to expand its labour force, while a declining firm will allow its wages to fall below average as it has no need to attract as many new recruits.

5.2.2 SEARCH THEORY AND UNEMPLOYMENT

We first consider a situation in which the level of aggregate demand is constant, and the average level of prices is stable. In such a situation, however, microeconomic changes are always taking place, with some firms growing and others declining or going out of business. In this picture, wages in individual jobs are moving up or down relative to one another, and workers who leave (or lose) their jobs search around in the manner described above until they find a new job at an acceptable wage.

This picture of unemployment seems consistent with Friedman's 'natural rate', and indeed is very similar to the familiar, and much earlier, concept of frictional unemployment (see for example Keynes, 1936, p.6). What distinguishes search theory is that the model that describes frictional unemployment in a situation of constant aggregate demand also explains fluctuations in unemployment in response to changes in demand. Before discussing the effect of changes in aggregate demand, there is a further implication of search theory for unemployment to be mentioned.

If unemployed workers are keen to find jobs, one would expect that they would be able fairly quickly to gain an accurate picture of the wage distribution they face. Once they have a realistic picture of their opportunities, if they continue searching they should soon find an acceptable job ('acceptable' in the sense that further search is unlikely to offer anything significantly better). Thus it is an implication of search theory that the length of time for which people are unemployed should be relatively short.

The evidence, both in the United States and in Britain, is to a large extent consistent with the search theory model. There are large flows of workers into and out of unemployment and the average duration of unemployment is quite short. The majority of people made unemployed find new jobs within two or three months (Perry, 1972). However, unemployment cannot be fully explained by the search theory model. In addition to the people who are unemployed for short periods, there are significant numbers of long-term unemployed who may remain unemployed for a year or longer. Nor can these long-term unemployed be regarded as 'unemployable', for the number of them rises in recession and falls in booms. The cyclical variation in the numbers of long-term unemployed seems very difficult to reconcile with search theory (Akerlof and Main, 1980).

5.2.3 CHANGES IN AGGREGATE DEMAND

We next consider what happens if, after demand has been held constant and prices remained stable, the government suddenly increases its spending on goods and services. Firms, on balance, will experience an increase in demand, and they will wish to recruit more labour. They will thus increase their wage offers. If workers' reservation wages do not change, a greater proportion of them will receive offers in excess of their reservation wage, and will hence take jobs. The outcome is that, in the economy as a whole, wages will have risen and unemployment fallen.

Similarly, if the government were to reduce its spending, firms would lower their wage offers and fewer workers (with given reservation wages) would accept jobs. Unemployment would then rise. This model then produces observations consistent with the Phillips Curve, that is an association between low unemployment and higher wage increases and between higher unemployment and lower wage increases (or wage reductions).

The effects on unemployment arise, however, because workers base their reservation wages on their perceived wage distributions, and their perceived wage distributions do not adjust (or do not adjust fully) to the actual changes in wage offers that result from the change in aggregate demand. It is because the change in aggregate demand succeeds in 'fooling' them as to the true distribution of wage offers that the government is able either to get them to take jobs that otherwise they would have refused (thereby achieving a temporary reduction in unemployment) or to turn down jobs they would otherwise have taken (with a consequential increase in unemployment). As workers adjust their perceived wage distributions in response to the new wage offers they observe, their reservation wages will be adjusted and the effects on unemployment will disappear.

5.2.4 UNEMPLOYMENT AND INFLATION

We now consider an economy in which inflation has been proceeding at a steady rate for a number of years, so that the actual and expected rates of inflation are the same. Workers anticipate continuing inflation, and hence, when unemployed, increase their reservation wages in line with their expectations of inflation. Wage offers are also increasing, with continuing inflation, so that the probability of a worker receiving a wage offer in excess of his reservation wage is independent of the rate of fully anticipated inflation. The rate of search unemployment is thus unaffected by fully anticipated inflation.

If the government, as in the previous case, increases its demand for goods and services, firms increase their wage offers and the actual rate of inflation rises. If workers' expectations do not immediately adjust, their reservation wages, which increase in line with their expectations of inflation, will increase only at the same rate as before, and hence more slowly than the rate of increase of the wages actually being offered. Thus a greater number of workers will receive offers in excess of their reservation wage, and hence take jobs. Thus a rise in the inflation rate (relative to expectations) will be associated with a reduction in unemployment. Once workers realize that the distribution of wage offers has changed, they will adjust their reservation wages, and unemployment will return to its original level.

Thus, on this theory unemployment is unaffected by any anticipated inflation rate, but it is inversely related to unanticipated inflation, precisely as suggested by equation (5.3). Search theory thus provides a rigorous analytical basis for the role of expectations and for the natural rate hypothesis. It suggests a short-run trade-off between inflation and unemployment, because in the short run the actual inflation rate can differ from that expected, but no long-run trade-off, because in the long run people's expectations will adjust to the actual inflation rate.

There are a number of serious objections to search theory, however. For example, it seems unable to account for phenomena such as lay-offs or redundancies; its predictions on the numbers voluntarily quitting their jobs are inconsistent with the evidence (Tobin, 1972); it assumes wages completely flexible, whereas wages are changed only occasionally; and, as noted above, it does not account for the numbers of long-term unemployed.

Search theory provides an explanation, both of the natural rate of unemployment and of short-run fluctuations in unemployment and inflation, which does not depend on arbitrary assumptions of wage or price inflexibility. In the search theory framework, prices and wages are perfectly flexible and markets always clear. Unemployment occurs because of voluntary decision by the unemployed to search rather than take the first job available. The weakness of the search theory approach is that, however difficult to explain in terms of economic theory, wage and price rigidities do exist and in consequence markets do not always clear.

5.3 EMPIRICAL EVIDENCE ON THE EXPECTATIONS HYPOTHESIS

The central proposition of the expectations hypothesis is that the coefficient on price expectations in equations such as (5.2) or (5.7) should be unity. This proposition was based, in Friedman's argument, on the *a priori* conviction that in the long run there is no money illusion; and it can also be derived from more rigorous microeconomic analysis of the labour market, as shown in section 5.2. We turn now to empirical tests of the expectations hypothesis.

Most empirical studies assume a fairly mechanical application of adaptive expectations. The procedure is to estimate an equation of the form

$$\dot{P}_t = f(U_t) + \phi \, \dot{P}_t^e \tag{5.9}$$

with

$$\dot{P}_t^e = (1 - \psi) \sum_j^\infty \psi^{j-1} \, \dot{P}_{t-j}. \tag{5.5}$$

The value of ψ is determined by trial and error; that is, a number of different series for $\dot{P}^e$ are calculated for different values of ψ in equation (5.5), and equation (5.9) is estimated for each of these different series. The chosen values for ψ is that which gives the best fit in equation (5.9).

The main focus of attention, however, is on the estimated value of ϕ in equation (5.9). Most early studies (e.g. Gordon, 1970; Turnovsky and Wachter, 1972; Cukierman, 1974) found values of ϕ significantly less than unity, and thus seemed to reject the 'strong' version of the expectations hypothesis. However, more recent work, including that of Gordon (1972), Turnovsky (1972), Parkin (1975), Parkin, Sumner and Ward (1976) and Wachter (1976), finds a value of ϕ close to, or not significantly different from, unity.

The tendency of the estimated value of ϕ to differ between studies and to float towards unity over time may cast some doubt on the expectations hypothesis. It is clear that, as inflation accelerated in the late 1960s and early 1970s, wages were able to keep up with the more rapid growth of prices without there being a sustained fall in unemployment. Studies of the expectations hypothesis incorporating data from this period will thus tend to find values for ϕ close to unity (whether or not the link between wage and price inflation increases in practice operates through expectations).

A second problem, particularly of UK studies, over this period is the changing relationship between unemployment and the pressure of demand in the labour market (see chapter 3 above, pp. 60–3). Studies that make no allowance for this shift can yield poorly defined results. In particular, with both inflation and unemployment rising over the period, some econometric studies find a positive coefficient on the unemployment term in an equation such as (5.9). Because such studies attribute part of the rise in inflation to higher unemployment, the coefficient on the price expectations term is biased downwards. (For example, Henry, Sawyer and Smith, 1976, find a positive coefficient on unemployment and a value for ϕ insignificantly differently from zero).

But the most serious problem with all these studies is that they assume a fixed adaptive expectations structure (as indicated by equation (5.5)). We have already noted (in section 5.1) that the way in which people use information on past inflation rates in order to forecast future inflation is itself dependent on the way the economy is behaving. An adaptive expectations scheme may give quite good forecasts if the inflation rate is relatively stable, but give extremely bad forecasts if the inflation rate is accelerating, or highly volatile. People are thus likely to change their method of forecasting inflation rather than to hold mechanically to one particular scheme.

These considerations have led economists to experiment with direct data on the state of price expectations. This marks a distinct departure from standard empirical practice, for little confidence has been placed in the past in data derived from questionnaire-type surveys. In particular, Carlson and Parkin (1975) have constructed a $\dot{P}^e$ series for the UK based on observations on the percentage of the population who believe it will fall as compared with the percentage who believe it will rise. Using this series, they regressed the equation

$$\dot{P}^e_t = \alpha_0 \, \dot{P}_{t-1} + \alpha_1 \, \dot{P}^e_{t-1}$$

and found that the adaptive expectations restriction (see equation (5.6)), that $\alpha_0 = (1 - \psi)$ and $\alpha_1 = \psi$, is not rejected. Their most satisfactory hypothesis however turned out to be a *second-order* error learning process which had been proposed by Rose (1972):

$$\dot{P}^e - \dot{P}^e_{t-1} = (1 - \psi)\,(\dot{P}_{t-1} - \dot{P}^e_{t-1}) + (1 - \psi_1)\,(\dot{P}_{t-2} - \dot{P}^e_{t-2}).$$

Direct evidence on price expectations in the USA has been collected by Livingston. As with the UK series, the Livingston series appears consistent with a two-stage process, in which expectations are influenced strongly by the immediate past, but with a tendency to regress to a long-term norm which itself changes only rather slowly (Brinner, 1977; Holden and Peel, 1977).

By contrast to the large number of studies examining the impact of price expectations on wage increases, there has been relatively little investigation of the effect of price expectations on the rate of price increase itself. An early study by Solow (1969) examined the responsiveness of price increases to both price expectations and wage increases. His results suggested a coefficient of significantly less than unity on price expectations. However, this study does not constitute a test of the expectations hypothesis because, as Parkin (1975) has argued, price expectations may affect prices not only directly but also through their effects on wage increases, and hence the proper test of the expectations hypothesis in the Solow model is that the sum of the coefficients on price expectations and wage increases should equal unity. Parkin concludes that, on this basis, Solow's results are consistent with the expectations hypothesis.

Laidler (1973) tested the hypothesis that the rate of price inflation is determined by the level of economic activity and the expected rate

of inflation using US data. His results were favourable to the expectations hypothesis with an estimated coefficient on the expected
inflation variable very close to unity.

Finally, a general difficulty with empirical tests of the expectations
hypothesis is that, as noted at the beginning of the chapter, the theory
assumes a closed economy. The actual economies on which the theory
has been tested are, of course, open economies with, in some cases,
large overseas trading sectors. The USA has a sufficiently large domestic market that it might be thought to approximate a closed economy;
but the European countries must be regarded as open economies, and
we consider the implications of this in chapter 7.

5.4 POLICY IMPLICATIONS

In this section we consider the implications of the expectations hypothesis, or of the natural rate of unemployment hypothesis, for:

(a) long-run macroeconomic policy;
(b) short-run macroeconomic policy;
(c) policies to influence expectations;
(d) microeconomic policy.

We continue to assume a closed economy, although, as we will argue
in chapter 7, most of the points made here will carry over to an open
economy with a freely flexible exchange rate.

5.4.1 LONG-RUN MACROECONOMIC POLICY

The main implication of the expectations hypothesis for long-run
macroeconomic policy is, of course, that in the long run macroeconomic policy cannot affect the unemployment rate. One might
argue that, in principle, with adaptive expectations, there is a trade-
off between unemployment and accelerating inflation, but, as argued
in section 5.1, it is likely that this trade-off would disappear if the
government were actually to embark on a policy of permanently
accelerating inflation.

If the natural rate of unemployment were known, the government
might be tempted to use fiscal and monetary policies to guide the
economy towards the natural rate, and hence attempt to minimize
fluctuations both in employment and in inflation. In practice,
however, the natural rate of unemployment is not known, and may
well change over time. This presents a very severe difficulty for any

policy based on unemployment targets, for if the government attempts to achieve a level of unemployment different from the natural rate, it will plunge the economy into ever-accelerating inflation (or deflation).

It follows that the government cannot base its monetary and fiscal policies on a target unemployment rate. It is perhaps easiest to describe the policy options open to the government if we first assume, by way of illustration, that the strict version of the quantity theory of money holds (see chapter 2). With the level of unemployment given by the natural rate, the level of output in the economy can be assumed to grow at a rate determined by supply-side factors (capital accumulation, the growth of the labour force, technical progress, etc.). Let us assume that these factors will lead to a growth of output of x per cent per annum. Then, according to the strict version of the quantity theory (with constant velocity of circulation of money), the rate of inflation is equal to the rate of growth of the money supply less the rate of growth of output:

$$MV = Py$$

implies that

$$\dot{M} + \dot{V} = \dot{P} + \dot{y}$$

(where $\dot{M}$ is the proportional growth rate of M, that is $1/M(dM/dt)$, etc.). V constant implies $\dot{V} = 0$, so

$$\dot{P} = \dot{M} - \dot{y}.$$

Thus, the government can determine the inflation rate through a control over the money supply. If we assume the government's preferred rate of inflation is zero, it should set the rate of growth of the money supply equal to the rate of growth of output (that is, x per cent per annum in this example).

The idea that the government should pursue a stable growth rate of the money supply consistent with long-run price stability has for a long time been advocated by Friedman (e.g. Friedman, 1948). But it is the expectations hypothesis that provides a rigorous theoretical justification for this policy rule (Friedman, 1968). Formally, we can argue that it is only if policy is related to a *nominal* variable (like the money supply) rather than a *real* variable (such as unemployment) that policy will be stabilizing in the face of unanticipated shocks.

As an example, assume that the natural rate of unemployment doubles, and that this change is not detected by the government. If it maintains an unemployment target equal to the earlier, lower, level of the natural rate it will, as we have seen, plunge the economy into ever-accelerating inflation. If, however, it pursues a Friedman money supply rule, the inflation will be temporary and self-correcting. Initially, there is excess demand in the economy and prices rise; but, with the growth of the money supply fixed, the rise in prices reduces real money balances and hence (as shown in chapter 2) reduces aggregate demand. Unemployment then rises, which in turn slows down inflation. The economy returns to equilibrium at the new, higher, level of the natural rate and with prices again stable.

We noted earlier that it was perfectly possible to accept the expectations hypothesis without at the same time holding a 'quantity theory' view of the macroeconomic system. If the velocity of circulation varies erratically, it may make more sense to relate policy to nominal magnitudes of direct interest (such as nominal GDP or the price level). Fiscal as well as monetary policies could be employed to maintain one or other of these nominal variables on some desired path. The expectations hypothesis does not, of itself, close off the traditional debates of stabilization policy (fiscal versus monetary measures; rules versus discretion; etc.): what it does imply, and it is a crucial difference, is that the target or objective of macroeconomic policy has to be a nominal rather than a real variable.

5.4.2 SHORT-RUN MACROECONOMIC POLICY

In the long run, as we have seen, fiscal and monetary policies should be so arranged as to reduce fluctuations of the economy away from the natural rate of unemployment and from the government's target inflation rate. Short-run policy may, however, be confronted with a more difficult problem. People's expectations — being determined by recent experience — may well be inconsistent with the government's long-run objectives.

In particular, an economy may be experiencing an undesirably rapid rate of inflation. While expectations of inflation persist, the government cannot achieve price stability, or any reduction in inflation, except at the expense of deflating the economy and forcing unemployment above the natural rate.

This problem is illustrated in figure 5.3, where we assume the economy is at the natural rate of unemployment at point A with the actual and expected rate of inflation equal to $\dot{P}_A$. The government wishes to reduce the inflation rate to zero, that is, to move the economy to point B. Initially it deflates demand by the use of fiscal or mone-

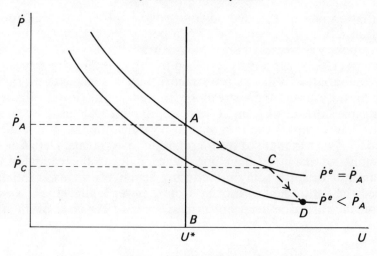

Figure 5.3

tary policy, so that, with a given state of price expectations, the economy is shifted to a point such as *C*, on the same short-run Phillips Curve as point *A*. The inflation rate therefore falls to P_C, which in turn reduces the expected rate of inflation. With reduced inflation expectations, the economy now moves on to a lower Phillips Curve, and hence, with continuing demand deflation in the next period, moves to a point such as *D*. This process continues until eventually both the actual and expected rates of inflation fall to zero, and the economy arrives at point *B*.

The reduction of inflation therefore entails a possibly large, but temporary, cost in the form of higher unemployment and lost output. Accepting that the reduction of inflation, within the context of this theory, necessarily involves such costs, it is natural to ask whether different deflationary strategies impose different costs, and whether, therefore, a least-cost strategy can be identified.

It seems clear that, the more severe the deflationary policies the government adopts, the more rapidly both the actual and the expected rate of inflation will fall. There is thus a choice between a severe, but short-lived, depression or a milder, but much more drawn-out, recession. Economic analysis does not have much to contribute to whether the 'short, sharp shock' or the 'gradualist' solution is to be preferred. We return to this issue in chapter 10.

A final question that can be asked in this context is whether it is worth incurring the costs of reducing inflation at all. If we 'inherit' an inflation rate of $\dot{P}_A$, one possible policy option is to maintain an inflation rate of $\dot{P}_A$ as an objective of policy. We thus avoid the need for temporary increases in unemployment.

Phelps (1978) has recently returned to this question. He argues that reducing inflation is like an investment: there is a current cost (in the form of lost output) and a stream of future benefits (lower inflation). As an investment, we can, at least in principle, calculate its rate of return, and compare the rate of return on investment – in reducing inflation – with the rate of return on other investments. Deflating the economy lowers investment and hence reduces the capital stock. Deflation is desirably only if the future benefits from lower inflation exceed the future loss of income from a lower capital stock. We will not pursue this issue here, but discuss some of the costs of inflation in chapter 9.

5.4.3 POLICIES TO INFLUENCE EXPECTATIONS

If the government decides to reduce the rate of inflation, the economy suffers a period of unemployment (in excess of the natural rate) while inflation expectations adjust to the new, lower, rate of inflation. If, however, at the same time inflation expectations could be reduced, the inflation rate could fall with no increase in the unemployment rate.

On a strict reading of the adaptive expectations hypothesis, expectations are a product only of past experience of inflation and hence cannot be affected other than by altering the inflation rate itself. But more generally it is plausible to think that people's expectations will be affected by government policy. In this section we briefly consider arguments for incomes policies and for indexation in this context.

If the government introduces an incomes policy, which for example limits increases in wages and other incomes to some given amount, and people expect that most wage settlements will in fact fall within that limit, and they further believe that prices are largely determined by wages, then the introduction of an incomes policy will alter expectations of future inflation. Because it lowers expectations, each group of workers will be willing to settle for a lower wage increase than otherwise, and it will then be possible to reduce inflation without increasing unemployment.

Thus, incomes policies can in principle produce a virtuous circle, in which each group of workers is prepared to accept a lower wage increase for themselves because they believe others will do likewise and that the rate of inflation will then fall, so that they will suffer no loss in real wages. Clearly crucial to this approach is the requirement that the incomes policy be credible: that each group of workers believes that other groups of workers will abide by it, and that the slower growth of costs, supported by a slower growth of nominal aggregate demand, will slow down price increases. The evidence that incomes policies do affect expectations is, however, not very strong. Carlson and Parkin (1975) found no perceptible impact of any incomes policy on their measure of expected inflation, while Holden and Peel (1977) found that incomes policies did reduce inflation expectations, but only by 1½ percentage points. Impressionistically, one could perhaps argue that incomes policies combined with demand deflation (such as that of the Labour Government in the UK from 1975 to 1977), which serve to push expectations towards equilibrium, have been effective and helped achieve a reduction in inflation. By contrast, incomes policies combined with demand expansion, which attempt to push expectations away from equilibrium, have broken down and reduced the credibility of subsequent incomes policies.

A different approach, based not so much on attempting to lower inflation expectations as on attempting to remove their impact altogether, is that of indexation. If workers' expectations of inflation are too high, relative to the rate of expansion of nominal aggregate demand, and wage claims are thus too high, indexation offers a possible solution. If workers were to agree to a wage settlement indexed to the price level, their wages would in the outcome rise only at the actual, rather at their expected, rate of inflation. Thus if price increases were immediately reduced by deflationary government policy, the rate of wage increases would also fall, and there would be no cause for unemployment to rise above the natural rate.

As the above account makes clear, the case for indexation in this context depends crucially on the assumption that, in response to a deflationary policy, the rate of price inflation falls quickly relative to the rate of wage increases. If, on the other hand, prices are a mark-up on wage costs (as the normal cost pricing hypothesis — chapter 3, appendix 1 — suggests) the rate of price inflation will start to fall only after the rate of wage increases slows down, and in such a model indexation will not help.

5.4.4 MICROECONOMIC POLICY

If macroeconomic policy cannot move unemployment away from the natural rate, except temporarily and at the cost of accelerating inflation, the only way of achieving a permanent reduction in unemployment is through reductions in the natural rate itself, through microeconomic or labour market policies. It is beyond the scope of this book to discuss such policies in any detail, but it may be useful to indicate the types of policies that might reduce the natural rate.

First, it seems likely that institutional impediments to job mobility may raise the natural rate of unemployment. In the UK it is often argued that occupational mobility is hindered by trade union, or other, restrictive practices, and that geographical mobility is restricted by housing policies which have all but eliminated a free rental market in housing. As a result, labour shortages in one sector or part of the country may co-exist with unemployment in another sector or part of the country, and the more difficult is mobility, the longer the imbalance will persist. Similarly, institutional practices that fix relative wages according to 'comparability' or some other non-market criterion can prevent equilibrating relative wage adjustments (Brittan, 1975). From an efficiency viewpoint, these impediments and rigidites are in any event undesirable, and there is therefore a strong case for government policies aimed at reducing or removing them.

However, if there were no rigidities or other market imperfections, it is by no means clear that government policy should attempt to reduce the natural rate. Alchian (1971), for example, is in no doubt that the equilibrium unemployment rate in a search model is socially optimal. Less unemployment means less search, which in turn means that some people will end up in less appropriate jobs than they could have got had they been unemployed for longer, and thus searched for longer. But Alchian's assertion that the natural rate is socially optimal is not supported by any analysis, and Phelps (1972) and Tobin (1972) have suggested a number of reasons — mostly based on externalities — for thinking that the equilibrium rate may be higher than is socially optimal. Such arguments suggest a role for government, for example in the provision of information on job vacancies or of training, to reduce the natural rate below its free market equilibrium level.

Finally, unemployment, and related social security benefits, clearly 'subsidize' search relative to work, and are thus likely to extend the duration of unemployment especially for workers whose pay in work is little more than the benefit rate (Nickell, 1979). Thus there is an efficiency case for reducing unemployment benefits (or converting them into loans). If, however, equity or distributional criteria rule out any change in unemployment benefits, a 'second-best' policy is to subsidize the pay of the low paid. In the UK, the family income supplement (FIS) scheme provides such a subsidy. (For a theoretical analysis of this argument, see Jackman and Layard, 1980.)

5.5 SUMMARY AND CONCLUSIONS

In this chapter we have argued that, if wage increases depend not only on the pressure of demand in the labour market but also on the expected rate of inflation, the trade-off between inflation and unemployment disappears. There is, in the short run, a trade-off between unanticipated inflation and unemployment, but, in the long run the actual and anticipated rates of inflation must be equal and there is then no trade-off between inflation and unemployment. In the long run unemployment is determined by the characteristics of the labour market and inflation by the growth of aggregate demand (in monetary terms) in the economy.

A microeconomic theory of the labour market consistent with the expectations hypothesis is search theory, which we described briefly in section 5.2. Search theory remains rather controversial, and seems unable to account for a number of labour market phenomena. It does, however, offer the most systematic attempt to model the relationship between wages and employment decisions at the level of the individual worker or firm.

More generally, it can be argued that the assumptions of rationality or the absence of money illusion are sufficient to justify the expectations approach. We will discuss this further in chapter 8, where we consider theories in which wage increases compensate for past, rather than anticipated future, inflation.

In section 5.3 we outlined the evidence from empirical studies on the expectations hypothesis. Overall, the evidence seems reasonably consistent with the theory. Section 5.4 set out the main implications of the expectations hypothesis for policy. The main point is that the government can no longer base its macroeconomic policy on some target value of a 'real' variable such as unemployment, output or growth. Instead, macroeconomic policy has to focus on some nominal, or monetary, target such as money GDP, the rate of inflation or the money supply. We examined the choice between different policies for reducing the rate of inflation. With the expectations hypothesis it seems difficult to avoid the conclusion that reducing inflation entails a temporary increase in unemployment above the natural rate. Finally, and very briefly, we mentioned a number of microeconomic policies aimed at reducing the natural rate of unemployment.

CHAPTER 6

Inflation and Monetarism

Explanations of inflation based on the Phillips Curve (with or without expectations) treat variations in the pressure of demand as an exogenous factor influencing the rate of change of wages and prices. The Phillips Curve approach is not committed to any particular view or to the determinants of aggregate demand. By contrast, a central tenet of the monetarist position is that variations in nominal income are best explained by variations in the rate of growth of the quantity of money.

We discussed the classical quantity theory of money in chapter 2. The quantity theory view that the rate of inflation was determined by the rate of growth of the money supply was based on three propositions, which modern monetarists have attempted to re-establish and to make more rigorous:

(a) that the velocity of circulation of money is stable, or, equivalently, that the demand for money is a stable function of a relatively small number of variables;

(b) that, while monetary factors may have a short-run impact on the level of real income, in the longer run the growth of real income is determined by real factors, such as population growth, capital accumulation and technical progress;

(c) that the supply of money can be controlled independently of the demand for money (or, at least, is determined by a different set of factors).

The quantity theory identity $(MV \equiv Py)$ can be written, in terms of rates of change, as

$$\dot{M} + \dot{V} \equiv \dot{P} + \dot{y}$$

or

$$\dot{P} \equiv \dot{M} + \dot{V} - \dot{y}.$$

If we can assume, from propositions (a) and (b), that V and y are

114

constant (so $\dot{V} = \dot{y} = 0$), and from proposition (c) that the growth of the money supply is determined by some factors independent of the demand for it, then those factors that determine the growth of the money supply will, in consequence, also determine the rate of inflation.

In this chapter we take up these issues in more detail. Section 6.1 is concerned with the stability of the velocity of circulation, but abstracts from the complications that can arise if inflationary expectations affect the demand for money. This problem is addressed in section 6.2, which also considers empirical evidence from experiences of 'hyper-inflation'. In section 6.3 we discuss the monetarist approach to the determination of real output and a recent development of this argument based on the idea of 'rational expectations'. Section 6.4 examines the question whether the supply of money has been (or can be) determined independently of the demand for it, and includes some comments on the lessons that can be learned from the monetarist experiment carried out in the UK since 1979.

Here again we assume a closed economy, leaving monetarist theories of the international transmission of inflation, and of the determinants of world inflation, to chapter 7. We will argue, however, that international factors are of major importance only in an economy with a fixed exchange rate, and that the analysis in this chapter will apply not only to a closed economy but also to an open economy that maintains a flexible exchange rate.

6.1 THE STABILITY OF THE VELOCITY OF CIRCULATION

The revival of the quantity theory of money took place largely under the guidance of Milton Friedman and other economists working in the Chicago tradition. Their first study to challenge fundamentally the postwar Keynesian orthodoxy was an empirical investigation by Friedman and Meiselman (1964), which purported to show that, as an empirical matter, the velocity of circulation of money was more stable than the Keynesian 'multiplier'. The methodology of the Friedman–Meiselman paper is relatively straightforward. The simple Keynesian model predicts that the level of total expenditure in general, and consumer expenditure in particular, varies with the level of autonomous expenditure such as autonomous investment and government expenditure. In symbols, the Keynesian hypothesis states that

$$C_m = C_1 (E_m)$$

where the m subscripts on C and E refer to the money values of consumer expenditure and autonomous expenditure respectively. The monetarist hypothesis, in contrast, states that variations in consumption expenditure are more adequately explained in terms of variations in the stock of money. In symbols,

$$C_m = C_2 \ (M).$$

Not surprisingly, Friedman and Meiselman's econometric testing found that the monetarist hypothesis was better determined statistically for all periods apart from the depression years.

Ando and Modigliani (1965), on the other hand, found that a theoretically more satisfactory definition of autonomous expenditure yields the contrary conclusion – that fiscal variables were more effective in explaining variations in consumption expenditure. Their principal objection to the Friedman–Meiselman approach is however of a methodological nature. They register the familiar Keynesian objection to highly simplified regression equations in which the apparently independent variables may not in fact be independent at all. They regard the application of partial equilibrium techniques to a general equilibrium problem as being less than useful.

For the UK Barrett and Walters (1966) produced inconclusive results on the basis of first-difference reduced-form equations. Monetary and fiscal variables, when considered separately, performed poorly, but when they were both included in the same equation they produced superior results. A more intricate study by Artis and Nobay (1969) once again produced rather ambiguous findings. Their results indicate that, on balance, fiscal policy is more effective than monetary policy.

The Friedman–Meiselman study proved very effective in dramatizing the issues in the form of a conflict between monetarist and Keynesian approaches (sometimes known as the 'gladiatorial approach' to economics). But to many economists it was not clear why, in terms of the standard neo-Keynesian analysis, the subject should degenerate into a sort of battle between the *IS* curve and the *LM* curve when, of course, the standard model already incorporated both.

It is a standard textbook result that, within the *IS–LM* model, the steeper the *LM* curve, the greater the impact of monetary factors on income and the smaller the impact of changes in autonomous expenditure. The *LM* curve is steep if both the demand for and the supply of money are interest-inelastic. For the present we focus on the demand for money (leaving the supply to section 6.4). If the demand for money is stable (in the sense that variables other than money income have only a relatively small impact on the demand for money), there will, in the *IS—LM* model, be a close association between the quantity of money and the level of money income. Stability of the velocity of circulation is thus equivalent to there being a stable demand function for money. Therefore we next consider, very briefly, the monetarist position on the demand for money.

6.1.1 FRIEDMAN ON THE DEMAND FOR MONEY

We have seen from chapter 2 that the proponents of the Cambridge cash-balance equation for the demand for money ($M = kPy$) typically assumed that k, though influenced by other variables, would, as an empirical matter, tend to be relatively stable. In the *General Theory*, Keynes argued that the pressure of a speculative motive for holding money could lead to a highly unstable (or highly interest-elastic, for any given state of expectations) demand function for money. Friedman's (1956) 'restatement' of the quantity theory assimilates the Keynesian approach into orthodox microeconomic choice theory.

Friedman's approach is based on the idea that people will allocate their wealth between different assets in such a way as to maximize their utility. Assets can yield pecuniary returns (such as interest or dividends) or non-pecuniary returns (such as the services provided by household durable goods). Money yields non-pecuniary services in the form of convenience (of effecting transaxtions) and security. A necessary condition for utility maximization is that, at the margin, the return from all assets must be equal. Thus money balances will be held up to an amount where the marginal utility of the services they provide is equal to the return available on other assets.

The most important implication of Friedman's approach is that money was regarded as a substitute not only for bonds but for equities, physical capital and durable goods. It follows that the expected rate of inflation will now affect the demand for money. The faster the expected rate of inflation, the higher the proportion of their wealth will people choose to hold in the form of durable goods and physical assets — which maintain their real value — rather than in money balances, which are eroded in value by inflation. (We return to the implications of this in section 6.2.)

As far as substitution between money and bonds is concerned, Friedman follows Keynes in defining the return on bonds to allow for both income and expected capital gains (or losses). The difference between Friedman and Keynes in this respect is purely one of empirical magnitudes. There is not space here to go into the now extensive empirical literature concerned with the demand for money (for a survey, see Laidler, 1977). While, of course, results differ between studies, there seems little doubt that, on balance, the evidence does point to a well identified demand for money function and, generally, to a relatively low interest elasticity. The first requirement of the monetarist approach – a stable demand-for-money function – does appear to exist for many countries and over most of the periods studied.

An apparent exception is the recent monetary history of the UK, where demand-for-money functions estimated on data prior to 1970 have 'broken down' during the 1970s. Recent work by Coghlan (1978) and Hendry (1980) has established that, with a more careful dynamic specification, a stable demand function for transactions balances (that is, currency and non-interest-bearing current account bank deposits, known as M1) can be identified for the UK over the period. It has not yet proved possible however to identify a demand function for the broader monetary aggregate, M3 (which includes interest-bearing deposit accounts at banks). We return to this particular problem in section 6.4, and in the meantime assume a stable demand function for money.

6.1.2 THE TRANSMISSION MECHANISM

We have already (in chapter 2) discussed the mechanisms whereby a change in the quantity of money affects the real economy. There we argued that the main channel of transmission was through the interest rate, and this is of course also the transmission mechanism in the *IS–LM* model. If the demand for money is stable, any change in the money supply must entail a movement of interest rates.

Clearly, for this mechanism to work it is essential that expenditure does respond to changes in interest rates. In the Keynesian model it is assumed that investment, and in particular business fixed investment, would be the most interest-sensitive component of expenditure. However, many empirical studies of investment have failed to detect any influence of interest rates (for a recent survey, see Savage, 1978). It is the alleged inability of the monetarists to produce an empirically well substantiated transmission channel for the impact of monetary policy that is one of the major factors behind continuing Keynesian scepticism. It is often claimed that the monetarists have a 'black box' approach, in which they are claiming that changes in money, as it were, go in at one end and changes in income come out at the other, but it is impossible to tell what goes on in between.

In response, monetarists argue that the interaction between monetary variables, real rates of return and aggregate expenditure is extremely complex. All such relationships can be part of the transmission mechanism of monetary policy. Monetarists criticize the Keynesian emphases on business fixed investment and on interest rates on government bonds. Friedman (1972) writes:

> *The major difference between us and the Keynesians is less in the nature of the process (of portfolio substitution) than in the range of assets considered. The Keynesians tend to concentrate on a narrow range of marketable assets and recorded interest rates. We insist that a far wider range of assets and interest rates must be taken into account − such assets as durable and semi-durable consumer goods, structures and other real property. As a result, we regard the market rates stressed by the Keynesians as only a small part of the total spectrum of rates that are relevant. . . . [Friedman, 1972]*

Writing of the apparent strangeness of the monetarist approach, he continues:

> *After all, it is most unusual to quote houses, automobiles, let alone furniture, household appliances, clothes and so on, in terms of the 'interest rate' implicit in their sales and rental prices. Hence the prices of these items continued to be regarded as an institutional datum, which forced the transmission process to go through an extremely narrow channel. [Friedman, 1972]*

The channels of transmission of monetary policy are thus many and diffuse, and some of the relevant variables are unobservable. Friedman offers the analogy of water running down a beach, arguing that it is very difficult in advance to predict the channel it will take, but one can be confident that it will ultimately get down to the sea. Similarly, money will affect expenditure though the precise mechanism may not be easy to identify. It is therefore better to focus on the major issue − the relationship between money and money income − rather than to become involved in the intricacies of the transmission mechanism.

The 'water on the beach' argument seems a more appropriate analogy for the case where the *LM* curve is vertical and hence there is a close association between money and money income irrespective of any instability in the *IS* curve. If the *LM* curve is not vertical, the monetarist argument must rest on some 'law of large numbers' principle, to the effect that, while expenditure on each particular type of capital good is subject to various random disturbances, in aggregate these will tend to cancel out, so that the aggregate effect will be better defined than the effects on individual expenditure components. While there is no doubt some truth in this line of argument, it is not a tremendously convincing basis for any claim that a stable relationship must exist between money and money income.

Nor can one argue that the observed stability of the velocity of circulation itself demonstrates the stability of the transmission mechanism. In section 6.4 we shall consider the argument that velocity is stable because money is endogenous (that is, the authorities supply whatever quantity of money people demand). The absence of a convincing account of the transmissions mechanism would be a relevant consideration in this context.

6.2 INFLATIONARY EXPECTATIONS, INTEREST RATES AND THE DEMAND FOR MONEY

In section 6.1 we introduced the idea that money as an asset could be regarded as a substitute not only for bonds but also for real assets. Consequently, the opportunity cost of holding money would depend not only on the real income produced by such real assets but also on the expected rate of inflation. We may write the total monetary return on real capital $i_k \equiv r^* + \dot{P}^e$, where r^* is the real rate of return and $\dot{P}^e$ the expected rate of inflation. In equilibrium, and neglecting risk premia, etc., the monetary return on bonds (i) will equal the monetary return on real capital (and both will measure the opportunity cost of holding money balances).

For the present we will assume that the real return on capital (r^*) is independent of the rate of inflation, though we will return to examine this assumption in more detail in chapter 9. It then follows that the nominal return on bonds, and the opportunity cost of holding money balances, increase by the full extent of any increase in the expected rate of inflation ($i = r^* + \dot{P}^e$). In section 6.1 we have argued that the demand for money is influenced by the nominal interest rate. It follows that an increase in the expected rate of inflation will raise interest rates and hence reduce the demand for money.

We may write the demand for money equation in standard form as

$$M_d = Pyi^{-\gamma} \tag{6.1}$$

Taking proportional time derivatives gives

$$\dot{M}_d = \dot{P} + \dot{y} - \gamma \; \frac{1}{i} \frac{di}{dt} \; . \tag{6.2}$$

But, given that $i = r^* + \dot{P}^e$, it follows that

$$\frac{di}{dt} = \frac{dr^*}{dt} + \frac{d\dot{P}^e}{dt} = \frac{dP^e}{dt}$$

since we may take r^* as constant. With adaptive expectations we can write

$$\frac{d\dot{P}^e}{dt} = \beta(\dot{P} - \dot{P}^e)$$

that is to say, people adjust their expectations as to the inflation rate by a fraction of the extent to which the actual inflation rate differs from their expectations. Making these substitutions in equation (6.2) gives

$$\dot{M}_d = \dot{P} + \dot{y} - \gamma \; \frac{1}{i} \; \beta(\dot{P} - \dot{P}^e). \tag{6.3}$$

In equilibrium, the level of real income will be determined by real factors (as described in chapter 5), and for simplicity we may assume it constant ($\dot{y} = 0$). Furthermore, in equilibrium the actual and expected rates of inflation are equal. It follows that, in equilibrium, the demand for money grows at the same rate as the (actual and anticipated) inflation rate.

In equilibrium, the supply of money and the demand for money must, of course, grow at the same rate. It follows therefore that, if there is an economy in which the supply of money is increasing at, say, 10 per cent per annum, that economy will be in equilibrium with a steady, fully anticipated, inflation rate of 10 per cent per annum.

There is, however, a difficulty in ensuring the stability of such an equilibrium. Still assuming an economy in which the money supply is increasing at 10 per cent per annum, and where inflation has been proceeding at 10 per cent, we now consider what happens if, for a short time and for whatever reason, the inflation rate rises above 10 per cent. What mechanism ensures the inflation rate returns to 10 per cent? One might argue that, with inflation for a short time above 10 per cent, the demand for money will also rise more rapidly than 10 per cent and hence more rapidly than the supply of money. There will then be excess demand for money; interest rates will rise; demand will be depressed and inflation thus restrained. But a glance at equation (6.3) shows that matters are more complicated. An increase in the inflation rate does indeed increase the demand for money through the direct effect of higher prices (the first term on the right-hand side of equation (6.3)), but at the same time higher inflation raises the expected inflation rate, thus increasing the opportunity cost of holding money balances and so reducing the demand for money (the final term in equation (6.3)). The system is stable only if an increase in the inflation rate raises the demand for money, that is, if

$$\frac{d\dot{M}_d}{d\dot{P}} = 1 - \frac{1}{i} \, \gamma \beta > 0.$$

Most empirical studies of the demand for money find relatively small interest elasticities (normally substantially less than one), and, by definition, $0 < \beta < 1$, so that the stability condition seems likely to hold.[1] If the stability condition does not hold, a chance inflationary disturbance can lead to ever-accelerating inflation with no increase in monetary growth. Sufficient fuel for the higher rate of inflation will always be forthcoming, not from increases in the rate of monetary expansion, but from the continual depletion of desired real balances.

6.2.1 EVIDENCE FROM HYPER-INFLATIONS

A rather extreme test of the stability of the monetarist system is the evidence from hyper-inflations. If the stability condition is satisfied, a hyper-inflation must be accompanied by an explosive growth in the quantity of money. The most celebrated analysis of the monetary dynamics of hyper-inflation is that of Cagan (1956).

Cagan operates with a model basically similar to that we have just set out.[2] He argues that 'the cost of holding money . . . during hyper-inflation is for all practical purposes the rate of depreciation in the real value of money or, equivalently, the rate of rise of prices', and hence he substitutes the expected rate of inflation for the interest rate or the opportunity cost of holding money. He also assumes that

the effects of variations in real output on the demand for money are
negligible compared with the effects of variations in the price level in
times of hyper-inflation.

Cagan examined seven European countries that had experienced
hyper-inflations. He found that in no case was the stability condition
violated, so that in each case the hyper-inflation was fuelled by an
ever-accelerating growth in the money supply and could in principle
have been halted by a curtailment of the rate of monetary expansion.
Cagan also found that the speed of adjustment of expectations itself
tended to increase as inflation became more rapid. (This finding is
consistent with our argument in chapter 5 that the process of forming
expectations would itself be affected by the inflation rate.)

We return to a more general discussion of the affects of hyper-
inflation in chapter 9. In this section we have been concerned only
with the evidence of hyper-inflation on the effect of inflation expectations on the stability of the velocity of circulation. The evidence
from hyper-inflations supports that from the demand for money
studies to the effect that an increase in the rate of inflation can be
expected, on balance, to raise rather than lower the demand for
money.

6.3 THE THEORY OF NOMINAL INCOME

> *I regard the description of our position as 'money is all that matters
> for changes in nominal income and for short-run changes in real
> income' as an exaggeration but one that gives the right flavour of
> our conclusions. . . . Changes in the quantity of money as such in
> the long run have a negligible effect on real income. . . . The price
> level (in the long run) is then a joint outcome of the monetary forces
> determining nominal income and the real forces determining real
> income. [Friedman, 1970a]*

If we accept that the velocity of circulation of money is stable (for
the reasons discussed in sections 6.1 and 6.2), it follows immediately
from the basic quantity theory equation that, with V stable, changes
in nominal income are determined largely by changes in the quantity
of money (M). From a quantity theory perspective, the next question
to consider is how changes in nominal income are split up between
changes in prices and changes in real income.

This question is discussed in Friedman's (1970a) paper, 'A Theoretical Framework for Monetary Analysis'. There Friedman argues

that the *IS–LM* framework for the determination of aggregate demand might be taken as common ground for both Keynesians and monetarists. The crucial difference between the two groups lay instead in their assumptions as to price flexibility. Monetarists tend to assume prices (and wages) perfectly flexible, with output maintained at its full employment equilibrium. Keynesians on the other hand assume prices (or, more precisely, money wages) fixed, so that fluctuations in demand affect output. But, Friedman argues, such assumptions are no more than assertions that come from outside the theoretical system determining aggregate demand. What is needed is to supply the 'missing equation', which describes how changes in nominal income are divided between price changes and output changes.

Friedman suggests that the division of a change in nominal income between prices and output depends on two factors: price expectations and the pressure of demand. A specific linear form is given by:

$$\dot{P} = \dot{P}^e + a\,(\dot{Y} - \dot{Y}^e) + \gamma\,(\log y - \log y^*) \tag{6.4}$$

$$\dot{y} = \dot{y}^* + (1 - a)\,(\dot{Y} - \dot{Y}^e) - \gamma\,(\log y - \log y^*) \tag{6.5}$$

where $Y(\equiv Py)$ is nominal income, y^* is full employment real income, and the e superscripts are expected values. (It will be noted that adding the two equations gives $\dot{P} + \dot{y} = \dot{P}^e + \dot{y}^* + (\dot{Y} - \dot{Y}^e)$, consistent with our definition that $\dot{P} + \dot{y} = \dot{Y}$ and the equivalent expectational equation $\dot{P}^e + \dot{y}^* = \dot{Y}^e$.)

It is immediately apparent that the 'missing equation' is in fact the familiar Phillips Curve (Tobin, 1972). If we set $a = 0$, equation (6.4) is no different from the expectations-augmented Phillips Curve discussed in chapter 5, except that the pressure of demand is measured in terms of deviations of output from its full employment level rather than of deviations of unemployment from its 'natural rate'. Allowing values of a greater than zero generalizes the equation to permit unexpected changes in nominal income in part to affect prices directly, rather than through an intermediate stage affecting real output. However, the monetarist position is not distinguished from the standard Phillips Curve approach by the assumption of a high value of a. For example, Friedman writes: 'A changed rate of growth of nominal income typically shows up first in output and hardly at all in prices' (1970c, p. 23).

We may summarize the monetarist position thus far in two statements. First, variations in aggregate demand are largely attributable to variations in the money stock. Second, such variations in demand affect output primarily in the short run, but in the longer run work through to prices, with no ultimate affect on output, via the mechanism of the expectations-augmented Phillips Curve. It follows that inflation is determined by the growth rate of the money supply, but only in the long run.

The important practical question is the time span of the short run and the long run in this context. The extensive empirical studies undertaken by monetarists find that, on average, a change in the monetary growth rate affects real output with a lag of about six to nine months, and the effect on prices follows with a further lag of up to a year. The closest correlations between monetary growth and inflation are those found with a time lag of about two years (Friedman, 1970c). This rather mechanical monetarism, with predictable time lags, is of course very attractive to those involved in economic policy, for it offers precise policy prescription for achieving specific economic objectives.

It should, therefore, be stressed that this mechanical view of monetarism is specifically repudiated by Friedman (1968, 1970c), who instead stresses that there is much leeway and slippage in the relationships involved and that what is true on average need not be true in each individual case. There may, in a celebrated phrase, be 'long and variable lags' between a change in the monetary growth rate and the resultant change in the inflation rate. For this reason, Friedman warns against the use of monetary policy as an instrument of short-run economic stabilization, and instead argues for a monetary rule, and specifically for a steady rate of growth of the money supply.

None the less, the monetarist position at this point seems rather confused. For, in essence, the whole approach is based on empirical regularities — the stability of the velocity of circulation, for example. If there are 'long and variable lags', one would not expect to observe such stable relationships; indeed, taken to the extreme, long and variable lags can deprive monetarism of any empirical content whatsoever. If the monetarist model set out in this section is the best available representation of the economy, it is hard to avoid the conclusion that the authorities should make use of its predictions in designing monetary policies. It seems sensible, in formulating policy, to make use of all relevant knowledge and available information, rather than be tied to some pre-ordained rule. (Of course, in formulating policy the authorities have to take account of the constraints imposed by the expectations hypothesis which we discussed in section 5.4.)

The case for a monetary policy rule, rather than discretionary monetary policy, can however be made on the basis of two rather different arguments. The first is political. One can argue that the authorities should be deprived of policy instruments that could in principle be used for the benefit of the people, because in practice such instruments will be misused for the benefit of the authorities themselves. For example, discretionary monetary policy will be used not for economic stabilization but instead to stimulate artificial economic booms at election times (Nordhaus, 1975; Frey and Schneider, 1978). We do not pursue this argument — which obviously raises political as much as economic issues — further here.

The second argument for a monetary policy rule derives from the theory of rational expectations. This has been the most important theoretical innovation in macroeconomics in recent years. We can only sketch out some of its implications here; most importantly, it seems to provide a rigorous theoretical justification for some aspects of the monetarist approach to inflation.

6.3.1 RATIONAL EXPECTATIONS

It is convenient to start by returning to equation (6.4), to set a equal to zero (for simplicity) and to rearrange with the level of output on the left-hand side, to give

$$\log y = \log y^* + \frac{1}{\gamma} (\dot{P} - \dot{P}^e). \tag{6.6}$$

Equation (6.6) states that output deviates from its 'full employment' equilibrium level only if there is a difference between the actual and expected rates of inflation. The models we have so far been considering assume typically that expectations are adaptive. Then, if there is an increase in the rate of monetary growth, the actual rate of inflation temporarily rises above the expected rate and output rises above its equilibrium level, as indicated in equation (6.6). That is, the adaptive expectations mechanism assumes that the authorities can systematically, through the use of monetary policy, 'fool' people into making incorrect inflation forecasts, and hence can affect real output.

The rational expectations approach is based on the supposition that one cannot fool people systematically because they will soon learn from their mistakes. In the present context, they will soon realize that they can forecast inflation better if they base their forecasts not only on past rates of inflation but also on the rate of monetary growth. Expectations are said to be 'rational' if they are based on the best available model of the economy. Thus, if one believes that the monetarist model provides the best representation of the economy, consistency requires that one assumes that people form their expectations on the basis of the predictions of the monetarist model (Muth, 1961). Thus, in a rational expectations model, the expected rate of inflation is determined by exactly the same factors that determine the actual rate of inflation. But if people correctly anticipate the affects of policy on the inflation rate, it follows that government policies cannot systematically create a gap between the actual and expected rates, and hence cannot affect real output.

It would of course be absurd to suppose that people always forecast inflation correctly. In rational expectations models people can make mistakes, but they do not persist in making the same mistakes over and over again. Once they have come to realize that inflation is determined largely by monetary growth, they will base their expectations on that relationship, and changes in the monetary growth rate will no longer have even temporary effects on real output.

There is not space to discuss the extensive recent literature on the rational expectations hypothesis here (for a summary, see Shiller, 1978). The important implication in the present context is that attempts by the monetary authorities to vary the monetary growth rate for purposes of economic stabilization will not be successful in stabilizing output but instead will lead to greater variability and uncertainty in the inflation rate. By contrast, a monetary rule specifying a steady growth rate of the money supply can be expected to lead to a more stable inflation rate (and hence to a monetary environment conducive to economic efficiency). The authorities cannot exploit empirical regularities of the past for policy purposes, because if they do so people will adjust their expectations accordingly and the empirical regularity will no longer hold.

6.4 MONEY, INFLATION AND CAUSALITY

An observed close correlation between the rate of inflation and the rate of monetary growth could be interpreted either as confirmation of the monetarist approach (that monetary growth causes inflation) or as evidence that the monetary authorities allow the supply of money to respond passively to the demand for it (so that inflation causes monetary growth). It is important to distinguish between these hypotheses because, if the observed correlation in the past has been the result of passive monetary policies, it cannot be presumed that a stable relationship will continue if the monetary regime is altered.

There are two main approaches to the causality question, one based on statistical analysis and the other on institutional evidence. We consider them in turn.

6.4.1 STATISTICAL ANALYSIS OF CAUSALITY

The statistical approach is based, essentially, on a careful and sophisticated use of the *post hoc ergo propter hoc* principle. Some exogenous and unanticipated change may alter the course of events in the future, but it cannot alter the past. An autonomous (and unanticipated) change in the growth rate of the money supply can affect the future rate of inflation, but it cannot change past inflation. If changes in the growth rate of the money supply typically precede changes in the inflation rate, it seems plausible to argue that it is the monetary change that causes the inflation rate change.

On the other hand, if monetary policy is passive, changes in the money supply follow (or at least do not precede) changes in the inflation rate. It follows that, by examining the timing of the relationship between changes in monetary growth and changes in inflation, one may gain some insight into the direction of cuasality.

The most straightforward approach is to plot the monetary growth rate and the inflation rate against time on a graph and to observe whether turning points in the monetary growth rate precede, follow or are contempraneous with turning points in the inflation rate. However, such evidence can hardly be regarded as conclusive (see, for example, Tobin, 1970, or Kaldor, 1970). One problem is that turning points, both in money and in inflation, tend to be cyclical. Friedman (1970b) summarizes the objections neatly in his comment on Kaldor (1970): 'pins move with the cycle, money moves with the cycle; this is evidence of neither a pin theory of the cycle nor of a monetary theory of the cycle but of the pervasive influence of cyclical fluctuations'.

Friedman goes on to stress the importance of direct historical (i.e. institutional) evidence. However, since 1970 there have been significant developments in statistical techniques for 'causality testing', first applied in this context by Sims (1972). The approach taken by Sims (based on an econometric technique devised by Granger, 1969) first separates the variation in money and in money income into two components: that part of the variation that can be predicted from the past values of that variable, and the remainder, which cannot (which is, in other words, the residual in a regression of the variable on its own past values). We may describe the latter component (which cannot be predicted on the basis of past values) as the 'innovation' in the series. We can then test whether innovations in money income are associated with past innovations in money, and vice versa. The point of this procedure is to remove the 'pervasive influence of cyclical fluctuations' and other systematic factors. The innovations can then represent autonomous and unanticipated changes in the causal variable, and induced changes in the dependent variable. Using this approach, Sims carried out an empirical investigation of the relationship between money and money income in the USA between 1948 and 1968. He found that innovations in money income were correlated with previous innovations in the money stock, but innovations in the money stock were uncorrelated with previous innovations in money income. Thus he concluded that money could be treated as exogenous.

A study based on the same principles but applied to the UK economy was carried out by Williams, Goodhart and Gowling (1976). They found that, in the UK, the evidence seemed to suggest that money income was the exogenous variable and the money stock the dependent variable. However, as they point out, the UK can be regarded as a small, open economy which had maintained, over the period they studied, a fixed exchange rate. In such an economy, for reasons we discuss in more detail in chapter 7, money is necessarily endogenous.

The main problem with causality testing, however, is that for all its econometric sophistication it is essentially based on the supposition that timing indicates causality. A counter-example suggested by Kaldor (1970) is the relationship between spending and the money supply in the weeks before Christmas each year. The demand for money rises to finance higher volume of spending, and there is an accommodating increase in the money supply. But, Kaldor argues, 'Nobody would suggest (not even Professor Friedman, I believe) that the increase in note circulation in December is the cause of the Christmas buying spree'. The point of the example is that, as a general possibility, people planning to increase their spending may first add to their money balances in order to be able to finance the proposed additional expenditure. If monetary policy is passive, a growth in the money stock may precede an increase in planned spending, while an increase in output (and hence income) will lag behind it. Thus, as in the Christmas example, monetary changes may well lead, but not be the cause of, changes in income.

6.4.2 INSTITUTIONAL EVIDENCE ON CAUSALITY

If one observes a change in the growth rate of the money supply at a particular point in time, it may be possible, by an examination of all the historical circumstances of the period, to decide whether that change in monetary growth is attributable to some change initiated by the monetary authorities, or whether the money stock responded passively to some other economic change. The *locus classicus* of this approach is the great work, *A Monetary History of the United States, 1867–1960* by Milton Friedman and Anna Schwartz (1963). Friedman and Schwartz believe the evidence indicates that, more often than not, monetary changes are autonomous, in the sense of being initiated by policy changes by the monetary authorities or by other monetary developments.

The most important example is that of the Great Depression of 1929–33. The Wall Street Crash of 1929 was followed by large numbers of bankruptcies and a consequent loss of confidence in the banking system with many bank failures. People withdrew their money from the banks, and in consequence the money stock fell by about one-third during this period. Friedman and Schwartz regard the collapse of confidence in the banks as an autonomous monetary shock, and the fall in money supply as the cause of the economic depression of the 1930s. They blame the depression on the monetary authorities' failure to stabilize the money stock. While as a policy prescription it would no doubt have been desirable for the Federal Reserve Bank to have attempted to maintain the money stock, and thus to have helped avoid the succession of bank failures, it does not follow that the Depression was caused by the monetary contraction. One could equally well argue that the bankruptcies and bank failures led to a collapse in trade, which in turn reduced the demand for money.

The recent monetary history of the UK appears at first sight to provide a much more clear-cut example. In 1972, following changes in the methods of regulating the banking system (described in the Green Paper, *Competition and Credit Control*, 1971) and the floating of the exchange rate, the money stock started to grow very rapidly. The broad money measure, M3, which consists of currency plus all bank deposits, recorded an annual growth rate in the range of 25–30 per cent between 1972 and 1973. This was followed by a sharp upturn in economic activity in 1973, which was in turn followed by a rapid acceleration in inflation, which reached a peak of just over 25 per cent in 1975. In this case, the behaviour of the money stock, output and prices appear to follow the textbook monetarist pattern, following a change in monetary policy, with such precision that there can be no doubt as to the direction of causation.

But even this experience cannot be regarded as conclusive evidence. The rapid growth of M3 in 1972–73 could be largely attributable to a distortion in the monetary statistics known as 'round-tripping'.[3] The rapid rise in economic activity in 1973 could be ascribed, on orthodox Keynesian grounds, to the huge government budget deficit of that period. And the inflation of 1974–75 might be, at least in part, a result of the sharp increase in oil prices in late 1973, combined with the 'threshold' provisions in wage agreements in force at this time. While monetary policy was undoubtedly loose in 1972–73, it is not clear to what extent this was the cause of the subsequent inflation.

6.4.3 IMPLICATIONS OF THE CAUSALITY DEBATE AND MRS THATCHER'S EXPERIMENT

It can be argued that the question whether monetary policy in the past has been autonomous or passive is not really important. Provided velocity is stable and output tends to its natural rate, the authorities always have the policy option of controlling inflation by controlling the money supply, whether or not they have done so in the past. Such an argument must, however, be subject to two important qualifications.

First, there is the question whether, given existing monetary arrangements and the instruments at their control, the authorities can in fact control the supply of money. If they cannot, institutional arrangements can be changed but such changes may of themselves upset the relationship between money and money income that is at the centre of the monetarist approach. Second, the observed stability of money demand functions may be a consequence of passive money supply policies and may break down if the government were to operate a policy based on controlling the money supply.

These matters have been put to the test in the UK since 1979 by Mrs Thatcher's government, which has made the control of the money supply the centrepiece of its economic strategy. While it is too early at the time of writing (December 1980) to judge the experiment as a whole, the most obvious early lesson has been the almost complete inability of the government to control its chosen measure of the money stock (sterling M3). During 1980, the target growth rate of the money stock has been 7–11 per cent, while the actual growth rate has been well in excess of 20 per cent. Given the importance that the government has attached to the control of the money supply, its failure to do so seems strong evidence that present institutional arrangements in the UK do not, in fact, permit the authorities to control the supply of money.

The second major lesson to be learnt from the experiment is that, despite the acceleration of monetary growth, the economy has plunged into a deep recession, with unemployment rising from 1.35 million in December 1979 to 2.24 million in December 1980. One possible interpretation is that the sharp rise in interest rates introduced in November 1979, with the intention of restraining the growth rate of the money supply, has been extremely effective in depressing demand, but has had a perverse effect on monetary growth. The very high interest rates may have encouraged people to increase their holdings of interest-bearing bank deposits (which form part of sterling M3).

These two early lessons from the montarist experiment seem to indicate rather strongly that, at least in the UK, it makes little sense to interpret any past association between monetary growth and inflation as evidence that autonomous monetary changes have been the main cause of changes in the inflation rate. In the past, with accommodating monetary policy, the quantity of money may have been a reliable leading indicator of changes in demand; but, Mrs Thatcher's experiment suggests, such relationships may well break down if the government makes the direct control of the money supply the basis of its economic policies.

6.5 CONCLUSIONS

At the start of the chapter we stated that monetarism was based on three propositions:

(a) that there is a stable demand function for money;
(b) that output tends to its full employment equilibrium level; and
(c) that the money supply is exogenous.

In this chapter we have found that theory and evidence support the first of these propositions − the stable demand function for money − which is, in any event, also part of the standard Keynesian *IS−LM* model. The second proposition has, in essence, already been established by the expectations hypothesis discussed in chapter 5. In this chapter we have done no more than trace out some monetarist developments of the expectations approach.

These first two propositions, taken together, imply that there will be a reasonably close correlation, even in the short run, between inflation and the rate of growth of the money supply. The most contentious question – which we discussed in section 6.4 – is whether the money supply is exogenous and determines the price level, or whether the money supply is endogenous and responds passively to changes in the demand for it. As we saw, the evidence here is mixed. In the USA the bulk of empirical studies suggest that, by and large, money has been exogenous. In the UK on the other hand, the evidence is less clear-cut, with the initial results of Mrs Thatcher's monetarist experiment strongly suggesting that institutional agreements in the UK do not permit the authorities to control the money supply directly.

Whether or not the authorities can control the money supply directly, one can argue a case for basing policy on monetary targets. In chapter 5 we argued that the expectations hypothesis implied that policy had to be based on nominal rather than real variables. If changes in stock of money tend to lead other nominal variables (such as money income or prices), as suggested by many of the studies discussed in section 6.4, a monetary target may provide a useful basis for policy. The reason is that changes in the money stock anticipate changes in economic activity and hence permit policy changes to be made in time to influence the course of activity. By contrast, if policy is based on the level of nominal income (or prices), it will always take effect too late to influence the level of income in relation to which the change has been made; by the time the policy change takes effect conditions may be very different, and the policy consequently inappropriate. Against this, there are a number of practical difficulties with monetary targets (not least the fact that different definitions of the money supply tend often to move in different directions in the short run).

NOTES

1. The presence of the interest rate itself in the stability condition may appear strange. The reason is that the interest elasticity of demand for money, γ, is defined as $(dM_d/M_d)/(di/i)$, so that, for a given γ, a 5 percentage point increase in the interest rate, from 10 to 15 per cent, has a much larger effect on the demand for money than a 5 percentage point increase from, say, 50 to 55 per cent. The proportional change in the demand for money for a given percentage point change in the interest rate, $(dM_d/M_d)/di$, is equal to γ/i. See also n. 2.

2. Cagan in fact assumed a rather unconventional form of the demand for money function, namely

$$\log M_d = \log P - k\,(\dot{P}^e) + \text{constant}$$

It follows that

$$\dot{M}_d = \dot{P} - k'(\dot{P}^e)\,\frac{d\dot{P}^e}{dt}$$

$$= \dot{P} - k'(\dot{P}^e)\beta(\dot{P} - \dot{P}^e).$$

In Cagan's formulation the stability condition is therefore $k'(\dot{P}^e)\beta < 1$. If one were to assume a constant value of k (so the stability condition would reduce to $k\beta < 1$), Cagan's demand-for-money function implies that the elasticity of demand for real balances is an increasing function of the expected rate of inflation. We can write the demand for money function in the form

$$\log (M/P) = \text{constant} - k\dot{P}^e$$

$$\frac{d \log (M/P)}{d\dot{P}^e} = -k$$

$$\frac{d\,(M/P)}{(M/P)\,d\dot{P}^e} = -k.$$

The elasticity of demand, by definition, is given by

$$\frac{\dot{P}^e\,d\,(M/P)}{(M/P)\,d\dot{P}^e} = -k\dot{P}^e$$

and thus increases (in absolute magnitude) with $\dot{P}^e$.

3. The interest rate charged on bank overdrafts is, conventionally, linked to the Bank of England's Bank rate, or minimum lending rate (MLR). At this time MLR was itself determined by the market interest rate on Treasury bills. In 1973 the interest rate on Treasury bills fell relative to other market interest rates, making it profitable for firms to borrow money on overdraft from banks and re-lend it, at higher interest rates, in the money market. The commercial banks then had to borrow the money back from the money market in order to finance their additional overdraft lending. This sequence of transactions, known as 'round-tripping', increases the bank deposit component of the M3 measure of the money stock, but there is no reason why it should have any effect on firm's spending plans or hence on economic activity.

CHAPTER 7

Inflation in an Open Economy

In this chapter we examine the impact of external, as opposed to domestic, influences on a country's inflation rate. In particular, we focus on world monetary developments, and on changes in the system of exchange rates. It is generally thought that, if a country wishes to maintain a fixed exchange rate with the rest of the world, its inflation rate cannot deviate at all substantially from the 'world inflation rate'. If, on the other hand, its exchange rate is flexible, the country can determine its own inflation rate, relying on exchange rate adjustments to maintain trade competitiveness.

These ideas are based on the theory of purchasing power parity (PPP). In section 7.1 we show that, if PPP holds,

(a) with fixed exchange rates, a country's inflation rate depends only on the world inflation rate and is independent of domestic conditions (e.g. monetary policy);

(b) with flexible exchange rates, a country's inflation rate is completely insulated from the world inflation rate and depends only on domestic factors.

The evidence, which we review very briefly in section 7.1, suggests that PPP may be regarded as a long-run equilibrium relationship, but it very clearly does not hold in the short run.

We next consider the determinants of inflation in the long run, assuming that PPP holds. With fixed exchange rates, the inflation rate of each country is determined by the world inflation rate, but it remains to establish what determines world inflation. Section 7.2 describes the monetary theory of the balance of payments, and provides a basis for the analysis of the determinants of world inflation in section 7.3. Section 7.3 includes a brief discussion of the 'international monetarist' explanation of the upturn in inflation experienced by many countries in the late 1960s and early 1970s.

We go on to consider the international transmission of inflation in the short run, that is over a period when PPP cannot be assumed to hold. In the short run with fixed exchange rates, the domestic pressure of demand in an economy may push its inflation rate above or below the world rate (section 7.4). With flexible exchange rates, domestic inflation will not be completely insulated from world economic developments in the short run (section 7.5).

7.1 PURCHASING POWER PARITY

The theory of purchasing power parity (PPP) is generally attributed to Cassell (1916), although earlier references to it can be found in the writings of the classical economists, particularly Wheatley and Ricardo (for a brief historical survey of the PPP doctrine, see Frenkel, 1978).

According to PPP, exchange rates equate the purchasing power of the different currencies; or, equivalently, the ratio of the price levels in two countries will equal the reciprocal of the exchange rate between their currencies.

For example, if, in the foreign exchange market, one can buy $2.40 for £1, then PPP asserts that one will be able to purchase the same volume of goods in the USA for $2.40 as one could in the UK for £1; or, equivalently, that the general level of prices in the USA (measured in dollars) will be 2.4 times as high as the level in the UK (measured in pounds).

The PPP result is based on the argument that, if there is free international trade in goods, the price of goods in each country, after adjustment to a common currency measure at prevailing exchange rates, must be approximately equal. For if not, traders will attempt to profit by buying in the cheap markets and selling where the goods are expensive, which will tend to equalize the prices in the different markets.

The form the price equalization takes will, however, depend on the exchange rate regime. Assume, for example, that American goods at the prevailing exchange rate are cheaper than equivalent British goods. Traders will shift their demand in favour of American goods. But to purchase American goods they require US dollars. If exchange rates are fixed, the US central bank is obliged to buy or sell dollars in exchange for foreign currencies in order to maintain the exchange rate. Hence it will supply the traders with the dollars they require at the fixed exchange rate. The traders are then able to purchase the American goods, but this raises the demand for, and hence the price of, such goods. The price in terms of US dollars rises until PPP is restored.

With flexible exchange rates, the process is different because the central bank would not intervene in the foreign exchange market. Thus, if traders wished to purchase additional US dollars, they would, taken together, be unable to do so: the additional demand for dollars would not be met by the central bank, but instead, in a free market for foreign exchange, would raise the price of dollars in terms of other currencies. The appreciation of the exchange rate raises the prices of American goods, in terms of other currencies, until PPP is restored. The price of American goods in terms of US dollars does not rise during this process because the traders, taken together, were unable to purchase additional US dollars and were thus unable to add to the demand for the American goods. With flexible exchange rates and no central bank intervention, PPP is therefore restored entirely by exchange rate adjustments.

Formally, PPP states that

$$eP = P^* \qquad (7.1)$$

where e is the exchange rate (the number of units of a foreign currency, say, US dollars, that can be purchased per unit of domestic currency) and P^* is the 'world price level' (measured in terms of the same foreign currency, US dollars in this case). Equivalently, $\dot{e} + \dot{P} = \dot{P}^*$. In a system of fixed exchange rates, $\dot{e} = 0$, and so $\dot{P} = \dot{P}^*$; the domestic inflation rate is determined by the world inflation rate.

In a system of flexible exchange rates, $\dot{e} = \dot{P}^* - \dot{P}$, the exchange rate appreciates or depreciates at a rate equal to the difference between the world inflation rate and the domestic inflation rate.

We next consider the empirical evidence on purchasing power parity. The theory is based on the idea that there exists the equivalent of a perfectly competitive world market for each of the different goods, so that there is a single price for each good throughout the world. This proposition is often now termed the 'law of one price'. The law of one price clearly holds for those goods that are, in fact, traded in a single world market such as metals and primary commodities. But the law of one price does not appear to hold at all closely for manufactured goods, and the evidence suggests that quite large changes in the relative prices of say German as against American exports of manufactured goods can persist for a substantial period of time (see, for example, Isard, 1977; Kravis and Lipsey, 1978; and Genberg, 1978).

Under a fixed exchange rate system, PPP implies that inflation rates should be equalized across countries. In practice, of course, inflation rates differ, but, given imperfections in the data and so on, it is not clear what degree of variability in the inflation rates could be regarded as broadly consistent with PPP. Another approach would be to test equation (7.1) directly. Writing (7.1) in logarithms gives

$$\log P = -\log e + \log P^* \qquad (7.1')$$

with e constant.

If we test a regression equation of the form

$$\log P_t = \alpha_0 + \alpha_1 \log P_t^* + u_t \qquad (7.2)$$

purchasing power parity implies that $\alpha_1 = 1$. Estimates of equations such as (7.2) frequently yield values of α_1 that are not significantly different from unity, but the fit of the equation is often poor, suggesting that PPP holds in the long run but not in the short run (Gailliot, 1970; Genberg, 1977).

In a flexible exchange rate system, PPP implies not a convergence of prices but that exchange rates adjust to offset differential price movements between different countries. There has been relatively little experience of flexible exchange rates before the 1970s. Frenkel (1978) has examined the floating exchange rate period in the early 1920s and has shown that exchange rate movements appear consistent with PPP. The experience of the 1970s appears rather different. Exchange rates have been highly unstable, and have fluctuated very much more than relative prices. Over a longer time horizon, say up to ten years, trends in exchange rates consistent with PPP can be observed (Genberg, 1978).

This brief account of PPP under fixed and floating exchange rates (for a fuller discussion and review of the literature, see Officer, 1976) suggests that PPP may be regarded as a long-run equilibrium characteristic, but that it is not a valid assumption for short-run analysis.

7.2 THE MONETARY THEORY OF THE BALANCE OF PAYMENTS

The monetary theory of the balance of payments derives all its essential features from David Hume's analysis of the operation of the gold standard. Hume writes:

> *Suppose that all the money of Great Britain were multiplied fivefold in a night, must not all labour and commodities rise (in price) to such an exorbitant height that no neighbouring nations could afford*

to buy from us; while their commodities, on the other hand, became comparatively so cheap, that, in spite of all the laws which could be formed, they would be run in upon us, and our money flow out; till we fall to a level with foreigners. . . . [Hume, 1752]

In more familiar terminology, we can restate Hume's argument in four stages:

(a) assume an exogenous increase in the stock of money in one country; then,
(b) on the basis of the quantity theory, the higher stock of money will tend to raise prices in that country, which in turn
(c) will divert demand abroad, which will lead to a deficit in the balance of trade; and
(d) the trade deficit will be financed by net monetary payments to foreigners, which reduce the money stock and hence prices until international competitiveness is restored. Since this requires that prices return to their original level, the money stock must also return to its original level, so that all the new money has flown out abroad.

This process is known as the specie-flow mechanism, whereby balance of payments equilibrium is restored by flows of specie (money) which adjust relative prices to restore trade competitiveness. It will be noted that, within each country, the price level is still proportional to the money supply, as in the quantity theory, but the quantity of money itself now depends on the balance of payments.

In its simplest form, as set out here, the specie-flow mechanism seems to depend on two, rather restrictive, assumptions. First, in identifying a trade deficit with an outflow of money, it appears to ignore international capital mobility. Second, in assuming an outflow of money will lead to a fall in the domestic money stock, it seems to require that the same currency is used for both domestic and international transactions.

The modern monetary theory of the balance of payments (Johnson, 1972; Frenkel and Johnson, 1976) overcomes these difficulties, first by focusing on disequilibrium in the money market (rather than in the trade balance), and second by defining the domestic money stock as the sum of international reserves and domestically created credit. As with the specie-flow mechanism, the monetary theory of the balance of payments implies that any exogenous increase in a country's money stock will flow out abroad through a balance of payments deficit. But the process operates slightly differently from Hume's approach:

(a)   assume an exogenous increase in the stock of money in one country; then
(b)   the supply of money in that country will exceed the demand for it, so that
(c)   people reduce their holdings of money by net purchases of goods or assets from residents of other economies, which implies a balance of payments deficit and an outflow of international reserves; and
(d)   with a given quantity of domestically created credit, a loss of reserves means a reduction in the domestic money supply. This process continues until all the newly created money has flown out abroad and the domestic money supply is again equal to the demand for it.

The monetary theory of the balance of payments can be summed up in three equations.

$$M_s \equiv R + C. \tag{7.3}$$

The domestic money supply is defined to consist of two components, international reserves (R) and domestically created credit (C).

$$M_d = M_d \, (P, y, i). \tag{7.4}$$

The demand for money is a conventional function of prices, real income and interest rates.

$$B \equiv \Delta R = B(M_d - M_s). \tag{7.5}$$

The balance of payments surplus (B), which is equal to the increase in reserves, is determined by the imbalance between the demand for, and the supply of, money.

Equations (7.3)–(7.5) are quite general. The monetary theory goes on to assume that, in equilibrium, all the factors affecting the demand for money in equation (7.4) are determined exogenously. The price level is determined in world markets according to the law of one price. The interest rate is determined in international capital markets by the requirement that, with international capital mobility, rates of return on assets denominated in different currencies must be equalized. We assume a 'small country' that cannot, by its own actions, affect world prices or interest rates. And real output y is determined by real forces independent of monetary factors or the balance of payments.

Writing the demand for money as exogenous in equation (7.4) and substituting from equation (7.3), gives

$$\Delta R = B(\bar{M}_d - R - C). \tag{7.6}$$

This equation has an equilibrium, with given $\bar{M}_d$ and C with

$$R = \bar{M}_d - C \tag{7.7}$$

such that, if there is a shift in $\bar{M}_d$ or C, there will be balance of payments disequilibrium and reserves will adjust according to equation (7.6) until the new equilibrium level of reserves (given by (7.7)) is achieved.

We can also write (7.7) in dynamic form:

$$\Delta R = \Delta \bar{M}_d - \Delta C \tag{7.8}$$

stating that, if equilibrium is to be maintained between the supply of the demand for money, there will need to be a balance of payments surplus, or deficit, according to whether the exogenous growth in the demand for money is greater than, or less than, the rate of domestic credit expansion. (Note that equation (7.8) is an equilibrium condition, and is not to be confused with (7.6), which is a disequilibrium adjustment equation.)

It will be seen that the monetarist theory of the balance of payments rests on the same basic assumptions as the monetarist model discussed in chapter 6. The assumptions are: that there is a stable demand function for money; that income tends to its full employment level; and that the supply of money (or, more precisely in this context, of domestic credit) is exogenous. In closed economy monetarist models, the growth of the money supply determines the inflation rate. In fixed exchange rate, open economy monetarist models, world inflation determines domestic inflation, which in turn determines the growth of the demand for money. The growth of money supply is adjusted to the growth of the demand for money by monetary inflows or outflows across the foreign exchanges.

7.3 THE DETERMINANTS OF WORLD INFLATION

We have argued that, under a fixed exchage rate system with purchasing power parity, each individual country cannot, in the long run, determine its own inflation rate but must follow the world inflation rate. But what then determines the world inflation rate? From a monetarist standpoint, it seems logical to start from the proposition that the world, as a whole, can be regarded as a closed economy, and that therefore the world rate of inflation will be determined in the simplest case (taking output and velocity as constant) by the rate of growth of the 'world money supply'.

When gold was the only form of money for both domestic and international payments, it was straightforward enough to identify the world money supply with the gold stock, and to link the growth of world money with annual gold production. For example, the gold the Spanish brought back from South America in the sixteenth century increased the stock of gold sharply and led to rapid inflation throughout Europe (the gold flowing out of Spain to sustain high prices throughout Europe through the specie-flow mechanism discussed in section 7.2).

In modern conditions, with paper currencies and banking systems, the world money supply consists of the aggregate of the domestic money stocks of each country. But we have just argued, in section 7.2, that each country's money stock is determined endogenously by, among other things, world prices. To resolve this apparent difficulty, we note that the growth of the money stock in each country equals the change in reserves *plus* the increase in domestic credit. Summing over all countries, the change in reserves must net out to zero, so that the increase in the world money stock is equal to the increase in 'world' domestic credit.

The demand for money in each country will then rise at the world inflation rate, which is itself determined by the world rate of domestic credit expansion. According to the monetarist theory of the balance of payments, a country will gain reserves if its rate of domestic credit expansion is below the world average (so the domestic money supply grows more slowly than the increase in demand for it). Likewise, if the country's rate of domestic credit expansion is above the world rate it will lose reserves. Thus a country will restrict its domestic credit expansion if it wishes to add to its holdings of international reserves, and will increase domestic credit expansion if it holds more reserves than it requires.

In aggregate, the change in the rate of domestic credit expansion will thus depend on whether, on balance, international reserves are adequate or whether there is a shortage. If there is a shortage of international reserves, countries typically will be attempting to increase their own holdings by means of maintaining a slow growth of domestic credit. But if there is an expansion of international liquidity, countries will feel able to expand domestic credit at a faster rate, the world money supply will increase, and with it the world inflation rate. It follows that, in a fixed exchage rate system, the rate of inflation depends largely on the rate of increase in international liquidity.

We have thus far assumed output and velocity constant in order to focus on the monetary mechanisms. In practical application, we would need to take account of changes over time in output or velocity, which, particularly in this context, means allowing for any growth in world trade. As world trade expands, nations will want to hold more reserves in order to be able to meet trading fluctuations in the demand for their currency. The key issue. therefore, is whether the supply of international reserves is increasing sufficiently to meet the increase in demand. If not, each nation will attempt to increase its own stock of reserves by reducing domestic credit expansion, with the result that world money stocks will decline. According to the global quantity theory approach there will then be a fall in the world inflation rate, which will bring the growth in the demand for reserves into balance with the growth of supply.

7.3.1 THE POSTWAR EXPERIENCE OF FIXED EXCHANGE RATES

At the end of the Second World War, the Western nations adopted a set of international monetary arrangements drawn up at Bretton Woods in 1944 and supervised by the International Monetary Fund (IMF). The system was based on fixed exchange rates, and although in principle it allowed countries to make exchange rate adjustments from one fixed rate to another (the 'adjustable peg' principle), in practice few such adjustments were made. The system was adopted in 1945, but in the immediate postwar period international trade and capital movements were so restricted that it was not until the mid-1950s that an effective fixed exchange rate system could reasonably be said to be operating.

Within this system, international liquidity was provided by gold, by IMF drawing rights and by the US dollar (and initially, and to a lesser extent, by the pound sterling). In the immediate postwar period the US dollar was so much the dominant currency that central bankers (outside the USA) were prepared to hold US dollars as international reserves. Thus, when countries other than the USA ran balance of payments deficits, they lost reserves equal to the deficit. But when the USA ran a deficit, it did not lose reserves but instead issued dollars which the central banks of the creditor nations added to their reserves. It turned out that the bulk of the growth of international liquidity during the fixed exchange rate period took the form of increased holdings of US dollars arising from US balance of payments deficits.

Under this system, international liquidity grew slowly until the mid-1960s, and the outbreak of the Vietnam War. Indeed, until the mid-1960s, a 'shortage' of international liquidity was often regarded as a serious world economic problem. From a monetarist standpoint it should, of course, instead be regarded as the cause of the relatively low inflation rates prevailing throughout the world in the 1950s and early 1960s. With the onset of the Vietnam War, however, the US balance of payments swung into massive deficit, leading to a sharp increase in international reserves. It is this process that, on the monetarist interpretation, explains the acceleration in inflation throughout the Western world in the late 1960s.

The system of fixed exchange rates was itself unable to survive the experience of huge US deficits. Whereas at the end of the Second World War the US gold stock was worth three times the total value of US external liabilities, as a result of the balance of payments deficits by the end of the 1960s the figure was less than one half. Central banks outside the USA could in practice no longer convert their dollars into gold. The convertibility of the dollar was formally suspended in 1971, and with it the fixed exchange rate system came to an end.

If we can regard the period 1955–71 as one of effectively fixed exchange rates, it is interesting to ask whether during that period the world inflation rate can be explained, in monetarist terms, by the world rate of growth of the money supply relative to the growth of world output. As with the quantity theory applied to a domestic economy, we require first a stable world demand for money function, second a mechanism relating inflation to excess demand, and third an exogenous money supply process.

Empirical work on these questions is somewhat sparse. Gray *et al.* (1976) have identified a stable world demand for money function. Duck *et al.* (1976) have examined a world expectations-augmented Phillips Curve, linking average capacity utilization indicators in the major OECD countries to average inflation rates, with reasonably encouraging results. Parkin *et al.* (1975) have developed a world money supply model, relating the world money stock to changes in the world monetary base. Genberg and Swoboda (1975) have examined the issue of causality and find that, typically, changes in the world money stock precede changes in the inflation rate.

7.4 WORLD INFLATION AND THE PHILLIPS CURVE UNDER FIXED EXCHANGE RATES

In this section we examine the determinants of inflation in the short run in an open economy with fixed exchange rates. We have already seen (in section 7.1) that in the short run purchasing power parity does not hold, and that hence a country's inflation rate is not determined exclusively by the world inflation rate. We start by recalling the theoretical perspective that lies at the opposite extreme to the law of once price: the traditional Keynesian 'elasticities approach' to the balance of payments, which implicitly assumes that each country produces different types of products which are not close substitutes for other countries' products.

According to the elasticities approach, a rise in prices in the rest of the world will impinge on a country in part directly, through raising the price of its imports, but to a large extent indirectly, through its effect on the quantities of goods imported and exported. This indirect effect arises because the rise in world prices lowers the relative price of its exports and raises the relative price of its imports, the effect depending on the magnitude of the respective demand elasticities. These indirect effects will increase the demand for domestic production and hence the demand for labour. If the economy is originally in equilibrium, the additional demand will raise wages and prices, and this process will continue until domestic prices are again equal to world prices and the excess demand is thus removed.

In this approach, in the long run the domestic inflation rate will be equal to the world inflation rate, but the equalizing mechanism operates through the pressure of demand in domestic markets. The approach is thus consistent with the Phillips Curve model of the determinants of domestic inflation, provided that one allows that the pressure of demand can be influenced by external as well as internal factors. One might also want to include an import price index, as a further variable in the price determination process, to allow for the direct effect of changes in import prices. More generally, one might want to argue that a country's price index is a weighted average of components determined directly in world markets and of components determined by domestic demand pressures.

In chapter 5 we argued that a simple excess demand Phillips Curve was inadequate, and that it was necessary to incorporate expectations. In a closed economy, we argued, a major determinant of people's expectations of inflation would be their recent experience of it. But in a fixed exchange rate open economy, inflation expectations might rationally also be based on the rate of inflation prevailing in the rest of the world, because in the long run the domestic inflation rate must conform to the world rate.

An empirical investigation along these lines has been carried out by Cross and Laidler (1976) and Laidler (1976). They test equations essentially of the form:

$$\dot{P}_t = g\, y_{t-1} + v\, \dot{P}^e_{t-1} + (1 - v)\, \dot{\pi}^e_{t-1} \tag{7.9}$$

where y is the excess demand measure, and π the world price level. They assume that the expected rates of domestic and world inflation are each separately determined by a conventional adaptive expectations process (see chapter 5) on previous values of domestic and world inflation rates. While the empirical results do not appear entirely satisfactory, the evidence suggests that expected world inflation is at least as important as expected domestic inflation in its effect on the rate of price increase.

7.5 FLEXIBLE EXCHANGE RATES

In the long run, with purchasing power parity, a flexible exchange rate completely insulates one country's inflation rate from that of the rest of the world. Each country's inflation rate is determined by domestic factors (such as the rate of growth of its money supply) and exchange rates adjust to equate the rate of change of the prices of foreign goods (in terms of domestic currency) with the rate of change of the price of domestic goods. But in the short run purchasing power parity does not hold, and flexible exchange rates do not completely insulate one country's inflation rate from that of other countries.

To develop this argument, we again return to the traditional Keynesian elasticities approach to the balance of payments. We examine the impact of an expansion in economic activity in the rest of the world on the short-run Keynesian assumption of static prices.

Initially, also, we assume no capital mobility. Then, at the prevailing exchange rate, expansion in demand in the rest of the world raises the demand for the currency of the domestic economy, and hence leads to an appreciation of the exchange rate. The rise in the exchange rate (with given domestic and world prices) will make domestic goods relatively more expensive, thus reducing the demand for them. At some point, depending on the demand elasticities, the effect of the higher exchange rate in reducing demand will exactly offset the original increase in demand and the trade balance will again be in equilibrium.

It follows that, with flexible exchange rates, there is a perverse short-run mechanism whereby expansion in one country tends to depreciate its exchange rate, and hence reduce inflation rates in other countries. Likewise, a co-ordinated expansion in the rest of the world will tend to appreciate a country's exchange rate and thus reduce its inflation rate.

The introduction of international capital mobility complicates the picture a little, but does not alter the basic transmission mechanism. If we assume that international capital flows respond to interest rate differentials, and that, in the short run, the interest rate can be affected by fiscal and monetary policies (as in the standard Keynesian *IS–LM* model), a country can, in the short run, affect its exchange rate by the mix of fiscal and monetary policies it adopts.

The analysis of the impact on a flexible exchange rate economy of fiscal and monetary policies is due to Mundell (1963a). Mundell argued that expansionary monetary policy would (within the standard *IS–LM* model framework) tend to lower interest rates and hence encourage an outward flow of capital. This would lead to a fall in the exchange rate, which would in turn raise the price (in terms of domestic currency) of foreign goods. By contrast, a fiscal expansion would raise interest rates, and thus lead to an appreciation of the exchange rate and hence a fall in the domestic currency price of foreign goods.

It is easy to extend this analysis to examine the effect on an economy of expansionary policies in the rest of the world. Expansionary monetary policies in the rest of the world will lower foreign interest rates, thus encouraging an inflow of capital into the domestic economy. The exchange rate will thus rise, and inflation will fall. The capital account effects of a world monetary expansion reinforce the current account in leading to an appreciation of the exchange rate. By contrast, a world fiscal expansion will be associated with higher foreign interest rates, which will encourage an outflow of capital from the domestic economy and hence a fall in the exchange rate. In this case, the capital account effect will go in the opposite direction to the current account effect and the net effect on the exchange rate is indeterminate.

These examples indicate that, in the short run, foreign disturbances can affect the domestic price level because they can alter the exchange rate and hence the domestic price of foreign goods. In the longer run, however, foreign incomes and interest rates will return to their equilibrium levels, and the effects of disturbances to the foreign price level will be fully offset by exchange rate adjustments.

As a first approximation, we might expect the inflation rate in an open economy with flexible exchange rates to be determined by the same factors as in a closed economy, that is by the pressure of demand and expectations. One might argue a case for the inclusion of short-run deviations of the exchange rate from purchasing power parity, which would have a direct effect on the price level as noted above. However, and unlike the fixed exchange rate case, there is no argument for incorporating world inflation rates into the domestic inflation expectations variable. With flexible exchange rates the inflation rate is unaffected, in the long run, by the world inflation rate, and people's expectations of inflation should therefore, rationally, be unaffected by it also.

7.6 CONCLUSIONS

In earlier chapters we have developed theories of inflation on the assumption of a closed economy. In this chapter we allowed for the fact that economies engage in international trade and capital transactions, and we examined how this affects a country's inflation rate. We showed that, if an economy maintains a fixed exchange rate, its inflation rate will depend primarily on international rather than domestic factors. By contrast, if a country has a floating exchange rate, its inflation rate is largely insulated from that of other countries and is determined primarily by domestic factors.

The postwar economy of the Western world could be reasonably described as a fixed exchange rate system up to 1971. During this period, the argument suggests, the inflation rates of the different Western countries should move reasonably closely together, and the average level of world inflation should depend to a large extent on world monetary developments. In particular, the relatively slow growth of international liquidity during the 1950s and early 1960s could be a major factor behind the low inflation rates of that period. The acceleration of inflation rates in the late 1960s can be associated with the huge United States balance of payments deficits resulting from the financing of the Vietnam War, which flooded the international monetary system with US dollars.

Since the early 1970s the world economy has been characterized by flexible exchange rates, and the argument of this chapter suggests that inflation rates might become more dispersed with each country pursuing independent macroeconomic policies. In fact, the inflationary experience of the 1970s has continued to be dominated by international influences, though of a real rather than a monetary form. The inflation of the middle and late 1970s can, to a large extent, be attributed to the consequences of the massive increases in oil prices levied by the oil-producing states in the autumn of 1973. We return to this in the next chapter.

Finally, in this chapter we have examined the international transmission of inflation under two extreme assumptions: rigidly fixed and freely flexible exchange rates. In practice, the exchange rate system, at least since the end of the gold standard, has been a mixture of these two extremes. During the postwar fixed exchange rate period there were a limited number of exchange rate changes, for example the devaluation of the pound in 1967. Likewise, with flexible exchange rates, governments frequently intervene in an attempt to stabilize the exchange rate. In analysing particular historical episodes it may sometimes be difficult to discover what the government's exchange rate policy actually was. None the less, our basic conclusion remains valid. In so far as a government intervenes in the exchange market in order to maintain its exchange rate at some given level, it has to allow its inflation rate, and monetary growth rate, to be determined by those of its trading partners. And in so far as it allows its exchange rate to float freely in accordance with market forces, it insulates its inflation rate from that of the rest of the world.

CHAPTER 8

Inflation and Real Wages

The theories of inflation we have considered so far have been based, with various elaborations, on the 'law of markets' — that prices go up if there is excess demand and go down if there is excess supply. In this chapter we consider a rather different approach. One can envisage wage bargaining as a process of attaining some 'desired' level of wages, so that wage increases in any period are determined by the difference between the 'desired' wage level and the actual level of wages currently being paid.

In chapter 4, we suggested that trade unions have an important influence on wage bargaining; but, as we noted in that chapter, it seemed logical to think that trade unions would be concerned with the level of real wages, rather than with the rate of wage increases. In the first section of this chapter we formulate models based on the idea that in wage bargaining trade unions attempt to achieve some given 'target real wage' for their members. Such a target implies, of course, that trade unions seek wage increases sufficient to compensate for any increases in the cost of living. But with experience of steadily rising real living standards, trade unions may in fact attempt to achieve some target growth rate of real wages.

In section 8.2, we examine a line of argument that, in essence, claims that the target real wage approach is in fact empirically indistinguishable from the standard expectations-augmented Phillips Curve (chapter 5). Formally, one can argue that the excess demand approach can be reformulated in terms of a real-wage adjustment approach if the desired real wage is the market equilibrium wage. We go on to show that there are, in general, differences between the target real wage approach and standard excess demand models.

In section 8.3 we consider alternative explanations that have been proposed to account for the 'stagflation' of the middle and late 1970s. The unprecedented combination of accelerating inflation and severe recession appears inconsistent with the standard Phillips Curve approach. While, at the time of writing, there is no consensus as to how to account for the experience of stagflation, we suggest that an approach incorporating the target real-wage hypothesis appears most plausible. In this section we also consider the revival of the notion of classical unemployment: that is, that trade unions insist on a real wage so high as to make it unprofitable for firms to employ the whole of the labour force.

8.1 THE TARGET REAL-WAGE HYPOTHESIS

The idea that, in wage bargaining, trade unions are primarily concerned with obtaining some target level of real wages for their members has a long history. Classical economists took it for granted that workers would not suffer from money illusion, and that wage bargains were effectively struck in real terms. Thus they tended to blame the unemployment of the Great Depression on the insistence of the trade unions on maintaining 'too high' a real wage — that is to say, a real wage in excess of that consistent with labour market equilibrium. This theory as to the cause of unemployment was of course attacked by Keynes in the *General Theory*, but has recently been revived in an attempt to explain the high unemployment levels of the late 1970s. (see section 8.3).

Keynes's view was that trade unions would oppose cuts in money wages, but that they would be prepared to accept cuts in real wages brought about by an increase in the general price level (Keynes, 1936, pp. 14–15). But, in analysing the problems of inflation in *How to Pay for the War*, as we have seen in chapter 2, Keynes's (1940) views seems to have undergone quite a significant change. For there he assumes that workers will in fact achieve money wage increases to compensate for inflation, which will thus enable them to maintain a given real wage. In the model of *How to Pay for the War*, as we noted in chapter 2, wages rise at the same rate as prices, but, because wages always lag behind, the level of wages never catches up with the level of prices. Though the wage bargain always restores real wages to this prewar level, given the prices prevailing at the time of the bargain, the faster the rate of price increases subsequent to the wage settlement, the lower the average real wage over the period achieved *ex post*. Workers achieve full compensation for price increases that have occurred up to the time of the settlement, but no compensation for any price increases that might be expected to occur over the period for which the wage settlement will remain in force.

As noted in chapter 3, Phillips and Lipsey both included a rate of price increase variable in their empirical work on the argument that a more rapid increase in prices would lead to higher money wage claims as workers would attempt to maintain their living standards in the face of increases in the cost of living. In chapter 3, we noted that Lipsey had found a more significant impact for the price change variable in the postwar period, suggesting that workers were becoming increasingly concerned with securing increases in real rather than in money wages.

It was not, however, until the 1970s that systematic theories relating money wage claims to attempts by trade unions to achieve a target level of real wages for their members were put forward and tested. In this section we consider in particular the work of Sargan (1964, 1971, 1980a), Jackson *et al.* (1972), Johnston and Timbrell (1973), Henry *et al.* (1976) and Henry and Ormerod (1978).

8.1.1 ECONOMETRIC SPECIFICATION: THE SARGAN MODEL

We may start from the assumption that, at any moment in time t, the trade unions are attempting to obtain for their members some target real wage R_t. If the price level expected to prevail on average over the time period over which the negotiated wage will remain in force is P_t^e, the trade union target money wage, W_t is given by

$$W_t = P_t^e R_t. \tag{8.1}$$

It may seem appropriate to proceed to an equation for the rate of increase of money wages by differentiating equation (8.1) to give

$$\dot{W}_t = \dot{P}_t^e + \dot{R}_t. \tag{8.2}$$

Sargan's argument is that such a procedure is not, in general, valid, in that it assumes that expectations are always correct and real wages always at their desired level. More generally,

$$d \log W_t = \log W_t - \log W_{t-1}$$
$$= (\log P_t^e - \log P_{t-1}^e) + (\log R_t - \log R_{t-1}).$$

But the expected rate of inflation, $\dot{P}_t^e$, is defined by

$$d \log P_t^e = \log P_t^e - \log P_{t-1}.$$

Hence

$$d \log W_t = d \log P_t^e + (\log P_{t-1} - \log P_{t-1}^e) + d \log R_t.$$

However, equation (8.1) implies that

$$W_{t-1} = P_{t-1}^e R_{t-1}$$

so that

$$\log P_{t-1}^e = \log W_{t-1} - \log R_{t-1}$$

and

$$d \log W_t = d \log P_t^e + d \log R_t + [\log R_{t-1} - \log (W/P)_{t-1}]. \quad (8.3)$$

The novelty of equation (8.3) is the final term, which implies that, should real wages deviate from the desired level, money wage claims will be increased in order to restore the real wage to the desired level. This term is sometimes known as the 'real-wage catch-up' term, or, more generally, as an error correction mechanism.

To test equation (8.3), Sargan (1971) made three further assumptions. First, he assumed that the trade union target real wage could be represented by a time trend, or equivalently that the trade unions' objective was to achieve a given growth rate of real wages over time. Then

$$R_t = R_0 e^{\rho t}$$

so that

$$\log R_t = \log R_0 + \rho t$$

and

$$d \log R_t = \rho.$$

Second, he assumed that inflation expectations would be determined by the rate of inflation experience in the previous year, so that $\dot{P}_t^e = \dot{P}_{t-1}$. Third, he allowed for the possibility that excess demand, as measured by unemployment, might affect the trade unions' ability to attain their real wage objectives.

The resulting estimated equation (Sargan, 1971 p. 55) gave an implied value of ρ of 1.6 per cent per annum as an estimate for the trade union target growth rate of real wages. The real-wage catch-up term proved significant and correctly signed, and the unemployment, though just insignificant, was also 'correctly' signed. The expected inflation measure, by contrast, was insignificant and with the wrong sign. While Sargan's empirical results were thus not entirely conclusive, they were clearly sufficient to establish that the target real-wage hypothesis should merit serious consideration. The next step, however, was to incorporate the effects of taxation on wage determination.

8.1.2 TAXATION AND WAGE CLAIMS

In his empirical work, Sargan (1971) had measured real wages by dividing the index of money wage rates by the index of retail prices. This calculation gives the real value, or purchasing power, of the gross (before-tax) wage received by the worker. It takes no account of direct taxes (income tax and the employee's national insurance contributions) paid by the worker. Workers may reasonably be more concerned about the real value of this net wage (or take-home pay) than about their gross wage.

Jackson, Turner and Wilkinson (1972) argue that the increased burden of direct taxation and a major factor in the acceleration of inflation in the late 1960s. They assume that in wage bargaining trade unions attempt to maintain or increase real living standards, and claim wage increases to compensate not only for price increases but also for increases in direct taxation. (Indirect taxes are of course taken into account in the retail price index.) They show that, in the years of the Wilson government (1964–70) in the UK, there was a substantial increase in the direct tax burden on the average worker. In 1950, the net (take-home) pay of a worker paid the national average wage amounted to 96.3 per cent of his gross wage. The proportion fell gradually in the late 1950s and early 1960s, reaching 91.4 per cent by 1964. In the next six years the direct tax burden rose much more sharply, and the ratio of net to gross earnings had fallen to 82.4 per cent by 1970 (figures taken from Johnston and Timbrell, 1973).

Jackson *et al.* do not themselves attempt a direct test of the hypothesis that workers attempt to recoup tax increases through higher wage claims. Rather, they develop a number of implications of this line of thought. In particular, they point out that, if workers are to maintain their real living standards in the face of a tax increase, they must effectively be shifting the tax on to their employers through the mechanism of a higher wage claim. To the extent that firms try to maintain their profits by resisting the higher wage demands, the outcome will be a dispute between the firm and its workers, most likely in the form of a strike by the workers in support of a higher wage than the firm is prepared to concede. Jackson *et al.* point to the sharp increase in the number of strikes in the UK in the late 1960s as a confirmation of their approach. Thus, Jackson *et al.* do not regard the increase in strikes as an indicator of some exogenous increase in trade union power or militancy, which is itself also the cause of the higher wage claims: rather, in their view it is the increased tax burden that is the cause of both the higher wage claims and the increase in strikes.

Second, Jackson *et al.* point out that, with a progressive tax structure, a given percentage increase in gross wages implies a smaller percentage increase in net wages (assuming no change in the tax structure). It follows that, if workers are to achieve increases in net wages at least equal to the rate of price increases, they need to achieve increases in gross wages higher than the rate of price inflation. Thus, a progressive tax system seems to add a further twist to the inflationary spiral.

In practice, however, governments do alter the tax structure to allow for the effects of inflation, and thus it seems likely that, with experience of inflation, workers will allow for the probability of some change in the tax structure rather than base their wage claims on the assumption that the tax structure will be held constant. For example, in attempting to forecast future tax deductions, workers might plausibly extrapolate past trends. If their recent experience is that the proportion of their pay deducted has been increasing, they may assume that deductions will continue to rise and hence put in higher wage claims to compensate. The effect of such a variable on wage claims has been examined empirically by Johnston and Timbrell (1973), who find that an increasing tax deductions ratio has a significant impact in raising wage claims.

In the same study, Johnston and Timbrell construct a 'wage catch-up' variable in a manner similar to the Sargan model discussed above, except that they define the target wage as the real wage net of taxation. The results are moderately favourable, in that the catch-up variable is of the correct sign; but in a number of the regressions it is not significant, and regressions based on the catch-up variable consistently do less well than those based on the tax deductions variable (described in the previous paragraph).

8.1.3 RECENT EVIDENCE

Support for the target real-wage hypothesis has recently been provided by Henry, Sawyer and Smith (1976). Henry *et al.* take a number of different models of inflation that had been proposed during the 1960s and early 1970s, and compare their performance in accounting for the inflationary experience of the UK up to the end of 1974. They

conclude that, on the basis of their empirical estimates, they are able
to reject explanations of inflation based on the expectations-augmented
Phillips Curve, the monetarist model (as formulated by Laidler, 1973)
and the cost-push model proposed by Hines (1964). On the other
hand, they find 'impressive support' for the Sargan target real-wage
approach.

It must, however, be said that the actual equation proposed by
Sargan (1971), which was estimated on data from 1949—68, does not
account at all well for the inflation of the early 1970s. Indeed, in
estimating the Sargan equation on data from 1948 to 1974, Henry
et al. find the wrong sign on the crucial real-wage catch-up variable.
However, by redefining the catch-up variable in terms of real net
earnings rather than in terms of real gross wage rates, Henry *et al.* are
able to provide an equation that fits the data both for the period of
Sargan's estimates and for the whole period they consider (up to the
end of 1974). In addition to finding significant coefficients of the
correct sign on the real net earnings catch-up variable, Henry *et al.*
also find in the equation estimated for the whole period a significant
and positive effect for past price inflation, and an insignificant effect
of unemployment on wage increases.

Unfortunately, this variant of the Sargan equation, with the catch-up
variable appropriately defined, was not to last long. Henry and Ormerod
(1978) report that after the second quarter of 1975 the equation
produces unsatisfactory results, which they attribute to the supposition that, untypically, workers were willingly prepared to forgo real
wage increases during the period of the '£6 a week' incomes policy
introduced in the summer of 1975.

It might, incidentally, be noted that 1975 was a year of deep recession, and this might be expected to account for at least part of the
slowing down in the rate of increase of money wages. Henry and
Ormerod, however, continue to find the unemployment variable
insignificant. In appendix 2 to chapter 3 we have suggested a number
of reasons for believing that the relationship between unemployment
and the pressure of demand has altered in recent years, and it may be
that, had Henry and Ormerod employed other measures of the pressure
of demand, they would have been better able to account for the
experience of 1975—76.

In more recent estimates, Sargan (1980a) incorporates a number of
variables suggested by Johnston and Timbrell and others. One new
variable, which appears to have a significant effect on wage increases,
is the ratio of earnings to wage rates. Sargan suggests some possible
arguments for incorporating such a variable, for example that it

embodies the effect of workers trying to consolidate higher earnings into basic wages, or that it relates to the structure of differentials. However, it is well known that earnings are high relative to wages when demand is high, and it may be that the variable is simply representing pressure of demand effects. (The effect of unemployment are again found to be insignificant.)

We do not pursue detailed empirical analysis of the target real-wage hypothesis any further here. We return to the approach in section 8.3, where we suggest it may offer one possible explanation for the unprecedented combination of high unemployment and high inflation experienced since the oil crisis of 1973.

8.2 EQUILIBRIUM REAL WAGES

In the models discussed in section 8.1 it was assumed that the target real wage was determined exogenously — by the aspirations of workers as expressed through the trade unions. At the other extreme, one can consider models in which the target real wage is assumed to be the market equilibrium wage. Thus formulated, the real wage approach and the excess demand approach have much in common.

Figure 8.1 provides a standard representation of the neoclassical labour market, the derived demand for labour being a decreasing function of the real wage, and we assume the supply of labour increasing with the real wage. The equilibrium real wage is $(W/P)^*$,

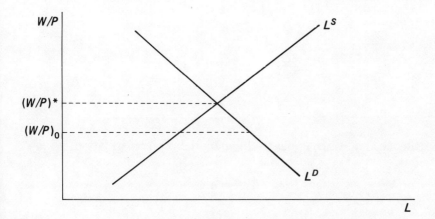

Figure 8.1

and the current value of the real wage $(W/P)_0$. We can now argue that wages will rise because the current real wage is below the desired (equilibrium) level. However, as is evident from the figure, a situation with the real wage below the equilibrium is always associated with market excess demand. An increase in wages could equally well be explained as a response to excess demand or as an adjustment of wages to the equilibrium, the two explanations being in this model indistinguishable from one another.

In this section we consider neoclassical models of this type. We discuss first a model proposed by Kuh (1967), and then the approach of Parkin, Sumner and Ward (1976). We conclude by examining the relationship between these models and the target real wage approach discussed in section 8.1.

8.2.1 THE PRODUCTIVITY APPROACH

Kuh (1967) developed a model of wage increases based on neoclassical production theory. If firms are competitive and maximize profits, it follows that the real wage will be equal to the marginal product of labour. If the labour force is to be fully employed, its marginal product is determined by the stock of capital and other factors of production, and the state of technical knowledge. The growth of real wages in equilibrium is determined by capital accumulation and technical progress.

Kuh assumed a Cobb-Douglas production function and neutral technical progress. Hence, output (Q) is given as a function of labour (L) and capital (K) by

$$Q = A L^\alpha K^{1-\alpha}. \tag{8.4}$$

Hence

$$\frac{\partial Q}{\partial L} = \alpha A L^{\alpha-1} K^{1-\alpha}$$

$$= \alpha \frac{Q}{L}. \tag{8.5}$$

Setting the real wage equal to the marginal product of labour gives

$$W/P = \alpha \frac{Q}{L}$$

or

$$W = P \left(\alpha \frac{Q}{L} \right) \tag{8.6}$$

and

$$\dot{W} = \dot{P} + \dot{Q} - \dot{L}.$$

But, from (8.4) we can write

$$\dot{Q} = \dot{A} + \alpha\dot{L} + (1-\alpha)\dot{K}.$$

Hence

$$\dot{W} = \dot{P} + \dot{A} + (1-\alpha)(\dot{K} - \dot{L}). \tag{8.7}$$

Kuh argues not that the market is always in equilibrium, but rather that equations such as (8.6) and (8.7) describe equilibrium relationships. Equation (8.7) determines the long-term trend of money wages, and Kuh accepts that other influences, and in particular cyclical factors such as unemployment, can cause fluctuations around the long-term path.

Clearly, Kuh makes a number of rather extreme assumptions (perfect competition, marginal productivity factor pricing, Cobb–Douglas production function, exogenous factor supplies and neutral technical progress), and this may seem to cast some doubt over the whole approach. However, some of these assumptions may be thought reasonable approximations in the long run, and others (e.g. the production function assumption) can be relaxed without altering the basic result in any important way. It may give more insight into the issues involved to compare Kuh's approach with that of Sargan (discussed in section 8.1).

Equations (8.6) and (8.7) are very similar in form to equations (8.1) and (8.2). The 'target real wage' of the Sargan model becomes the equilibrium marginal product of labour in Kuh's model. The trade union-determined target rate of real-wage growth in the Sargan formulation becomes the rate of productivity growth in Kuh's equation (8.7). It follows that an empirical test of equation (8.3) might be regarded as much a test of the Kuh model as of the Sargan model, the only difference being whether the term R is given a productivity or a target real-wage interpretation. (Indeed, Sargan, 1971, does test the Kuh productivity variable in addition to the target real wage approach, finding rather similar results.)

One way of distinguishing between the two hypotheses (suggested by Henry and Ormerod, 1978) is based on the idea that, in the target real-wage model, the relevant variable is the net wage, while in the Kuh model the relevant variable should be the gross wage (or, more strictly, the gross unit labour cost to the employer). We have already noted that Henry *et al.* (1976) find better results with the net wage variable, and this may offer some support for the target real-wage interpretation.

A more systematic attempt to resolve this issue is provided by Parkin, Sumner and Ward (1976). They propose a model in the neoclassical framework, as depicted in figure 8.1. The demand for labour depends on the real unit labour cost, which is gross wages plus taxes on employment paid by the employer (employers' national insurance contributions) divided by an index of prices received by producers (i.e. excluding indirect taxes). The supply of labour depends on net real wages, that is money wages net of tax deductions deflated by an index of consumer prices. The change in equilibrium wages thus depends on the change in these various prices and taxes.

In the framework of this model, one can represent the target real-wage hypothesis by the assumption of a horizontal supply curve of labour. In this case, only taxes and prices relevant to the supply side (the net real wage) affect the equilibrium real wage. Similarly, one can represent the Kuh model by the assumption of a vertical supply curve of labour, so that only taxes and prices relevant to the demand for labour affect the equilibrium real wage. More generally, one can argue that both supply side and demand side taxes and prices should be relevant, with the relative weights attached to each depending on the relative slopes of the supply and demand curves.

Parkin *et al.* argue that the rate of money wage increases at any time consists in part of the adjustment of the wage to its current equilibrium value and in part of an amount corresponding to the expected increase of the equilibrium wage during the wage contract period. The first (adjustment to equilibrium) component, they suggest, can be measured by the unemployment rate. The expected change in the equilibrium wage is held to depend on the expected changes in all the various taxes and prices that affect the demand for, or supply of, labour. Parkin *et al.* use survey data for price expectations, and assume that tax changes are always correctly foreseen. While the results reported by Parkin *et al.* are somewhat inconclusive, the general picture to emerge is that 'demand side' taxes and prices have a larger and better defined effect than that of taxes and prices on the supply side. This implies a relatively steep supply curve of labour, and these results are thus closer to the Kuh model than to the target real-wage approach.

Parkin *et al.* suggest that the wage catch-up variable may in fact be acting as a proxy for excess demand. If, they argue, the target real wage rises in line with labour productivity, and if the actual real wage falls below it, it follows that workers are being paid less than their marginal product, and hence there will be excess demand (as suggested in figure 8.1). In comparing the target real-wage approach with the equilibrium real-wage model, there thus appear to be two issues. First, is the trade union target real wage in fact the same as the equilibrium real wage? Second, is the real-wage catch-up variable indistinguishable from a proxy measure of excess demand?

To answer the first of these questions, it would seem that, if target real-wage growth were in fact determined exogenously by the trade unions, it would only by coincidence happen to be equal to the rate of productivity growth in the economy. Yet both Sargan (1971) and Henry *et al.* (1976) seem to take comfort from the fact that the target growth rate of real wages that they compute is in fact close to the rate of productivity growth. Indeed, it follows from equation (8.3) that the inflation rate is on a 'knife edge', with constant inflation possible only if actual real wages grow at the same rate as the trade union target real wage. If the target wage growth were more rapid than the actual real-wage growth (determined by productivity growth) the outcome would be ever-accelerating inflation. These considerations appear to suggest that, unless the trade union real-wage target is the same as the rate of productivity growth, the model breaks down; but, on the other hand, if the trade union target is equal to productivity growth, it can hardly be said to be determined exogenously. One could, perhaps, argue that, like expectations, trade union real-wage targets are determined by their past experience of real-wage growth. Then, in the long run, target wage growth will adjust to productivity growth, but in the short run the real wage target will be exogenous. We pursue this idea further in section 8.3.

The second question, as to whether the real-wage catch-up variable is indistinguishable from a proxy measure of excess demand, seems to depend primarily on the structure of the product market. The demand-for-labour curve in figure 8.1 is drawn on the assumption that firms are perfectly competitive and can sell as much output as they wish at prevailing market prices. Its position then depends only on the stock of capital, the state of technology and the prices of other variable inputs, which can all (normally) be taken as given in the short run.

If, however, we depart from the full competitive model, for example by assuming that product markets can be in disequilibrium, so that firms cannot sell all they wish at the prevailing market price (Barro and Grossman, 1971), firms' demand for labour no longer depends only on the real wage (with given capital stock, etc.) but also on the level of aggregate demand. In such models a fall in aggregate demand will reduce the demand for labour by firms even with no change in wages or prices (or, hence, in the real wage). There will be disequilibrium in the labour market, indicated say by unemployment, but no discrepancy between the actual and the equilibrium real wage.

In practice, it is well known that real wages do not move in the counter-cyclical manner implied by the neoclassical labour demand function of figure 8.1. In the short run there appears therefore to be no close correlation between the pressure of demand in the labour market and the real wage (relative to trend). It thus follows that, as an empirical matter, it should be possible to distinguish excess demand from real-wage catch-up effects.

8.3 INFLATION AND OIL PRICES

In the five years preceding the quadrupling of oil prices in the autumn of 1973, the average rate of inflation of the Western countries was just over 5 per cent per year. There was then a sharp increase in the inflation rate in every country, and over the next five years the inflation rate on average was more than double, at about 11 per cent per annum (Bruno, 1980). The inflation of the middle and late 1970s differed from previous inflationary experience not only because it was much more rapid, but also because it was accompanied not by a high level of demand but by a recession of a severity unparalleled in postwar experience. The combination of accelerating inflation and severe recession seems extraordinarily difficult to reconcile with the expectations-augmented Phillips Curve approach, and in this section we examine some alternative explanations.

There are three prima facie reasons for thinking that the increase in oil prices may be a major factor behind the 'stagflation' of 1970s. First, the fact that inflation has increased in all countries and at about the same time suggests a common cause. Second, as figure 8.2 indicates, the deterioration in performance after 1973 is so sharp and dramatic relative to earlier fluctuations that there seems no doubt that the problem set in at the time of the oil price increase. Third, the impact effect of an oil price increase is to raise prices and at the same time to depress demand, and this makes an explanation based on oil prices plausible.

In the first part of this section, we set out a simple expectations-augmented Phillips Curve model, within which we can analyse the impact of an increase in oil (or other intermediate input) prices. The model suggests that, if the government maintains control of the growth of the money supply, an oil price increase can generate only temporary inflation and temporary unemployment. The model seems incapable of explaining the persistence of higher inflation and recession that has been experienced.

We next consider explanations based on a revival of the idea of 'classical unemployment'. Such models, like those considered in section 8.1, assume that the real wage in the economy is determined by the trade unions. An increase in oil prices necessitates a fall in real wages if full employment is to be maintained. If trade unions refuse to accept a reduction in real wages, the outcome is 'classical' unemployment, which will persist for as long as the trade unions insist on 'excessive' real wages. It is, however, difficult to explain the persistence of inflation within a simple classical unemployment model, and in the last part of this section we suggest a 'generalized real wage' Phillips Curve approach which avoids some of the difficulties of the classical unemployment model.

8.3.1 THE EXPECTATIONS APPROACH

In discussing the expectations-augmented Phillips Curve in chapter 5, we assumed that prices are set as a mark-up on prime costs, and that prime costs consist only of wages. We now generalize this model by incorporating a second component of prime costs, namely intermediate inputs whose prices are determined independently of domestic wages. Thus we can write

$$\dot{P} = \alpha \dot{W} + (1 - \alpha) \dot{P}_E \qquad (8.8)$$

where $\dot{P}$ is the rate of change of domestic output prices, $\dot{W}$, the rate of change of money wages, and $\dot{P}_E$ the rate of change of intermediate input prices, with α being the proportion of labour cost in total prime costs.

We assume that money wages are determined according to a conventional expectations-augmented Phillips Curve:

$$\dot{W} = \dot{P}^e + \gamma (y - y^*) \qquad (8.9)$$

where y^* is the equilibrium level of real output.

Finally we adopt the simple monetarist model of aggregate demand, in which the equilibrium level of output and the velocity of circulation of money are assumed constant, and the money supply grows at a constant rate per annum. Then

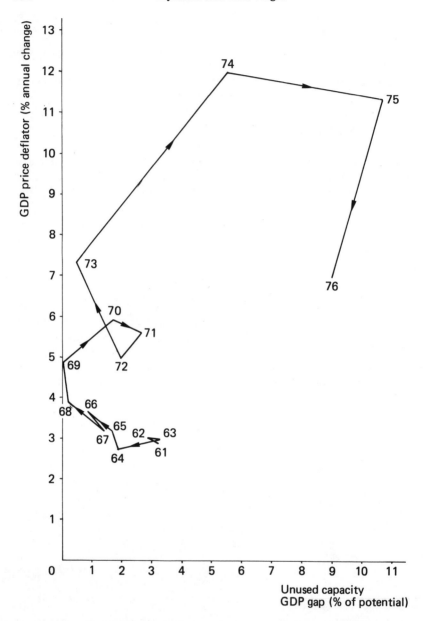

Figure 8.2 Inflation and Unused Capacity: Seven Major OECD Countries.
(Source: OECD, 1977)

$$\dot{M} = \dot{P} + \dot{y}. \tag{8.10}$$

The equilibrium of this system is given with $y = y^*$ and $\dot{P} = \dot{P}^e = \dot{W} = \dot{P}_E = \dot{M}$. Let us suppose we start from such an equilibrium, with the money supply, prices wages, etc., all growing at a steady rate, say 5 per cent per annum. We now assume a sharp jump in P_E in one year. (In 1973–74 the price of imported intermediate inputs rose by over 30 per cent, largely as a result of the increase in oil prices.)

From equation (8.8), the higher input prices will lead, with given money wage increases, to a faster rate of increase of output prices. From equation (8.10), with a given growth rate of the money supply, higher price inflation will cause a fall in output below its equilibrium level.

We next consider what will happen to money wages. The simplest case is that in which people assume that the jump in input prices was a once-and-for-all occurrence, so that their expectations as to the future rate of inflation are unaffected. Then, in equation (8.9), with given price expectations but a lower level of output, the growth rate of money wages will slow down. If there is no further jump in oil (or other input) prices, the rate of price increases will also slow down, to below its previous equilibrium level (because of the slower growth of money wages). Inflation is now slower than the growth of the money supply, and output will therefore start to recover. Equilibrium will be restored through this process, with output again at full employment equilibrium and the inflation rate again equal to the growth rate of the money supply.

Alternatively, one might assume expectations determined (rather mechanically) according to the adaptive expectations procedure described in chapter 5. Again, the impact effect of the oil price increase is to cause higher inflation and lower output, but now the effect on subsequent wage bargains is less straightforward. If, in formulating their expectations, people give a high weight to the immediate past, there will be a sharp increase in $\dot{P}^e$ in equation (8.9), and hence wage increases may be higher despite the lower level of output. But if there is no further jump in oil prices, the rate of price inflation will slow down, and this will in principle reverse the effect on expectations. If expectations are adaptive according to any systematic rule, a once-and-for-all price increase can affect expectations only temporarily.

One could, of course, introduce different expectations hypotheses. For example, there might be a 'ratchet effect', whereby people expect the future rate of inflation to be equal to the highest rate they have experienced in the past. On this hypothesis, a temporary jump in the inflation rate will be permanently embodied in people's expectations. If the government wishes to maintain an inflation rate below the previous peak, output must be held permanently below equilibrium, as can be seen from equation (8.9).

More generally, one can argue that it is possible to explain the persistance of stagflation on the expectations approach only by assuming that inflationary expectations have been 'too high' ever since 1974. While this is not impossible, it seems difficult to reconcile with the assumptions of economic rationality underlying the expectations approach. We therefore consider a completely different type of explanation.

8.3.2 CLASSICAL UNEMPLOYMENT

We must first distinguish Keynesian from classical unemployment. In figure 8.3 we depict the neoclassical labour market (as in figure 8.1) together with a Keynesian aggregate demand curve marked ZZ. The neoclassical labour demand curve (DD) indicates the number of workers that competitive profit-maximizing firms would choose to hire assuming they were able to sell as much output as they chose to produce at the given market price. The Keynesian aggregate demand indicates the number of workers required to produce a level of output equal to the level of aggregate demand for goods and services in the economy (which we assume, for simplicity, to be independent of the real wage). We start from a position of full employment equilibrium with employment L^* and real wage $(W/P)^*$.

In figure 8.3(a) we depict Keynesian unemployment. There is a fall in the level of aggregate demand, and as a result the curve ZZ shifts inwards to $Z'Z'$. There is unemployment at the equilibrium real wage, but the remedy is not to cut the real wage, but to restore the level of aggregate demand and so to shift the aggregate demand curve back from $Z'Z'$ to ZZ.

For comparison, in figure 8.3(b) we illustrate a case of classical unemployment. Assume that, for some reason, the demand curve for labour shifts inwards (for example, because a part of the economy's capital stock is destroyed in some natural disaster). The DD curve shifts to $D'D'$, and again there is unemployment at the previous equilibrium real wage. If equilibrium is to be restored it is, in this case, necessary to reduce the real wage to $(W/P)_1$. An increase in aggregate demand, the Keynesian remedy, will not help in this case (except in so far as it can be regarded as an indirect way of reducing the real wage).

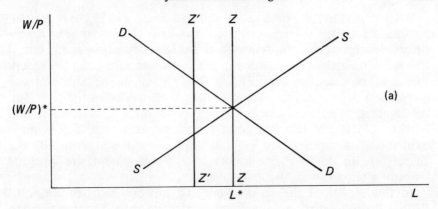

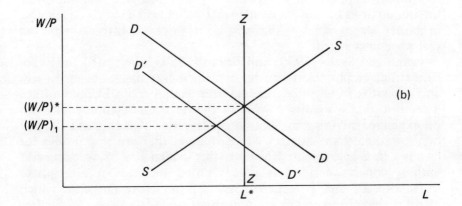

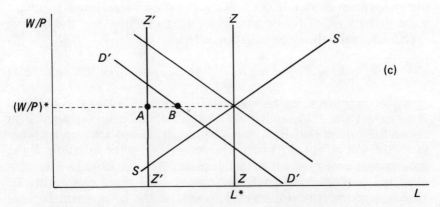

Figure 8.3 (a) Keynesian Unemployment. (b) Classical Unemployment.
(c) Effects of Oil Price Increase.

An increase in oil prices, as Bruno and Sachs (1979) have argued, has the effect of shifting both the ZZ and the DD curves. The higher prices depress aggregate demand, as we have already argued, but at the same time the higher price of oil (regarded as a complementary factor of production) reduces the firm's demand for labour at any given level of real wages.[1] The outcome is illustrated in figure 8.3(c). As depicted, the rise in unemployment (at point A) can be attributed to the 'Keynesian' fall in aggregate demand. However, if demand is expanded, unemployment will fall until we arrive at point B, and thereafter no further reductions in unemployment are possible without a reduction in the real wage.

In this model, if the government expands demand beyond point B, it will not be profitable, with the real wage at $(W/P)^*$, for firms to expand production. In consequence prices will rise, and the trade unions, anxious to prevent a fall in real wages, will insist on an increase in money wages equal to the increase in prices so as to maintain the real wage unchanged.

Bruno and Sachs (1979) and Bruno (1980) have tested the hypothesis that employment can be explained by changes in real wages and in relative input prices on data from a number of OECD countries. They find that a significant part of the variation in employment can be explained in this way, thus suggesting that it is shifts in the DD curve, rather than shifts in the ZZ curve, that are responsible for changes in employment. However, this evidence is of necessity not entirely conclusive since, as already noted, increases in input prices shift both ZZ and DD curves, and it is therefore not clear which effect the empirical results are reflecting.

We turn now to the determinants of inflation within the classical unemployment model. If the objective of wage bargaining is to obtain some given level of real wages, as argued in section 8.1, the correct specification for the wage equation is (8.3):

$$d \log W_t = d \log P_t^e + d \log R_t + [\log R_{t-1} - \log (W/P)_{t-1}] \quad (8.3)$$

If, for simplicity, we assume a static economy with a constant real wage target ($\dot{R} = 0$), and if we start in equilibrium (at point B in figure 8.3(c)), so that $R_{t-1} = (W/P)_{t-1}$, it follows that money wage increases will be equal to the expected rate of price inflation. If the government now expands demand, prices will rise more rapidly than expected, real wages will fall, and money wage demands will then be raised to restore the real wage. Likewise, if the government reduces demand, prices will rise more slowly than expected and real wages will rise. Money wage demands will be moderated because real wages are now above the target level. Changes in aggregate demand feed directly into changes in the inflation rate, in this model, with only very transitory effects on output or employment.

It is, therefore, hard to account for the persistence of inflation within the classical unemployment model. Attempts by government to reduce inflation by restraining the growth of aggregate demand should, on this model, have been successful. Of course, it might be that governments have incorrectly diagnosed the problem as one of Keynesian unemployment, and hence have expanded rather than contracting it. There is, however, an alternative explanation, based on a synthesis of the target real wage and Phillips Curve approaches.

8.3.3 A GENERALIZED REAL-WAGE PHILLIPS CURVE

We next assume that wage claims may be affected both by target real wages and by the level of demand. Neglecting time subscripts, and again assuming a static economy, we can write

$$\dot{W} = \dot{P}^e + \gamma(y - y^*) + (R - W/P). \tag{8.11}$$

For any constant rate of inflation, $\dot{W} = \dot{P}^e$, and hence

$$y = y^* - \frac{1}{\gamma}(R - W/P). \tag{8.12}$$

The level of output at which inflation will be held constant thus depends on the discrepancy between the desired and the actual real wage.

The implications of this approach are that, if the oil price increase lowers the actual real wage, money wage claims will rise in an attempt to restore real wages. If the government wishes to prevent an acceleration of inflation, it must depress demand sufficiently to counteract the wage-push effect, as indicated by equation (8.12). In this model, unemployment is not a consequence of actual real wages being too high, and it therefore being unprofitable for firms to hire the whole labour force: rather, it is a consequence of money wage claims being excessive, as a result of a loss of real wages, and a high level of unemployment being needed to prevent the wage-push developing into an accelerating inflationary spiral.

On this approach, we assume not a sudden exogenous increase in trade union real wage demands, but rather that the trade unions maintain existing real wage targets at a time when the increase in oil prices requires a real wage cut. Even so, it might be expected that trade unions would come to realize that the attainable level of real wages had fallen, and would adjust their wage targets accordingly. There is, however, another factor to take into account. Higher oil prices reduce the profitability of new investment, and they may be expected to slow down the rate of capital accumulation and hence the growth rate of productivity. Whether or not other factors have been involved as well, there has in fact been a slowdown in productivity growth during the 1970s. This could account for the persistence of target real wages in excess of the wage levels actually attainable.

This model suggests that governments face a policy dilemma: they can restrain the growth of aggregate demand in order to control inflation, with the consequence of persistently high unemployment (as indicated by equation (8.12)) for as long as real wage targets remain excessive; or they can expand demand, with the result that inflation will accelerate. As in the expectations-augmented Phillips Curve models, there is no long-run trade-off between inflation and unemployment. As in those models, there is a short-run trade-off, but it is located around a higher level of unemployment.

NOTE

1. The impact of an increase in the relative price of oil on the demand for labour at a given real wage is rather more complicated than suggested in the text. There is an output effect and a substitution effect. The output effect, most simply, states that, with given factor proportions, the rise in total input prices relative to the output price causes a reduction in production, and hence in demand for the variable factors such as labour. The substitution effect states that the change in the relative price of labour as against oil will cause a substitution from oil to labour at any given level of output, hence raising the demand for labour. As an empirical matter, it is generally thought that in the short run the substitution effect is very small, and the output effect dominates (see Bruno and Sachs, 1979).

CHAPTER 9

The Effects of Inflation

Up to this point we have assumed that inflation is an unambiguously evil phenomenon, and that it is one of the principal tasks of a responsible government to take the appropriate steps to reduce the rate of inflation. Nevertheless, despite the highly emotional rhetoric that issues from politicians and journalists alike, it is by no means obvious to the economist that inflation is a bad thing. It has often been argued, for example, that a price level that is changing at a constant proportional rate and is fully anticipated and acted upon by all economic agents will have negligible effects upon economic welfare. That is, the addition of 'noughts' at the end of *nominal* quantities at regular periods may have no effect on *real* quantities.

In the first two sections of this chapter we shall attempt to gauge the effect of a fully anticipated inflation on (a) the real interest rate and investment, and (b) the level of economic welfare. By a fully anticipated inflation, we mean a situation in which all movements in the general price index are (and have been) correctly foreseen by economic agents, and in which prices adjust perfectly flexibly. In the third section of the chapter, we examine how inflation affects an economy where these conditions do not hold.

In the first two sections we show that even a fully anticipated inflation can have real effects, but that these effects all emanate from a particular institutional assumption, namely that no interest is paid on money. Because of this assumption, changes in the expected rate of inflation alter the real return on money balances, leading to real resource allocation effects. If the banking system were competitive, interest would be paid on money balances (bank deposits) and it would then follow that a fully anticipated inflation would have no real effects.

Unanticipated inflation is more difficult to analyse in general theoretical terms. In section 9.3 we indicate some of the more important ways in which the failure to correctly anticipate, or adjust to, inflation appears to affect the economic system. We suggest some reasons why inflation may be a disruptive influence on economic activity and can have serious effects on economic welfare.

9.1 THE EFFECTS OF ANTICIPATED INFLATION ON INVESTMENT AND REAL INTEREST RATES

Most of the monetarist models of inflation that we have so far encountered have depended heavily upon the Fisherine theory of nominal interest, whereby the money interest rate is the sum of the real interest rate, r (often assumed to be constant, especially in the longer run) and the expected rate of inflation, $\dot{P}^e$. That is:

$$i = r + \dot{P}^e. \tag{9.1}$$

There is not normally supposed to be a relation between the expected rate of inflation and the equilibrium real interest rate. (In the short run, of course, a failure to anticipate inflation adequately may depress the real rate of interest, but this disequilibrium will not persist into the long run.) Keynes (1936) attacked this theory in the *General Theory*, arguing that part of the impact of a higher rate of inflation would be on the marginal efficiency of capital. Even Fisher himself had doubts about the *empirical* validity of equation (9.1):

> *When prices are rising, the rate of interest tends to be high but not so high as it should be to compensate for the rise; and when prices are falling, the rate of interest tends to be low, but not so low as it should be to compensate for the fall. . . . The erratic behaviour of real interest is evidently a trick played on the money market by the 'money illusion' when contracts are made in unstable money.*
> *[Fisher, 1930]*

And there the matter rested until R.A. Mundell (1963b) took up the question of the relation between the real interest rate and the expected rate of inflation.

9.1.1 MUNDELL'S MODEL

We shall assume a closed economy with only two assets, money and equity shares. Total wealth is the sum of the real value of equities, E^*, and real money balances (M_0/P), the supply of money being fixed at M_0. Wealth will be allocated between E and (M_0/P), the exact division depending upon the difference between the nominal return on shares (which is the nominal interest rate, i) and the nominal return on money, σ. Real income and employment are assumed to be at their full employment equilibrium levels and are suppressed into the functional forms of the following equations. The demand for money may therefore be written:

$$\frac{M_0}{P} = L\,(i - \sigma). \tag{9.2}$$

For the moment we shall follow Mundell in assuming that the nominal return on money is zero so that $\sigma = 0$ and equation (9.2) may be rewritten:

$$\frac{M_0}{P} = L\,(i). \tag{9.3}$$

Following Fisher, it is assumed that $i = r + \dot{P}^e$, and we assume that $\dot{P}^e$ is exogenously determined. If $\dot{P}^e = 0$, equation (9.3) describes the relation between (M/P) and r, which we shall label LM_1 (see figure 9.1).

For each value of $\dot{P}^e$, a new LM relation holds. The greater the expected rate of inflation, the further to the south-west will be the relevant LM curve lie. Thus LM_2 corresponds to a positive expected rate of inflation.

So far we have considered only the factors that determine the demand for real balances. It is now necessary to consider the factors

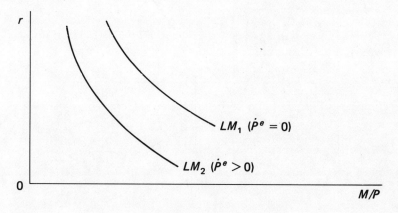

Figure 9.1

that determine the demand for and supply of loanable funds, i.e. the factors that determine savings and investment. Investment, I, varies inversely with the real interest rate; i.e.,

$$I = I(r), I'(r) < 0.$$

We assume saving an increasing function of the real interest rate and a decreasing function of wealth. (For purposes of the present analysis, we may ignore government spending and taxation.) We can then write total savings as

$$S = S(r, E^* + M_0/P). \tag{9.4}$$

In equilibrium,

$$I(r) = S(r, E^* + M_0/P). \tag{9.5}$$

The two variables that concern us at the moment in the equilibrium condition (9.5) are r and M_0/P. A rise in r will reduce desired investment ($I'(r) < 0$), but may in fact stimulate saving ($S_r > 0$). In all events, so long as $I'(r) < S_r$, a rise in r will have to be accompanied by a rise in M_0/P if the equilibrium condition (9.5) is to be satisfied. From the point of view of saving–investment equilibrium, therefore, a rise in r will be associated with a rise in M_0/P. The locus of such equilibrium combinations is the *IS* curve illustrated in figure 9.2.

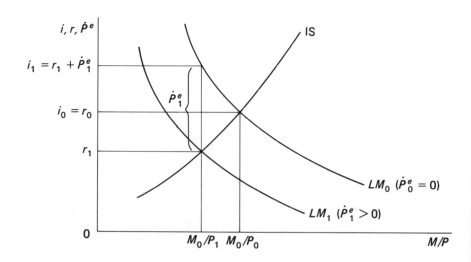

Figure 9.2

It should be borne in mind that we are making the assumption that the level of real income does not vary as a result of various monetary and fiscal policies. The *IS* and *LM* curves that are referred to in this chapter do not therefore relate the interest rate to the level of *real income*: they relate to the holding of *real balances*. The labels have been retained in order to emphasize the notion that an *IS* curve is a locus of points of equilibrium in the product market and the *LM* curve the locus of points of equilibrium in the money market. The choice of variables for the horizontal and vertical axes will depend upon the nature of the problem to be solved (figure 9.2).

Full equilibrium occurs at the intersection of the *IS* curve and the relevant *LM* curve. For example, if the expected rate of inflation is zero, the equilibrium real (and nominal) rate of interest will be r_0 and the equilibrium level of real balances will be M_0/P_0. But should the expected rate of inflation rise to $\dot{P}_1^e$, full equilibrium requires that both r and M_0/P should fall to r_1 and M_0/P_1 respectively. The nominal interest rate will rise from r_0 to $r_1 + \dot{P}_1^e$; i.e. i will indeed rise, but not by as much as the rise in $\dot{P}^e$.

The mechanics of the process are as follows. A higher expected rate of inflation raises the nominal interest rate for each real interest rate; individuals attempt to run down their holdings of real balances by substituting shares for real balances in their transactions portfolio: but since it is assumed that the economy is at full employment, any increase in the demand for capital will simply bid up prices; the fall in the value of real balances that accompanies this price increase will curtail consumption and stimulate saving at each rate of interest, which in turn will stimulate investment and drive down the real yield on shares.

9.1.2 SOME EXTENSIONS OF THE MUNDELL MODEL

One crucial assumption of the Mundell model is that money bears no interest ($\sigma = 0$). To the extent, however, that money consists of bank deposits, which banks are able to lend out at the nominal rate of interest, one would expect that, if the banking system were competitive, banks would pay interest on their deposits. In the limiting case of perfect competition banks should pay on their deposits an interest rate equal to the nominal interest rate in the rest of the economy less some differential to pay for the cost of banking services provided to depositors. In this case the differential between σ and i is unaffected by the level of nominal interest rates, and hence by the expected rate of inflation. The *LM* curve in figure 9.2 is then vertical.

It follows that changes in the expected rate of inflation have no effect on the real interest rate. This confirms the point made in the introduction to this chapter, that the effects of fully anticipated inflation arose only where restrictive practices in the monetary system permitted banks and governments to avoid paying interest on money.

Second, we have assumed that the expected rate of inflation is altered exogenously. With a model of this type it is natural to think that, after a period of price stability, the government will suddenly announce that the money supply from now and for ever will expand at a steady rate of growth of say, x per cent per annum. The price level then starts rising at x per cent per annum, and the actual and expected rates of inflation are then both x per cent. This picture seems to suggest that the government scatters money across the economy, as from one of Professor Friedman's helicopters.

In practice, the increase in the money supply necessary to sustain an inflation can arise either through a persistent fiscal deficit or through open market operations. We next analyse these two cases, following Phelps (1965). In the former case, a fiscal deficit will shift the *IS* curve of figure 9.2 upwards. Incorporating the government budget, we would rewrite equation (9.5)

$$I(r) + (G - T) = S(r, E^* + M_0/P) \qquad (9.6)$$

and an increase in government spending less taxation $(G - T)$ must be accompanied by an increase in r (for given M_0/P), or by a fall in M_0/P (for given r) if equilibrium is to be maintained. With given real income, a constant real fiscal deficit constitutes a constant proportion of real income, and hence, if it is financed entirely by money creation, it will provide a constant rate of growth of the money supply. Thus a monetary expansion effected through a fiscal deficit leads to a once-and-for-all shift in the *IS* curve.

What happens to the real interest rate depends upon the relative displacement of the *IS* and *LM* curves. In figure 9.3, the real interest rate falls slightly from r_1, to r_3, but this need not necessarily occur. If the upward displacement of the *IS* function for a given M/P exceeds the consequent downward displacement of the *LM* function, the rate of interest will in fact rise. The essential point is that, when inflationary expectations are induced by an expansionary budgetary policy, the real rate of interest will not necessarily fall, as is implied in Mundell's model where expectations are exogenously given. And even if it did fall, the decline in r would be very much smaller in magnitude than would be predicted by Mundell's model, in which the economy

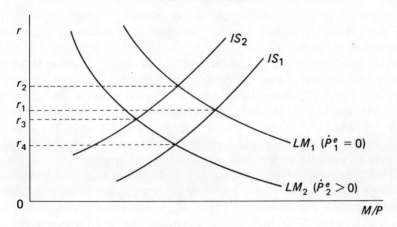

Figure 9.3

moves along a *given IS* function to a new point of equilibrium at r_4.

By contrast, if the money enters the system by means of open market operations, the government purchases equities, and hence the expansionary monetary policy implies lower private sector holdings of equities. As indicated by equation (9.5), a fall in E^* requires either a rise in M_0/P or a fall in the rate of interest if equilibrium is to be maintained. Thus the *IS* curve shifts to the right, as shown in figure 9.4. In equilibrium, the real interest rate falls further than had been the case in figure 9.2.

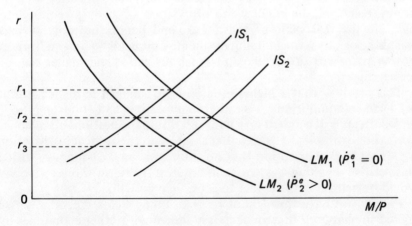

Figure 9.4

Phelps thus concludes that the effect of a fully anticipated inflation on the real interest rate depends on how the associated monetary expansion is financed. It can be regarded as a variant on a familiar proposition: that even in a model in which money is neutral (in the sense that an equal proportional increase in the quantity of money and in all prices leaves all real variables unchanged), a change in the quantity of money necessarily entails a change in one of the other components of the government budget, and because these other components have non-neutral effects, a change in the money supply cannot be brought about with entirely neutral effects.

Third, the analysis may appear rather short-run in nature. Returning to figure 9.2, at the new equilibrium (with the higher expected inflation rate), the real interest rate is lower and saving and investment are higher. It follows that the new equilibrium is characterized by a more rapid rate of real capital accumulation, and hence the real stock of equities and real income will grow more rapidly.

To analyse the long-run consequences of a change in the anticipated rate of inflation, it is necessary to reformulate the problem in the framework of an equilibrium growth model. The basic argument in this context (Tobin, 1965; Johnson, 1967) is that, along any given steady-state growth path, the higher the (fully anticipated) inflation rate the smaller the stock of desired real money balances and hence, with a given savings ratio, the greater the capital stock per worker. The mechanism is essentially similar to that of the Mundell model. A high rate of inflation means that people attempt to reduce their holdings of money balances, with the result that the price level rises and the stock of real money balances falls. The lower the stock of money balances, the smaller the proportion of savings required to maintain the real value of that stock, and hence the more savings available for physical capital investment. This leads to an equilibrium growth path with a higher capital–labour ratio, and higher output per head.

This result — that a higher inflation rate can lead to higher output per head in equilibrium — is rather unappealing, and Johnson (1967) shows that it is dependent on a number of rather questionable assumptions. For example, he argues that there is no theoretical justification for the crucial assumption that no interest is paid on money. With a competitive banking system, and interest paid on money, money would be neutral with respect to economic growth.

Finally, we have throughout been assuming a closed economy. We argued in chapter 7 that an economy linked with other economies by means of fixed exchange rates cannot, except in the short run, pursue an independent monetary policy, and that its inflation rate must follow that of its trading partners. One could, however, analyse a group of economies linked by fixed exchange rates as a single closed economy and apply the analysis of the effects of inflation to the group of economies taken as a whole.

If, however, the economy has a flexible exchange rate, it will be able to follow an independent monetary policy. If anticipated inflation has the effect of lowering the real rate of interest, however, and capital is perfectly mobile between countries, savings will flow out of the domestic economy to purchase higher-yielding capital overseas. This process will continue until the domestic real interest rate is restored to the level of international rates.

One may put this point a different way by arguing that savers in one country face a virtually infinitely elastic array of investment opportunities throughout the world; or, equivalently, that a small change in domestic savings will not alter the 'world' interest rate. We may then regard the *IS* curve in figure 9.2 as horizontal, so that, again, a shift in price expectations does not alter the real interest rate.

9.2 ANTICIPATED INFLATION AND ECONOMIC WELFARE

The question now arises as to the possible welfare repercussions, if any, of a fully anticipated inflation.

Retaining the assumption that money bears no interest ($\sigma = 0$), the only welfare effect of anticipated inflation will be to induce asset-holders to economize on the holding of money in their transactions balances by participating in such socially wasteful activities as making more frequent trips to the bank to encash their equity shares. As long as there is a difference between the nominal yield on money and other riskless and easily convertible assets, there will exist an incentive to economize on money. This incentive will be the greater the higher the nominal interest rate.

This observation led Bailey (1956) to devise a measure of the welfare cost of a higher expected rate of inflation. Starting with the Fisherine assumption that a higher expected rate of inflation produces an equal rise in the nominal rate of interest, Bailey proposed that variations in i will mainly reflect variations in $\dot{P}^e$. That is, $i = r + \dot{P}^e$ where r is constant. We shall be interested in three rates of interest: $0, i_1$ and i_2. Corresponding to each interest rate will be three different rates of inflation: $\dot{P}^e_0 = -r$, $\dot{P}^e_1 = 0$ and $\dot{P}^e_2 > 0$ respectively.

In figure 9.5, the curve AB is the demand curve for real money balances as a function of the opportunity cost of holding money, i.

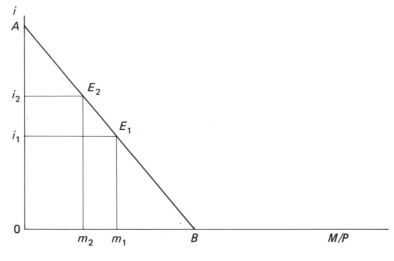

Figure 9.5

Following Friedman (1969), the demand curve is assumed to be derived from the utility the consumer enjoys from the 'non-pecuniary services' provided by real money balances (security, convenience and so on). The height of the demand curve corresponding to any level of real money balances thus measures the marginal utility of these non-pecuniary services at that point. Likewise, the total area under the demand curve represents the total utility derived by consumers from holding a given level of real money balances.

For example, in figure 9.5, if the interest rate is i_1 (corresponding to zero expected inflation), consumers will hold real money balances equal to m_1, and the total utility they derive from them is given by the area $AE_1m_1 0$. If now there is a positive expected rate of inflation, the interest rate will rise to i_2, and the total utility derived from holding money fall to $AE_2m_2 0$. The loss of utility consequent upon the higher expected rate of inflation is thus measured by the area $E_2E_1m_1m_2$.

It is crucial to note that, while there are opportunity costs to individual consumers incurred in holding higher money balances, there are no costs to society as a whole associated with maintaining a higher rather than a lower stock of real money balances in the economy. This is not because money is assumed costless to print, because we are here concerned with real rather than nominal money balances. Rather, it is because the public can, in this model, achieve the level of real money balances it desires by means of (costless) adjustments in the general price level. The opportunity cost of holding money balances for individuals is, from a social viewpoint, akin to a tax levied by the suppliers of money (the government and the banking system). This approach leads directly to the view of inflation as a tax on money balances.

Within this framework, the optimum quantity of money is given by point B in figure 9.5, at which point consumer utility is at a maximum. At this point, the marginal utility of the non-pecuniary services of money has been driven down to zero (equal to the social cost of provision of such services), and a state of 'full liquidity' is said to prevail. Full liquidity is achieved when the nominal interest rate is zero, which requires an expected rate of price deflation equal to the real interest rate ($\dot{P}^e = -r$).

Even apart from any practical difficulties that may be entailed in instituting a policy of price deflation to engender the appropriate expectations, as a policy recommendation the proposal has not been favourably received (Johnson, 1970). At a political level, it will be observed that, in a state of full liquidity, the government's tax revenues fall to zero. It seems unlikely that the government would be prepared to abandon a source of tax revenue, and it would probably be inefficient for it to reduce the tax on money balances to zero given that it levies taxes on holdings of most other assets.

Perhaps more fundamentally, in a freely competitive banking system, as we have already noted, interest would be paid on bank deposits, and the opportunity cost of holding such deposits would be independent of the general level of interest rates and would depend only on the services banks provide to their depositors. With a freely competitive banking system, full liquidity prevails at any expected rate of inflation. (Ideally, we would also need the government to pay interest on holdings of currency. Such payments are generally considered impractical, but currency holdings in any event amount to only a small proportion of the total money stock.) From this perspective, full liquidity is the state of affairs that would tend to prevail unless the authorities, by means of banking regulations, etc., attempt to prevent it. And if the objective of the authorities is to move the system away from full liquidity, it seems inconsistent, as Johnson points out, to then recommend them to institute a rate of price deflation in order to restore full liquidity.

We consider, finally, the magnitude of these welfare costs. We have argued that the loss of utility associated with an increase in the expected inflation rate can be measured by an area such as $E_2 E_1 m_1 m_2$ in figure 9.5. It is immediately apparent that, for any given increment in the inflation rate, the size of this area depends on the slope of the demand for money curve. Those who believe the interest elasticity of the demand for money to be low (a view traditionally associated with the monetarist camp) are obliged to infer that the welfare costs of anticipated inflation are also low. However, if the costs of anticipated inflation are solely those of economizing on money balances – more frequent trips to the bank and so on – it seems plausible to think that they will be small.

In periods of hyper-inflation, the value of money falls very rapidly indeed. To take an extreme example, in Hungary in July 1946 the price level rose by several thousandfold within a single week (Griffiths, 1976, p. 142). In such circumstances the incentive to economize on money balances is of course extremely strong. Firms pay wages daily (or even more frequently) rather than weekly. Once paid, workers rush out to the shops to buy goods, rather than hold on to money that will soon become worthless. When firms receive payment they immediately spend the money – on stocks of goods or, indeed, on anything that might retain its value better than money. Far more time is spent on transactions and, with the constant pressure to spend as quickly as possible, existing goods and output are allocated between consumers and firms in a much less efficient way than when people can allow the time to choose rationally what they want to purchase. It is none the less remarkable that, even in these cases of extreme hyper-inflation, people continue to use money for transactions rather than reverting to barter. This provides some further support for the view that the demand-for-money function is quite steep (see also our discussion in section 6.2 above). A good survey of hyper-inflations is provided by Griffiths (1976, chapter 10).

9.3 THE EFFECTS OF UNANTICIPATED INFLATION

In reading the first two sections of this chapter, the reader may be wondering precisely why inflation is regarded as the process undermining the economic stability of Western economies. If the only effects of inflation are to force economic agents to economize on their holdings of real balances by making more frequent trips to the bank, and if even this inconvenience can be obviated by allowing money to bear interest, why should anyone worry about inflation at all? But then the reader will recall that the sort of inflation that was being referred to was a fully anticipated inflation with two essential characteristics: (a) that all movements in the general price index were correctly foreseen by everyone, and (b) that all prices adjusted perfectly flexibly. In this section we examine what may happen if these conditions are not satisfied.

9.3.1 UNANTICIPATED INFLATION AND LONG-TERM CONTRACTS

At any time there exist in an economy a large number of contracts, entered into at some period in the past, specifying that monetary payments be made from one economic agent to another. Examples of such contracts include pensions and annuities, government bonds, corporate debentures and the like. In the event of unanticipated inflation, the real value of the monetary payment specified in the contract is different from that which the parties to the contact had expected when the contract was entered into. If inflation is more rapid than expected, there is a windfall gain to net monetary debtors and a corresponding loss to net monetary creditors.

Unanticipated inflation can be regarded as unjust because it arbitrarily falsifies contracts − as, for example, with the pensioner who has saved during his lifetime to provide adequately for his old age, but finds the provision he had made suddenly reduced by inflation. Correspondingly, the man to whom he had lent his savings benefits because of the reduced real value of the repayments.

These direct redistributive effects of inflation are widely deplored, in part because they are unjust (in the sense of falsifying the contract), and in part because those who lose often seem more 'worthy' than those who gain. It is, for example, one of the most serious consequences of hyper-inflation that speculators and profiteers grow rich at the expense of ordinary citizens. The latter group, seeking only to provide a safe home for their savings to provide for their old age, invest in bank deposits on government stocks which quickly become worthless in a hyper-inflation. In Germany, for example, the middle classes were completely impoverished by the hyper-inflation of the early 1920s.

By contrast, it is generally thought that the middle classes do rather well out of inflation in the UK, because they typically own real assets (houses) and have net monetary debts (mortgages). More generally, the pattern of monetary credits and debts is not at all straightforward. The government is by far the largest monetary debtor, and is therefore a major beneficiary of unanticipated inflation. But most firms, and many households (i.e. those with mortgages) are also monetary debtors. The main monetary creditors are the pension funds and life assurance companies, that is to say, households at one remove. Thus a typical household may benefit from unanticipated inflation as a taxpayer, and through reduced mortgage debts, but may lose in terms of its pension entitlements.

It is sometimes thought that these redistributive effects, however unjust, are irrelevant from the viewpoint of economic efficiency because they can be regarded as lump-sum transfers. Such an inference is not correct, however, for the prospect of further unanticipated movements in the price level will mean that any long-term debt contract currently entered into will have associated with it a much higher degree of uncertainty as to the real value of the future monetary payments specified in the contract. Such uncertainty is a deterrent to borrower and lender alike, and thus may severely limit the market in long-term loans (as people do not wish to hold assets or liabilities of such uncertain real value). Indeed, since the onset of more rapid inflation in the UK in the early 1970s, new issues of corporate loan stock have virtually disappeared.

Perhaps most fundamentally in this context, the prospect of a highly uncertain future price level deprives people of a secure home for their savings. Even if, in the outcome, inflation is no worse than people expect, the uncertainty and insecurity that results from there no longer being a safe asset for people to hold is a severe cost in terms of economic welfare.

9.3.2 INSTITUTIONAL MONEY ILLUSION

A second major cost of unanticipated inflation arises from the failure of various types of arrangements to be adjusted to take account of inflation. The most immediate example is the tax system. There is, in principle, nothing to stop the tax system being adjusted each year to maintain the real burden of each tax unchanged. Most obviously, income tax allowances, set in nominal money terms, can be increased each year in line with inflation. Less obvious, however, is the point that capital gains tax and taxes on nominal interest payments, in times of inflation, tax nominal income, which serves only to maintain the real value of an asset. If no allowance is made for this in the tax system, the effective burden of taxation on capital is increased. Such inflation-induced increases in taxation may be a serious source of inefficiency — for example, by providing a strong incentive to invest resources in tax-advantaged forms (such as owner-occupied housing).

There are many examples one might cite of what we have termed 'institutional money illusion'. One concerns the 'front-loading' of loan contracts. Normally, a person who borrows money, for example in the form of a mortgage, is expected to repay a constant monetary amount per annum over the life of the loan. If prices are stable, this implies a constant repayment stream in real terms. With inflation, and given the same type of loan contract, the real value of the repayments falls over time. Repayments, in real terms, tend to be higher in the early years of the loan and lower towards the end of its life. Again, real magnitudes are affected by inflation.

More generally, inflation confuses the distinction between income and capital. In a complex financial system, established ways of thinking and sound business practices often seem to be based on the assumption that the value of money is stable. People cling to these principles even when the value of money becomes unstable. One might instance the difficulty of the accounting profession in reaching agreement as to how corporate profits should be measured in times of inflation. In the UK, government fiscal policy seems still to be measured in terms of the public sector borrowing requirement – a measure that takes no account of the effects of inflation on the public finances.

Established financial practices persist even though, with inflation, they are no longer appropriate. People continue to use money as the measuring rod for economic activities without recognizing that, if the measuring rod itself is liable to change unpredictably, actions based on it are likely to lead to the wrong results.

9.3.: RELATIVE PRICE VARIABILITY

In ciscussing fully anticipated inflation we assumed that prices were perfectly flexible. If changing prices is costly, so that prices are changed only infrequently, in times of inflation relative prices may move away from their equilibrium levels with a consequent loss of allocative efficiency. The greater variability of relative prices may also be a source of increased uncertainty.

The objection to this argument is that, even in times of zero inflation, relative prices will generally be changing, and if price changes are costly to make, the equilibrating changes may well be delayed. While it seems likely that unanticipated inflation will exacerbate the problem, there is no proof that it will do so. For example, if prices are much easier to increase than to reduce, inflation may actually assist in achieving equilibrating relative price adjustments, since it makes it possible to change relative prices without having to cut any price in money terms.

9.3.4 INDEXATION

By indexation we mean the practice whereby contracts for future payment would be denominated not in terms of a given sum of money, but instead in terms of a sum of money multiplied by the general price index. Such index-linking of contracts maintains the real value of repayments irrespective of what happens to the general price level between the time of signing the contract and the time the repayments fall due.

It is clear that, if all contracts were indexed, unanticipated inflation would no longer have redistributive effects, since such effects arise from unanticipated changes in the general price level, altering the real value of payments denominated in money terms. Likewise, it would remove the uncertainty associated with inflation, for the holder of an indexed asset can be sure that it will retain its real value. Similarly, indexation can be applied to the tax system, and thus can help remove the distorting effects of inflation in this context. In general one can argue (Jackman and Klappholz, 1975) that in a fully indexed economy there are no costs of unanticipated inflation; or, equivalently, that indexation produces an outcome equivalent to that which would have occurred had inflation been correctly foreseen. Indexation does not reduce the costs of fully anticipated inflation: for example, if no interest is paid on money, we still have the costs discussed in section 9.2. Nor, of course, does indexation remove the uncertainties resulting from changes in relative prices brought about by real factors.

None the less, if the costs of unanticipated inflation are substantial, and we have argued that they are, there does seem a very strong case for the introduction of more widespread indexation to reduce or eliminate such costs. It can also be argued (Friedman, 1974) that indexation can reduce the costs, in terms of unemployment, of a deflationary monetary policy designed to achieve a given reduction in the rate of inflation. We have already touched on this point in section 5.4 above, where we argue that the argument depends on the assumption that prices are more flexible than wages, an assumption for which the evidence on pricing behaviour (chapter 3 appendix 1) seems to offer little support.

The main opposition to indexation derives from the view that, by making inflation less painful, it will reduce the incentive to governments to pursue anti-inflationary policies. Inflation serves no useful purpose, and price stability is clearly the ideal solution. It is a political, rather than an economic, judgement as to whether inflation would in fact be higher with indexation. (We have already noted that, as a large monetary debtor, in the absence of indexation the government is a substantial beneficiary from unanticipated inflation).

We return to indexation as a policy recommendation in section 10.2 below.

CHAPTER 10

Conclusions and Policy Recommendations

In this final chapter we shall attempt to summarize our main conclusions as to the factors determining inflation and the implications of our arguments for policies to control it. We do not summarize each of the theories we have discussed again here: there are such summaries at the end of most of the chapters. Instead, we focus on our overall conclusions on what appear to us to be the most important issues.

10.1 THE DETERMINANTS OF INFLATION

10.1.1 THE ROLE OF EXCESS DEMAND

We believe that the bulk of the empirical evidence supports the hypothesis, upon which most economic theory is built, that increases in wages and prices are affected by the pressure of demand in the market. Clearly, the breakdown of the Phillips Curve in the late 1960s gave rise to serious doubts on this score. And a number of more recent studies, particularly in the UK, have failed to detect a significant influence of unemployment on inflation. However, we argue that this conflicting evidence is not conclusive, in part because some of the early Phillips Curve studies are mis-specified because they do not include a price expectations variable (chapter 5), and in part because unemployment appears a rather unreliable indicator of the pressure of demand (chapter 3 appendix 2).

In claiming that empirical work has established a significant role for excess demand factors, there are two points we should make clear. First, the argument that excess demand matters does not rule out the possibility that cost-push factors may have an important influence also. We return to this below. Second, our claim that excess demand matters is not, in itself, linked to any specific theory as to the factors

188

determining excess demand. Indeed, in recent years fluctuations in demand have had more to do with international developments than with the traditional domestic fiscal or monetary measures. The inflationary boom of the early 1970s can be attributed to the massive increase in international liquidity associated with the financing of the Vietnam War (chapter 7). The stagflation of the mid-1970s can likewise be attributed to the OPEC oil price increase of the autumn of 1973 (chapter 8). Equally, however, domestic fiscal and monetary measures, and indeed other domestic factors, can affect the level of aggregate demand.

10.1.2 ABSENCE OF MONEY ILLUSION

The one common theme of all recent analyses of inflation is that people are not deluded by changes in money values, and that wage increases match price increases in full. This absence of money illusion is central both to the 'neoclassical' expectations hypothesis and to the 'cost-push' target real-wage approach (chapter 8).

In the absence of money illusion, sustained excess demand generates not simply inflation, but ever-accelerating inflation. There is no long-run trade-off between the pressure of demand (or unemployment) and inflation. The 'Keynesian' belief that the government could steer the economy to maintain some desired level of unemployment by means of demand management policies seems no longer correct. If the long-run Phillips Curve is vertical, output and unemployment are determined by 'real' forces and inflation by the growth of nominal aggregate demand.

10.1.3 COST-PUSH FACTORS

We believe that factors traditionally classified as 'cost-push' such as trade union militancy and 'real wage resistance' have an important influence on wage bargaining. However, if we accept that there is no money illusion in wage bargains, cost-push pressures cannot be accommodated by a faster, but still stable, rate of inflation, but must instead lead to an explosive acceleration of inflation.

If the demands of the trade unions are couched in real terms, as appears to be the case, the government cannot buy them off with a faster rate of inflation, because the trade unions will see through the pretence. But if inflation does not ease the problem, the pursuit of inflationary policies yields no benefit to the government, and there is therefore no reason why a government, faced with militant trade unions, should adopt more inflationary policies. In the absence of money illusion, the government has no alternative but to allow unemployment to rise sufficiently to curb the trade unions' wage demands. In the long run, cost-push pressures *must* raise the unemployment rate, but they need have no effect on inflation.

10.1.4 MONEY AND INFLATION

In chapter 6 we argued that, as an empirical matter, the velocity of circulation of money was reasonably stable, and that, in the long run, sustained inflation is impossible without an accompanying expansion in the quantity of money. Milton Friedman (1970c) has argued that 'inflation is always and everywhere a monetary phenomenon'. We think that the rather more precise statement that 'a necessary and sufficient condition for sustained inflation is an expansion of the money stock of approximately equal magnitude' conveys a more accurate picture. We prefer the more cautious statement because, as indicated in chapter 6, we are not convinced that the government can easily or directly control the supply of money. While the correlation between inflation and monetary growth, in the long run, is established, we believe the direction of causation is much more disputable than suggested by Friedman's statement.

10.2 RECOMMENDATIONS FOR POLICY

Our recommendations for policy are guided, first, by our main conclusions as to the determinants of inflation (summarized above) and, second, by our analysis of the economic costs of inflation (chapter 9). Our analysis suggests that moderately high rates of inflation, as have been experienced in the UK over the last twenty years or so, have severe costs in terms of economic welfare, and no benefits. The objective of policy should be to restore price stability, which means an inflation rate of no more than 2 or 3 per cent per year.

We have discussed the principles of policies to control inflation in an economy where excess demand matters, and there is no money illusion, in section 5.4 above. Here we return to these points, in the context of a policy package to restore price stability. We think the main features of such a package should be as follows.

10.2.1 BASE MACROECONOMIC POLICY ON A 'NOMINAL' MAGNITUDE

Our main conclusion in chapter 5 was that policy should be based on a 'nominal' economic variable, such as a measure of the money supply, the price level, or the exchange rate, rather than on a real variable such as output or employment. This raises the immediate question of which of the nominal variables to choose as the policy target. Many monetarists argue that the money supply is the best policy target, because it is a magnitude over which the government has direct control. As already indicated, we are not convinced by this argument. If the money supply is largely endogenous in the short run, the case for using it rather than the price level as the policy target becomes less strong.

The alternative is the exchange rate. The European Monetary System provides the opportunity for the UK to link the pound to the currencies of continental Europe, and hence to let its inflation rate be determined by the average rate of the European countries. We think this should be regarded as a serious policy option, but it has many other political and economic implications, which it would be inappropriate to go into here. For the rest of this section we will therefore assume a government pursuing an independent counter-inflationary policy by means of domestic policies based on a monetary, or price level, target, and maintaining a freely floating exchange rate.

The other main policy question is then the speed of deceleration of inflation towards price stability. Monetarists generally argue that the required reduction in the rate of monetary expansion should be undertaken gradually so as to avoid subjecting the economy to too violent a change in direction. We know too little about the precise mechanics of adjustment to be able to predict with any accuracy the reaction of the economic system to a sudden jerk occasioned by a dramatic reduction in the rate of monetary expansion.

On the other hand, it can be argued that the gradualist approach is very unappealing politically. It seems to require a long, drawn-out recession, while the gains in terms of reduced inflation are slow to appear. There must be doubts as to whether politicians will persevere along such an unrewarding road, and inflationary expectations may therefore not adjust downwards as required.

By contrast, a much sharper rate of deceleration offers the advantages of more immediate results, and therefore a better prospect of jolting expectations to a lower level. The recession is of course much more severe, but the prospect of recovery arrives much sooner. This leads to our second recommendation.

10.2.2 INTRODUCE AN INCOMES POLICY FOR A SHORT PERIOD

If the government pursues very sharply deflationary policies, the risk it faces it that wage bargains will be maintained at a high level, with the consequence of much unemployment. Of course, if the government announces its strategy, that may affect expectations and hence the level of wage settlements. But statements of policy intent by governments do not always (or even usually) provide accurate forecasts of how governments will in fact behave, and hence it is optimistic to assume that they will have much effect on expectations.

We believe therefore that the government, at the time it introduces a fiercely deflationary policy, should also introduce an incomes policy designed to reduce the growth rate of money wages to a rate consistent with its new (and much lower) target for monetary (or price level) growth. If an incomes policy can hold down wage settlements in the short run, it can play an important role in reducing the costs of adjustment (in terms of unemployment) of the economy to the lower rate of inflation.

From a monetarist perspective, an incomes policy in this context is something of an act of brute force designed to protect people who, rationally enough, disbelieve government policy pronouncements in circumstances where the government will actually carry out its plans. Once the lower rate of inflation had been acheived, expectations would adjust to it, and there would be no further role for the incomes policy.

10.2.3 ADOPT WIDESPREAD INDEXATION

We have suggested how, in our view, inflation can best be brought under control. But experience suggests it is unrealistic to expect immediate or permanent success. The short-term gains to expansionary policies are ever-present. We believe people should be protected against unanticipated fluctuations in the inflation rate. There is no reason why the community need suffer as much from the consequences of lapses from price stability in the future as it has in the past. Such costs could be substantially avoided if indexed contracts were widely available (section 9.3 above).

Finally, it seems to us that the main threat to price stability in the future lies in the fact that the rate of unemployment consistent with non-accelerating inflation is so high, and appears to have risen so rapidly in recent years. While unemployment is high, governments will be subject to continual pressure to expand demand, even though such policies ultimately have no effect on unemployment but serve only to raise the inflation rate. The causes of this rise in unemployment are not well understood, though we have suggested some possible factors (for example, the determination of the trade unions to maintain real wage growth despite the OPEC oil price increase). Until the causes of the high level of unemployment are understood, and effective measures to reduce unemployment introduced, the prospects for price stability must remain bleak.

Bibliography

Ackley, G. (1958) 'A Third Approach to the Analysis and Control of Inflation', in *The Relationship of Prices to Economic Stability and Growth*, Joint Economic Committee, Washington.

Addison, J. and Burton, J. (1979) 'The Identification of Market and Spillover Forces in Wage Inflation: A Cautionary Note', *Applied Economics*, 11, March, 95–103.

Akerlof G.A. and Main, B.G.M. (1980) 'Unemployment Spells and Unemployment Experience', *American Economic Review*, 70, December, 885–93.

Alchian, A.A. (1971) 'Information Costs, Pricing and Resource Unemployment' in Phelps (1971).

Ando, A. and Modigloani, F. (1965) 'The Relative Stability of Monetary Velocity and the Investment Multiplier', *American Economic Review*, 55, September, 693–728.

Archibald, G.C. (1969) 'Wage–Price Dynamics, Inflation and Unemployment: The Phillips Curve and the Distribution of Unemployment', *American Economic Review*, 59, May, 125–34.

Artis, M.J. and Nobay, A.R. (1969) 'Two Aspects of the Monetary Debate', *National Institute Economic Review*, 49, August, 33–51.

Ashenfelter, O.C. and Johnson, G.E. (1969) 'Bargaining Theory, Trade Unions and Industrial Strike Activity', *American Economic Review*, 59, March 35–49.

Ashenfelter, O.C. and Pencavel, J.H. (1974) 'A Note on Estimating the Determinants of Changes in Wages and Earnings', Working Paper 46, Industrial Relations Section, Princeton University.

Bailey, M.J. (1956) 'The Welfare Cost of Inflationary Finance', *Journal of Political Economy*, 64, April, 93–110.

Barrett, C.R. and Walters, A.A. (1966) 'The Stability of Keynesian and Monetary Multipliers in the United Kingdom', *Review of Economics and Statistics*, 48, November, 395–405.

Barro, R.J. and Grossman, H.I. (1971) 'A General Disequilibrium Model of Income and Employment', *American Economic Review*, 61, March, 82–93.

Baumol, W.J. (1951) *Economic Dynamics.* New York, Macmillan.

Bhatia, R.J. (1961) 'Unemployment and the Rate of Change in Money Earnings in the United States, 1900–58', *Economica*, 28, August, 286–96.

Bodkin, R.G. (1966) *The Wage-Price-Productivity Nexus.* Philadelphia, Pennsylvania University Press.

Bowen, W.G. (1960) *The Wage-Price Issue: A Theoretical Analysis.* Princeton University Press.

Bowen, W.G. and Berry, R.A. (1963) 'Unemployment Conditions and Movements of the Money Wage Level' *Review of Economics and Statistics,* 45, May, 163–72.

Bowers, J.K. *et al.* (1970) 'The Change in the Relationship between Unemployment and Earnings Increase: A Review of Some Possible Explanations', *National Institute Economic Review,* 54, November, 44–63.

Brechling, F.P.R. (1968) 'The Trade-off between Inflation and Unemployment', *Journal of Political Economy,* 76, July/August, 712–37.

Brechling, F.P.R. (1972) 'Wage Inflation and the Structure of Regional Unemployment', University of Essex Discussion Paper no. 40, mimeographed. Reprinted in Laidler and Purdy (1974).

Brinner, R.E. (1977) 'The Death of the Phillips Curve Reconsidered', *Quarterly Journal of Economics,* 91, August, 389–418.

Brittan, S. (1975) *Second Thoughts on Full Employment Policy.* Chichester, Centre for Policy Studies.

Bronfenbrenner, M. and Holzman, F.D. (1963) 'A Survey of Inflation Theory', *American Economic Review,* 53, September, 593–661.

Bruno, M. (1980) 'Import Prices and Stagflation in the Industrial Countries: A Cross-section Analysis', *Economic Journal,* 90, September, 479–92.

Bruno, M. and Sachs, J.D. (1979) 'Supply versus Demand Approaches to the Problem of Stagflation', Discussion Paper no. 796. Jerusalem, Falk Institute.

Cagan, P. (1956) 'The Monetary Dynamics of Hyperinflation', in Friedman (1956a).

Cagan, P. (1969) 'Theories of Mild, Continuing Inflation: A Critique and Extension', in S.W. Rousseas (ed.) *Inflation: Its Causes, Consequences and Control.* Wilton Conn., Calvin K. Kazanijian Economics Foundation.

Carlson, J.A. and Parkin, J.M. (1975) 'Inflation Expectations', *Economica,* 42, May, 123–38.

Cassel, G. (1916) 'The Present Situation of the Foreign Exchanges', *Economic Journal,* 22, March, 62–65.

Coghlan, R.T. (1978) 'A Transactions Demand for Money' *Bank of England Quarterly Bulletin,* 18, March, 48–60.

Cross, R. and Laidler, D. (1976) 'Inflation, Excess Demand and Expectations in Fixed Exchange Rate Open Economics: Some Preliminary Empirical Results', in M. Parkin and G. Zis (eds). *Inflation in the World Economy.* Manchester University Press.

Cukierman, A. (1974) 'A Test of the "No Trade-off in the Long Run" Hypothesis', *Econometrica,* 42, November, 1069–80.

de Menil, G. (1971) *Bargaining: Monopoly Power Versus Union Power.* Cambridge, Mass., MIT Press.

Department of Employment (1976) 'The Changed Relationship between Unemployment and Vacancies', *Department of Employment Gazette,* 84, October, 1093–9.

Desai, M. (1975) 'The Phillips Curve: A Revisionist Interpretation', *Economica,* 42, February, 1–19.

Dicks-Mireaux, L.A. (1961) 'The Interrelationship Between Cost and Price Changes, 1948–59. A Study of Inflation in Post-War Britain', *Oxford Economics Papers,* 13, October, 267–92.

Dicks-Mireaux, L.A. and Dow, J.C.R. (1959) 'The Determinants of Wage Inflation: in the United Kingdom, 1946–1956', *Journal of the Royal Statistical Society,* Series A, 122, 145–74.

Dicks-Mireaux, L.A. and Shepherd, J.R. (1962) 'The Wages Structure and Some Implications for Incomes Policy', *National Institute Economic Review,* 22, November, 38–44.

Dow, J.C.R. (1956) 'Analysis of the Generation of Price Inflation, A Study of Cost and Price Changes in the United Kingdom, 1946–1954', *Oxford Economic Papers,* 8, October, 252–301.

Duck, N.W., Parkin, J.M., Rose, D. and Zis, G. (1976) 'The Determination of the Rate of Change of Wages and Prices in the Fixed Exchange Rate World Economy: 1956–70', in J.M. Parkin and G. Zis (eds) *Inflation in the World Economy.* Manchester University Press.

Duesenberry, J. (1950) 'The Mechanics of Inflation', *Review of Economics and Statistics,* 32, May, 144–9.

Eatwell, J., Llewellyn, J. and Tarling, R. (1974) 'Money Wage Inflation in Industrial Countries', *Review of Economic Studies,* 41, October, 515–23.

Eckstein, O. (ed.) (1972) *The Econometrics of Price Determination.* Proceedings of a conference sponsored by the Federal Reserve System and the Social Science Research Council, Washington.

Eckstein, O. and Wilson, T.A. (1962) 'The Determination of Money Wages in American Industry', *Quarterly Journal of Economics,* 76, August, 379–414.

Fisher, I. (1920), *The Purchasing Power of Money: Its Determination and Relation to Credit, Interest and Crises.* New York, Macmillan.

Fisher, I. (1930) *The Theory of Interest.* New York, Macmillan.

Flemming, J. (1976) *Inflation.* Oxford University Press.

Frenkel, J.A. (1978) 'Purchasing Power Parity: Doctrinal Perspective and Evidence from the 1920s', *Journal of International Economics,* 8, May, 169–91.

Frenkel, J.A. and Johnson, H.G. (eds.), (1976) *The Monetary Approach to the Balance of Payments.* London, George Allen and Unwin.

Frey, B.S. and Schneider, F. (1978) 'A Politico-economic Model of the United Kingdom', *Economic Journal,* 88, June, 243–53.

Friedman, M. (1948) 'A Monetary and Fiscal Framework for Economic Stability' *American Economic Review,* 38, June, 245–64.

Friedman, M. (1951) 'Some Comments on the Significance of Labor Unions for Economic Policy', in D. McC. Wright (ed.) *The Impact of the Union.* New York, Harcourt and Brace.

Friedman, M. (ed.) (1956a) *Studies in the Quantity Theory of Money,* Chicago University Press.

Friedman, M. (1956b) 'The Quantity Theory of Money: A Restatement', in Friedman (1956a).

Friedman, M. (1959) 'Statement on Monetary Policy', in *Employment, Growth and Price Levels.* Washington, US Government Printing Office.

Friedman, M. (1968) 'The Role of Monetary Policy', *American Economic Review,* 58, March, 1–17.

Friedman, M. (1969). *The Optimum Quantity of Money.* London, Macmillan.

Friedman, M. (1970a) 'A Theoretical Framework for Monetary Analysis', *Journal of Political Economy,* 78, March/April, 193–238.

Friedman, M. (1970b) 'The New Monetarism: Comment', *Lloyd's Bank Review,* 98, October, 52–3.

Friedman, M. (1970c) *The Counter-Revolution in Monetary Theory.* Institute of Economic Affairs, Occasional Paper no. 33.

Friedman, M. (1972) 'Comment on the Critics', *Journal of Political Economy,* 80, September/October, 906–50.

Friedman, M. (1974) *Monetary Correction.* Institute of Economic Affairs, Occasional Paper no. 41.

Friedman, M. and Meiselman, D. (1964) 'The Relative Stability of Monetary Velocity and the Investment Multiplier in the United States, 1897–1958', in *Stabilization Policies: A Series of Research Studies Prepared for the Commission on Money and Credit,* Englewood Cliffs, NJ, Prentice-Hall.

Friedman, M. and Schwartz, A.J. (1963) *A Monetary History of the United States, 1867–1960.* Princeton University Press for the National Bureau of Economic Research.

Gailliot, H.J. (1970) 'Purchasing Power Parity as an Explanation of Long-term Changes in Exchange Rates', *Journal of Money, Credit and Banking,* 2, August, 348–57.

Genberg, H. (1977) 'Policy Autonomy of Small Countries', in E. Lundberg (ed.) *Inflation Theory and Anti-inflation Policy.* London, Macmillan.

Genberg, H. (1978) 'Purchasing Power Parity under Fixed and Flexible Exchange Rates', *Journal of International Economics,* 8, May, 247–76.

Genberg, H. and Swoboda, A.K. (1975) 'Causes and Origins of the Current Worldwide Inflation', Discussion Paper, Ford Foundation International Monetary Research Project, Graduate Institute of International Studies, Geneva.

Gilbert, C.L. (1976) 'The Original Phillips Curve Estimates', *Economica,* 43, February, 51–7.

Godfrey, L.G. (1971) 'The Phillips Curve: Incomes Policy and Trade Union Effects' in Johnson and Nobay (1971).

Godley, W. and Nordhaus, W.D. (1972) 'Pricing in the Trade Cycle', *Economic Journal,* 82, September, 853–82.

Gordon, R.J. (1970) 'The Recent Acceleration of Inflation and its Lessons for the Future', *Brookings Papers on Economic Activity,* 1, 8–41.

Gordon, R.J. (1972) 'Wage Price Controls and the Shifting Phillips Curve', *Brookings Papers on Economic Activity,* 2, 385–421.

Granger, C.W.J. (1969) 'Investigating Causal Relations by Econometric Models and Cross-Spectral Methods', *Econometrica,* 37, July, 424–38.

Gray, M.R., Ward, R. and Zis, G. (1976) 'The World Demand for Money Function: Some Preliminary Results', in M. Parkin and G. Zis (eds) *Inflation in the World Economy.* Manchester University Press.

Griffiths, B. (1976) *Inflation: The Price of Prosperity.* London, Weidenfeld and Nicolson.

Hahn, F.H. (1971) 'Professor Friedman's Views on Money', *Economica,* 38, February, 61–80.

Hansen, B. (1951) *A Study in the Theory of Inflation.* London, George Allen & Unwin.

Hansen, B. (1970) 'Excess Demand, Unemployment, Vacancies and Wages' *Quarterly Journal of Economics,* 84, February, 1–23.

Hendry, D.F. (1980) 'Predictive Failure and Econometric Modelling in Macroeconomics: The Transactions Demand for Money', in P. Ormerod (ed.) *Economic Modelling.* London, Heinemann.

Henry, S.G.B. and Ormerod, P. (1978) 'Incomes Policy and Wage Inflation: Empirical Evidence for the U.K. 1961–77', *National Institute Economic Review,* 85, August, 31–9.

Henry, S.G.B., Sawyer, M.C. and Smith, P. (1976) 'Models of Inflation in the United Kingdom: An Evaluation', *National Institute Economic Review,* 77, August, 60–71.

Hicks, J.R. (1968) *The Theory of Wages* (2nd ed. London, St Martin's Press.

Hieser, R.O. (1970) 'Wage Determination with Bilateral Monopoly in the Labour Market: A Theoretical Treatment', *Economic Record,* 46, March, 55–72.

Hines, A.G. (1964) 'Trade Unions and Wage Inflation in the United Kingdom: 1893–1961', *Review of Economic Studies,* 31, October, 221–52.

Hines, A.G. (1971) 'The Determinants of the Rate of Change of Money Wage Rates and the Effectiveness of Incomes Policy', in Johnson and Nobay (1971).

Holden, K. and Peel, D. (1977) 'An Empirical Investigation of Inflationary Expectations', *Oxford Bulletin of Economics and Statistics,* 39, November, 291–9.

Holt, C.C. (1971) 'Job Search, Phillips' Wage Relation, and Union Influence: Theory and Evidence', in Phelps (1971).

Holzman, F.D. (1950) 'Income Determination in Open Inflation', *Review of Economics and Statistics,* 32, May, 150–8.

Hume, D. (1752) 'Of the Balance of Trade' in *Essays, Moral, Political and Literary* vol. 1 reprinted London, Longman Green (1898).

Isard, P. (1977) 'How Far Can We Push the "Law of One Price"?' *American Economic Review,* 67, December, 942–8.

Jackman, R.A. and Klappholz, K. (1975) *Taming the Tiger.* Hobart Paper no. 63. London, Institute for Economic Affiars.

Jackman, R.A. and Layard, P.R.G. (1980) 'The Efficiency Case for Long-Run Labour Market Policies', *Economica,* 47, August, 331–49.

Jackson, D., Turner, H.A. and Wilkinson, F. (1972) *Do Trade Unions Cause Inflation?* University of Cambridge Department of Applied Economics Occasional Paper no. 36. Cambridge University Press.

Johnson, H.G. (1967) 'Money in a Neoclassical One Sector Growth Model', *Essays in Monetary Economics.* London, George Allen & Unwin.

Johnson, H.G. (1970) 'Is There an Optimal Money Supply?' *Journal of Finance,* 25, May, 435–42.

Johnson, H.G. (1972) *Inflation and the Monetarist Controversy.* Amsterdam, North-Holland.

Johnson, H.G. and Nobay, A.R. (eds) (1971) *The Current Inflation.* London, Macmillan.

Johnston, J. (1972) 'A Model of Wage Determination under Bilateral Monopoly' *Economic Journal,* 82, September, 837–52.

Johnston, J. and Timbrell, M. (1973) 'Empirical Tests of a Bargaining Theory of Wage Rate Determination', *Manchester School,* 41, June, 141–67.

Kaldor, N. (1959) 'Economic Growth and the Problem of Inflation', *Economica,* 26, November, 287–98.

Kaldor, N. (1970) 'The New Monetarism', *Lloyds Bank Review,* 97, July, 1–18.

Keynes, J.M. (1936) *The General Theory of Employment, Interest and Money.* London, Macmillan.

Keynes, J.M. (1940) *How to Pay for the War.* London, Macmillan.

Klein, L.R. and Ball, R.J. (1959) 'Some Econometrics of the Determination of Absolute Prices and Wages', *Economic Journal,* 69, September, 465–82.

Kravis, I.B. and Lipsey, R.E. (1978) 'Price Behaviour in the Light of Balance of Payments Theories', *Journal of International Economics,* 8, May, 193–246.

Kuh, E. (1967) 'A Productivity Theory of Wage Levels – An Alternative to the Phillips Curve', *Review of Economic Studies,* 34, October, 333–60.

Laidler, D.E.W. (1971) 'The Phillips Curve, Expectations and Incomes Policy', in Johnson and Nobay (1971).

Laidler, D.E.W. (1973) 'The Influence of Money on Real Income and Inflation: A Simple Econometric Model', *Manchester School,* 41, December, 367–95.

Laidler, D.E.W. (1976) 'Inflation – Alternative Explanations and Policies: Tests on Data Drawn from Six Countries', in K. Brunner and A. Metzler (eds) *Institutions, Policies and Economic Performance.* Carnegie-Rochester Conference Series on Public Policy, no. 4.

Laidler, D.E.W. (1977) *The Demand for Money: Theories and Evidence* (2nd ed). New York, Harper and Row.

Laidler, D.E.W. and Purdy, D.L. (eds) (1974) *Inflation and Labour Markets.* Manchester University Press.

Layard, R., Metcalf, D. and Nickell, S. (1978) 'The Effect of Collective Bargaining on Relative and Absolute Wages', *British Journal of Industrial Relations,* 16, November, 287–302.

Levinson, H.M. (1960) 'Pattern Bargaining: A Case Study of the Automobile Workers', *Quarterly Journal of Economics,* 74, May, 296–317.

Levinson, H.M. (1966) *Determining Forces in Collective Wage Bargaining.* New York, John Wiley.

Lipsey, R.G. (1960) 'The Relation Between Unemployment and the Rate of Change of Money Wage Rates in the United Kingdom, 1862–1957: A Further Analysis', *Economica,* 27, February, 1–31.

Lipsey, R.G. and Steuer, M.D. (1961) 'The Relation Between Profits and Wage Rates', *Economica*, 28, May, 137–55.

MacKay, D.I. and Hart, R.A, (1974a) 'Wage Inflation and Regional Wage Structure', in J.M. Parkin and A.R. Nobay (eds) *Contemporary Issues in Economics*. Manchester University Press.

MacKay, D.I. and Hart, R.A. (1974b) 'Wage Inflation and the Phillips Relationship', *Manchester School*, 42, June, 136–61.

Marshall, A. (1923) *Money, Credit and Commerce*. London, Macmillan.

Mortensen, D. (1971) 'A Theory of Wage and Employment Dynamics', in Phelps (1971).

Mulvey, C. and Trevithick, J.A. (1974) 'Some Evidence on the Wage Leadership Hypothesis', *Scottish Journal of Political Economy*, 21, February, 1–11.

Mundell, R.A. (1963a) 'Capital Mobility and Stabilization Policy under Fixed and Flexible Exchange Rates', *Canadian Journal of Economics and Political Science*, 29, November, 475–85.

Mundell, R.A. (1963b) 'Inflation and Real Interest', *Journal of Political Economy*, 71, June, 280–3.

Muth, J.F. (1961) 'Rational Expectations and the Theory of Price Movements', *Econometrica*, 29, July, 315–35.

Nickell, S. (1979) 'The Effect of Unemployment and Related Benefits on the Duration of Unemployment', *Economic Journal*, 89, March, 34–49.

Nield, P.R. (1963) *Pricing and Employment in the Trade Cycle*. Cambridge University Press.

Nordhaus, W.D. (1972) 'Recent Developments in Price Dynamics', in Eckstein (1972).

Nordhaus, W.D. (1975) 'The Political Business Cycle', *Review of Economic Studies*, 42, April, 169–90.

OECD (1970) *Inflation: The Present Problem*. Paris, OECD.

OECD (1977) *Towards Full Employment and Price Stability*. Paris, OECD.

OEEC (1961) *The Problem of Rising Prices*. Paris, OEEC.

Officer, L.H. (1976) 'The Purchasing Power Parity Theory of Exchange Rates: A Review Article', *IMF Staff Papers*, 23, March, 1–60.

Paish, F.W. (1968) 'The Limits of Incomes Policies', in F.W. Paish and J. Hennessy *Policy for Incomes*. Hobart Paper 29. London, Institute of Economic Affairs.

Parkin, J.M. (1975) 'The Causes of Inflation: Recent Contributions and Current Controversies', in J.M. Parkin and A.R. Nobay (eds) *Current Economic Problems*. Cambridge University Press.

Parkin, J.M., Richards, I and Zis, G. (1975) 'The Determination and Control of the World Money Supply under Fixed Exchange Rates', *Manchester School*, 43, September, 293–316.

Parkin, J.M. and Sumner, M.T. (eds) (1972) *Incomes Policy and Inflation*. Manchester University Press.

Parkin, J.M., Sumner, M. and Ward, R. (1976) 'The Effects of Excess Demand, Generalized Expectations and Wage–Price Cpntrols on Inflation in the U.K.: 1956–71', in K. Brunner and A.H. Meltzer (eds) *The Economics of Price and Wage Controls*. Amsterdam, North-Holland.

Patinkin, D. (1965) *Money, Interest, and Prices* (2nd ed.). New York, Harper and Row.

Pencavel, J.H. (1970) 'An Investigation into Industrial Strike Activity in Great Britain, *Economica*, 37, August, 239—56.

Perry, G.L. (1966) *Unemployment, Money Wage Rates and Inflation*. Cambridge, Mass., MIT Press.

Perry, G.L. (1970) 'Changing Labor Markets and Inflation', *Brookings Papers on Economic Activity*, 3, 411—41.

Perry, G.L. (1972) 'Unemployment Flows in the US Labor Market' *Brookings Papers on Economic Activity*, 2, 245—92.

Peston, M.H. (1971) 'The Micro-Economics of the Phillips Curve', in Johnson and Nobay (1971).

Phelps, E.S. (1965) 'Anticipated Inflation and Economic Welfare', *Journal of Political Economy*, 73, February, 1—17.

Phelps, E.S. (1967) 'Phillips Curves, Expectations of Inflation and Optimal Unemployment over Time', *Economica*, 34, August, 254—81.

Phelps, E.S. (ed.) (1971) *Microeconomic Foundations of Employment and Inflation Theory*. London, Macmillan.

Phelps, E.S. (1972) *Inflation Policy and Unemployment Theory*. New York, Norton.

Phelps, E.S. (1978) 'Inflation Planning Reconsidered', *Economica*, 45, May, 109—24.

Phillips, A.W. (1958) 'The Relation between Unemployment and the Rate of Change of Money Wage Rates in the United Kingdom, 1861—1957', *Economica*, 25, November, 283—99.

Phipps, A.J. (1977) 'Strike Activity and Inflation in Australia', *Economic Record*, 53, September, 297—319.

Pigou, A.C. (1917) 'The Value of Money', *Quarterly Journal of Economics*, 37, November, 38—65.

Posner, M.V. (1973) Letter to *The Times* (4 September).

Purdy, D.L. and Zis, G. (1973) 'Trade Unions and Wage Inflation in the UK: A Reappraisal', in J.M. Parkin and A.R. Nobay (eds) *Essays in Modern Economics*. London, Longman.

Purdy, D.L. and Zis, G. (1974) 'On the Concept and Measurement of Union Militancy', in Laidler and Purdy (1974).

Rees, R. (1970) 'The Phillips Curve as a Menu for Policy Choice', *Economica*, 37, August, 227—38.

Robinson, J. and Wilkinson, F. (1977) 'What Has Become of Employment Policy?' *Cambridge Journal of Economics*, 1, March, 5—14.

Rose, D. (1972) 'A General Error-learning Model of Expectations Formations', University of Manchester Inflation Workshop Discussion Paper 7210.

Ross, A.M. (1948) *Trade Union Wage Policy*. Berkeley, California University Press.

Santomero, A.M. and Seater, J.J. (1978) 'The Inflation—Unemployment Trade-Off: A Critique of the Literature', *Journal of Economic Literature*, 16, June, 499—544.

Sargan, J.D. (1964) 'Wages and Prices in the United Kingdom: A Study in Econo-
    metric Methodology', in P.E. Hart, G. Mills and J.K.Whitaker (eds) *Econometric
    Analysis for National Economic Planning*. London, Butterworth.

Sargan, J.D. (1971) 'A Study of Wages and Prices in the UK 1949–1968', in
    Johnson and Nobay (1971).

Sargan, J.D. (1980a) 'A Model of Wage–Price Inflation' *Review of Economic
    Studies*, 47, January, 97–112.

Sargan, J.D. (1980b) 'The Consumer Price Equation in the Post War British
    Economy: An Exercise in Equation Specification Testing', *Review of Economic
    Studies*, 47, January, 113–35.

Savage, D.L. (1978) 'The Channels of Monetary Influence: A Survey of the
    Empirical Evidence', *National Institute Economic Review*, 83, February,
    73–89.

Seltzer, G. (1951) 'Pattern Bargaining and the United Steelworkers', *Journal of
    Political Economy*, 59, August, 319–31.

Shiller, R.J. (1978) 'Rational Expectations and the Dynamic Structure of Macro-
    economic Models: A Critical Review', *Journal of Monetary Economics*, 4,
    January, 1–44.

Simler, N.J. and Tella, A. (1968) 'Labour Reserves and the Phillips Curve', *Review
    of Economics and Statistics*, 50, February, 32–49.

Sims, C.A. (1972) 'Money, Income and Causality', *American Economic Review*,
    62, September, 540–52.

Smithies, A. (1942) 'The Behaviour of Money National Income under Inflationary
    Conditions', *Quarterly Journal of Economics*, 56, November, 113–29.

Solow, R.M. (1969) *Price Expectations and the Behaviour of the Price Level*.
    Manchester University Press.

Taylor, J. (1970) 'Hidden Unemployment: Hoarded Labour and the Phillips
    Curve' *Southern Economic Journal*, 37, July, 1–16.

Taylor, J. (1972) 'Incomes Policy, the Structure of Unemployment and the
    Phillips Curve: the United Kingdom experience: 1953–70', in Parkin and
    Sumner (1972).

Thomas, R.L. and Stoney, P.J.M. (1970) 'A Note on the Dynamic Properties of
    the Hines Inflation Model' *Review of Economic Studies*, 37, April, 286–94.

Thomas, R.L. and Stoney, P.J.M. (1972) 'Unemployment Dispersion as a Deter-
    minant of Wage Inflation in the United Kingdom, 1925–1966', in Parkin and
    Sumner (1972).

Tobin, J. (1965) 'Money and Economic Growth', *Econometrica*, 33, October,
    671–84.

Tobin, J. (1968) 'Unemployment and Inflation: The Cruel Dilemma', in A. Phillips
    and O.E. Williamson (eds) *Prices: Issues in Theory and Public Policy*.
    Philadelphia, University of Pennsylvania Press.

Tobin, J. (1970) 'Money and Income: *Post Hoc Ergo Propter Hoc*', *Quarterly
    Journal of Economics*, 84, May, 301–17.

Tobin, J. (1972) 'Inflation and Unemployment' *American Economic Review*, 62,
    March, 1–18.

Trevithick, J.A. (1975) 'Keynes, Inflation and Money Illusion', *Economic Journal*, 85, March, 101—13.

Turnovsky, S.J. (1972) 'The Expectations Hypothesis and the Aggregate Wage Equation: Some Empirical Evidence for Canada', *Economica*, 39, February, 1—17.

Turnovsky, S.J. and Wachter, W.L. (1972) 'A Test of the "Expectations Hypothesis" Using Directly Observed Wage and Price Expectations', *Review of Economics and Statistics*, 54, February, 47—54.

Wachter, M.L. (1976) 'The Changing Cyclical Responsiveness of Wage Inflation', *Brookings Papers on Economic Activity*, 1, 115—59.

Ward, R. and Zis, G. (1974) 'Trade Union Militancy as an Explanation of Inflation: An International Comparison', *Manchester School*, 42, March, 46—65.

Wiles, P. (1973) 'Cost Inflation and the State of Economic Theory', *Economic Journal*, 83, June, 377—98.

Williams, D., Goodhart, C.A.E. and Gowling, D.H. (1976) 'Money, Income and Causality: The UK Experience', *American Economic Review*, 66, June, 417—23.

Author Index

Ackley, G. 81
Addison, J. 83
Akerlof, G. 101
Alchian, A.A. 112
Ando, A. 116
Archibald, G.C. 45, 49
Artis, M.J. 116
Ashenfelter, O. 52, 53, 75, 80

Bailey, M.J. 179
Ball, R.J. 57, 82
Barrett, C.R. 116
Barro, R.J. 161
Baumol, W.J. 66
Berry, R.A. 81
Bhatia, R.J. 50
Bodkin, R.G. 81
Bowen, W.G. 81
Bowers, J.K. 42, 49
Brechling, F.P.R. 49, 82
Brinner, R.E. 105
Brittan, S. 112
Bronfenbrenner, M. 31
Bruno, M. 162, 168, 170
Burton, J. 83

Cagan, P. 89, 94, 122, 123, 134
Carlson, J.A. 105, 111
Cassell, G. 136
Coghlan, R.T. 118
Cross, R. 146
Cukierman, A. 104

de Menil, G. 70
Department of Employment, 60, 61, 62
Desai, M.J. 47
Dicks-Mireaux, L.A. 52, 57
Dow, J.C.R. 52, 56
Duck, N.W. 144
Duesenberry, J. 67

Eatwell, J. 83
Eckstein, O. 59, 82, 83

Fisher, I. 10, 11, 12, 172, 173
Flemming, J.S. 95
Frenkel, J.A. 136, 138, 139
Frey, B.S. 126
Friedman, M. 1, 8, 12, 70, 89, 90, 96,
    99, 100, 103, 107, 108, 115, 116,
    117, 119, 123, 124, 125, 128, 130,
    180, 186, 190

Gailliot, H.J. 138
Genberg, H.A. 137, 138, 145
Gilbert, C.L. 47
Godfrey, L.G. 79, 80
Godley, W. 58
Goodhart, C.A.E. 129
Gordon, R.J. 104
Gowling, D.H. 129
Granger, C.W.J. 128
Gray, M.R. 144
Griffiths, B. 182
Grossman, H.I. 161

Hahn, F.H. 96
Hansen, B. 17, 28, 30
Hart, R.A. 49, 51
Hendry, D.F. 118
Henry, S.G.B. 79, 80, 85, 104, 152, 155, 156, 159, 161
Hicks, J.R. 74
Hieser, R.O. 75
Hines, A.G. 52, 57, 78, 79, 80, 156
Holden, K. 105, 111
Holt, C.C. 71
Holzman, F.D. 31, 67
Hume, D. 138, 139, 140

Isard, P. 137

Jackman, R.A. 112, 186
Jackson, D. 76, 82, 83, 152, 154, 155
Johnson, H.G. 139, 178, 181
Johnston, J. 75, 80, 152, 154, 155

Kaldor, N. 81, 128, 129
Keynes, J.M. 8, 10, 17, 18, 19, 20, 21, 24, 25, 31, 64, 75, 100, 117, 151, 172
Klappholz, K. 186
Klein, L.R. 57, 82
Kravis, I.B. 137
Kuh, E. 158, 159, 160

Laidler, D.E.W. 80, 105, 118, 146, 156
Layard, P.R.G. 84, 112
Levinson, H.M. 71, 75, 82, 83
Lipsey, R.E. 137
Lipsey, R.G. 6, 34, 35, 40, 42, 43, 45, 47, 48, 49, 50, 55, 56, 81, 89, 152

McKay, D.I. 49, 51
Main, B.G.M. 101
Marshall, A. 16
Meiselman, D. 115, 116
Modigliani, F. 116
Mortensen, D. 100
Mulvey, C. 49, 76, 82, 83

Mundell, R.A. 147, 172, 173, 174, 175
Muth, J.F. 127

Nickell, S.J. 63, 112
Nield, R.R. 57
Nobay, A.R. 116
Nordhaus, W.D. 58, 59, 126

OECD, 50, 164
OECD, 2, 6, 52
Officer, L.H. 138
Ormerod, P. 85, 152, 156, 159

Paish, F.W. 34
Parkin, J.M. 71, 85, 104, 105, 111, 144, 158, 160
Patinkin, D. 15
Peel, D. 105, 111
Pencavel, J. 52, 53, 75
Perry, G.L. 50, 51, 101
Peston, M.H. 49, 63
Phelps, E.S. 89, 96, 99, 110, 112, 176, 177, 178
Phillips, A.W. 6, 33, 43, 44, 45, 46, 50, 55, 56, 89, 152
Phipps, A.J. 80
Pigou, A.C. 12
Posner, M.V. 65
Purdy, D.L. 71, 79, 80

Rees, A. 88
Robinson, J. 79
Rose, D. 105
Ross, A.M. 75

Sachs, J.D. 169, 170
Santomero, A.M. 50
Sargan, J.D. 42, 49, 58, 82, 152, 153, 154, 155, 156, 159, 161
Savage, D. 118
Sawyer, M.C. 79, 104, 155
Schneider, F. 126
Schwartz, A. 130
Seater, J.J. 50

Seltzer, G. 82, 83
Shepherd, J.R. 52
Shiller, R.J. 127
Simler, N.J. 50, 51
Sims, C.A. 128, 129
Smith, P. 79, 104, 155
Smithies, A. 23, 30, 31
Solow, R.M. 59, 94, 105
Steuer, M.D. 81
Stoney, P.J.M. 49, 79, 82
Sumner, M.T. 85, 104, 158, 160
Swoboda, A.K. 145

Taylor, J. 51, 53, 80
Tella, A. 50, 51
Thomas, R.L. 49, 79, 82

Timbrell, M. 80, 152, 154, 155
Tobin, J. 99, 103, 112, 124, 128, 178
Trevithick, J.A. 22, 49, 76, 82, 83
Turner, H.A. 154
Turnovsky, S.J. 104

Wachter, W.I. 104
Walters, A.A. 116
Ward, R. 80, 104, 158, 160
Wiles, P. 86, 87
Wilkinson, F. 79, 154
Williams, D. 129
Wilson, T.A. 82, 83

Zis, G. 71, 79, 80

Subject Index

Adaptive expectations, 93–5, 103–6,
121, 123
administered prices, 56–60
aggregation, 28, 34, 40–3, 55
asset substitution, 118–20, 172–82
atomistic competition, 68
Australia, 80
autonomous expenditure, 23, 115–16

Balance of payments
disequilibrium, 2
and inflation, 2, 145–9
monetary theory of, 138–41
postwar problems, 2, 143–5
US deficits, 55, 144
bargaining models, 68–71, 64–75
Belgium, 80
bilateral monopoly, 70

Cambridge equation, 12–13, 117
Canada, 3
capacity utilization, 18, 31, 164
cash balances, 15–17, 172–82; see
also Money
causality, 127–32
Chile, 1
Cobb–Douglas production function,
158–9
collective bargaining
advantages of, 70–6
and conventions of equity, 67, 75
and inflation, 64–87
models of, 68–76

comparability criteria, 67, 75–6, 82–3
cost inflation, 3, 6, 64–87, 189–90
and expectations, 98
policy towards, 6, 64, 189–90
simple model of, 65–7
trade unions and, 6, 64–87
wage-push, 6, 64–87
costs,
of holding money, 117–18, 122,
172–82
normal, 57–60
unit labour, 56–7

Deflation, 2, 108–10, 181, 192
demand for goods, 20, 56–60, 118–20
demand for labour, 13–14, 32–56,
68–70
demand for money, 12–13, 15–16,
114, 117–18, 120–1, 132
demand-pull inflation, 3, 5–6, 17–30,
32–60, 64, 188–9
Hansen's model, 28–30
Keynes's model, 17–22
neo-Keynesian models, 22–30,
115–20
dynamic models of the labour market,
28–30, 34–45, 99–103

Earnings, 52–3
economic welfare, 179–87
equation of exchange, 10–11
equilibrium,
balance of payments, 145–9

full employment, 2, 21–3, 89–92, 124–7, 130–2
general, 89
level of income, 17–30, 124–7, 130–2, 163–70
real wages, 157–62, 163, 166–70
error-learning process, 93–5
excess demand,
aggregate, 17–30, 64, 188–9
and full employment, 17–30, 89–92
for goods, 28–30, 56–60, 64, 188–9
for labour, 6–7, 28–30, 32–56, 68–70
and prices, 15–30, 56–60, 64, 89–92, 188–9
and real wages, 157–62
and wages, 6–7, 28–30, 32–56, 64
exchange rates
and capital flows, 135–49
fixed, 7, 135–46, 148–9, 191
flexible, 7, 135–8, 146–9
expectations,
adaptive, 93–5, 103–6, 121, 123
and cost inflation, 98
hypothesis, 7, 8, 54–5, 88–113, 124–5, 171–82
of price changes, 54–5, 58–9, 88–113, 121, 123–5, 163–6, 171–82
rational, 126–7

Fiscal policy, 116, 131, 176–8, 185
flows,
of capital, 135–49, 179
of labour, 99–103
France, 80
frictional unemployment, 37, 100–1
full employment, 2, 11–14, 25–7, 89–92, 124–7, 130–2
meaning of, 89, 99–103
full liquidity, 181

Germany, 1, 80
government expenditure
and inflation, 18–24, 39, 116, 176–8
and the money supply, 176–8

Hidden unemployment, 51
hoarding of labour, 51
Hungary, 182
hyper-inflation, 1, 19, 122–3, 182
in Europe, 123
in Germany, 1
in Hungary, 182
and money, 122–3

Import prices, 46, 145–8
imported inflation, 135–49, 178–9
income,
and demand for money, 12–13, 15–16, 120–1
distribution of, 20–4, 182–5
equilibirum level of, 11–14, 17–30, 124–7, 130–2, 163–70
income velocity of circulation, 12, 114–15, 120, 123, 125
incomes policy, 6–7, 64, 84–6, 110–11, 192
effect of, 84–6
in the Netherlands, 6
role of, 64, 84–6, 110–11, 192
in the UK, 84–6, 156
indexation, 110–11, 186–7, 192–3
inflation,
accelerating, 3, 24, 89–95
anticipated, 9, 93–113, 171–82
and commodity prices, 7
constant, 24, 92–4
cost-push, 3, 6, 64–84, 189–90
creeping, 1
decelerating, 24, 191
definition, 1
and economic welfare, 179–87
effects of, 171–87
and expectations, 54–5, 58–9, 88–113, 120–7, 171–82, 189, 192

income/expenditure, models of,
  17–30, 115–17, 172–8
in industrialized countries, 2, 3
and interest rates, 16–17, 25–7,
  120–3, 172–9
and investment, 16–19, 172–9
monetarist model of, 10–17,
  114–33, 172–82
and money illusion, 23, 184–5, 189
and oil prices, 55, 162–71, 193
political consequences of, 1
and profits, 20–4, 65–7
and the real interest rate, 16–17,
  25–7, 120–3, 172–9
and resource allocation, 22, 171–87
and saving, 20–4, 172–9
and search, 102–3
and taxation, 154–5
and trade unions, 6, 8, 67–84
unanticipated, 9, 93–113, 182–7
and unemployment, 6, 32–56,
  88–113
wage, 6, 7, 32–56, 67–84
in the world, 50, 55, 142–9, 162–6,
  189
inflationary gap, 3, 5–6, 17–24
inflation rate,
  in Canada, 3
  in France, 3–5
  in Germany, 3–5
  in Japan, 3–5
  in UK, 3–5, 78–84, 131–2
  in USA, 3–5, 22, 50
inflation tax, 179–81
investment, 16–19, 172–9
Italy, 80

Japan, 1

Key bargain, 75–6, 82–3
Keynesian theory, 8, 17–22, 95–8,
  115–20, 151
Korean War, 2, 3

Labour Government (UK), 82, 154

labour market, 13–14, 28–30, 32–56,
  99–103
and inflation, 20–30, 32–56,
  64–84
models of, 99–103
and trade unions, 64–87
lags,
  in the Keynesian model, 21–2, 24
  and price adjustments, 56–60,
    124–6
  and wage adjustments, 21–2,
    43–5, 72–3
lay-offs, 103
liquidity trap, 26
'loops' (Phillips curve), 43–5

Marginal product of labour, 13–14,
  158–60
market power (of trade unions), 65–87
Monetarist models of inflation, 7, 8,
  10–17, 114–33, 171–82
Monetary policy, 7, 116, 118–20, 123,
  125–7, 130–3, 191–2
money,
  demand for, 12–13, 15–16,
    25–27, 114, 117–18, 120–1,
    132, 172–82
  illusion, 23, 96, 184–5, 189
  and inflation, 8, 10–17, 114–33,
    190
  in a Keynesian model, 25–27
  and prices, 10–17, 114–33, 190
  quantity theory of, 8, 10–17,
    114–15
  supply of, 10–17, 25–7, 114–17,
    127–33, 138–43, 191–2
  velocity of circulation of, 10–14,
    25–6, 114–15, 120–3
monopoly power (of trade unions)
  64–87
multiplier, 115–16

Natural rate of unemployment,
  89–113, 124
Netherlands, 6, 80
nominal income theory, 123–7

normal-cost hypothesis, 57—60

Open market operations, 176—8
opportunity cost (of holding money)
　117—18, 122
output,
　dynamic determination of, 123—7
　growth of, 2
　per man, 56—60
overtime, 52

Phillips Curve, 6—8, 30, 32—56,
　68—70, 88—113, 169—170, 188
Pigou effect, 24
policy, 3, 5—8, 64, 106—13, 123,
　125—7, 130—3
　recommendations for, 190—3
political variables, 76, 82
portfolio balance transmission
　mechanism, 118—20
postwar inflation, 2—5
price specie flow mechanism, 138—40
prices,
　determination, 10—17, 56—60,
　　123—33
　dynamics, 123—7
　and excess demand, 56—60, 64,
　　88—113
　expected changes in 54—5, 58—9,
　　88—113, 120—7, 172—82
　flexibility, 13
　and money, 10—17, 25—7, 114—33,
　　190
productivity, 56—9, 158—62
profit, 17—22, 56—9, 65—7, 81—2
profiteers, 17—22
profits,
　propensity to save from, 17—22
　and trade unions, 81—2
purchasing power parity, 135—8

Quantity Theory of Money, 8
　classical, 10—17, 114—15
　Friedman's restatement of, 117
quasi-fixed exchange rate, 149

Rate of interest,
　and demand for money, 16—17, 26,
　　117—18, 120—3, 172—82
　and investment, 118—20
　nominal, 120—3, 179—82
　real, 16—17, 25—7, 120—3, 172—82
rational expectations, 126—7
real balances, 12—13, 15—16, 25—7,
　122, 179—82
real wages, 13—14, 21—2, 28—30, 34,
　90, 150—70
reservation wage, 100—3

Savings, 20—4, 172—9
search theory, 99—103
strikes, 73—5, 80—1
supply of labour, 13—14, 32—56
Switzerland, 80

Target real wage, 151—8
　Sargan model, 152—4
taxes and inflation, 20—1, 154—5,
　176—8, 184
technical progress, 158—62
trade cycles, 43—5
trade unions,
　changes in membership, 78—80
　and collective bargaining, 64—84
　and cost inflation, 6, 64—87
　degree of unionization, 78—80
　impact on inflation, 6, 8, 64—84,
　　189—90
　and information, 71—3
　and the labour market, 64—84
　market power of, 67—76
　and market structure, 67—76
　militancy, 75—6, 83—4
　and political variables, 82
　and profits, 81—2
　and strikes, 73—5, 80—1
　and transfer mechanisms, 67, 75—6,
　　82—3
　union/non-union differential, 77,
　　82—3
　and wage drift, 52—3

transfer mechanisms, 67, 75–6, 82–3
transmission mechanisms, 14–17,
 118–20
two-gap models of inflation, 28–30

Unemployment,
 classical, 166–9
 dispersion of, 40–2, 45, 49–50
 duration of, 101
 and excess demand, 6, 32–56,
  60–3, 88–113
 frictional, 37, 100–1
 hidden, 51
 and key bargains, 75–6, 82–3
 and labour hoarding, 51
 measurement of, 51, 60–3
 and microeconomic policies,
  111–12
 natural rate of, 89–113, 124
 rate of change of, 43–5, 47–8
 and search theory, 99–103
 and vacancies, 36–7, 50–4, 60–3
unionization,
 change in, 78–80
 degree of, 78–80
United Kingdom,
 incomes policy in, 84–6
 inflation in, 1, 3–5, 78–84, 130–3
United States of America,
 balance of payments of, 144
 inflation in, 3–5, 22, 50, 81–2

Vacancies
 and excess demand, 36–37, 50–2,
  60–3

measurement of, 50–2, 60–3
velocity of circulation, 10–17, 25–7,
 114–15, 120, 123
 and demand for money, 12
 instability of, 11, 25–6
 stability of, 10–13, 114–20
 transactions, 10–11

Wage,
 bargaining, 64–87
 differentials, 67, 75–6, 82–3
 drift, 52
 indexation, 111, 186–7
 leadership, 75–6, 82–3
 measurement problems, 50–3
 policy, 6, 64
 rates, 52–3
 real, 13–14, 21–2, 28–30, 34,
  90, 150–70
 rigidity, 64–75, 150–70
 rounds, 75–6, 82–3
 share of national income, 65–7
 transfer mechanisms, 65–7, 75–6,
  82–3
Walrasian system, 89
war finance, 1, 18–22, 55, 144
wealth, 117
world inflation, 142–5, 148–9,
 162–6, 189
 and excess demand, 7
 and oil prices, 162–6, 189
 and US deficits, 7, 55, 144, 148–9
world liquidity, 7, 55, 142–5, 148–9,
 189